ALL ABOUT SPACE 3

BEYOND THE OBJECT

ALL ABOUT SPACE 3

BEYOND THE OBJECT

The Cube of Truth (Introduction) 7
Matthias Michel

HOUSE 2 – Counter City 18
Dieter Dietz & photographers Katalin Deér, Dylan Perrenoud, Anna Positano, ALICE Studio

I. 37

A BRIEF HISTORY OF SPACE

Matthias Michel

The Age of Magic Space 39
Ibram's Awakening 46
7 Cosmologies (Beginnings) 57
Magic Spaces (Conceptions)
The World – Space and Time – Architecture – The Spatiality of the Sexes
The Age of Poetic Space 69
The Legend of the Seven Architects 74
Two Letters 82
Poetic Spaces (Interventions) 89
The "Promethean Turn" – Inscriptions – Revaluations
The Holy Grail 98
The Age of Rational Space 105
Prometheus Bound 115
Rational Spaces (Abstractions) 122
"Renaissance" – Globality. Divisibility. Conceptuality. – A State of Mind – Empty Spaces
Blackmail 136
Confessions of an Exile 142
The Age of Spacisms Or The Black Square and the Blue Marble (Multiple Explications) 147
(Hemi-)Spherical Thinking 178

II. 181

ZURICH MAPS

Matthias Michel & Jonas Voegeli

III. 213

THE IMAGINATION OF SPACE

Zurich Spaces 215
Dylan Perrenoud

Zurich – A Drawing in Words 249
Dieter Dietz

Drawing For Real – A Quest into the Space of Imagination 259
Interior and Exterior – A Taste of Drawing for Real – Translations – Drawing and Time – "Denkraum" – To Draw into Space: Desire
Dieter Dietz & Daniel Zamarbide

Architectures of Contribution 291
Dieter Dietz & Daniel Zamarbide

HOUSE 3 297
Camille Vallet & photographers ALICE Studio, Victor Maréchal, Stephane Grandgirard, Aurélien Mole

As the true method of knowledge is experiment,[1]
the true faculty of knowing must be the faculty which experiences.
(William Blake; *All Religions are one – The Voice of One Crying in the Wilderness*, 1788)

The Cube of Truth

(Introduction)

10th of June 2017. Reception area of the Tower of Justice in Bhymbal, City of the Thousand Glass Towers, capital of the outer eastern World of Ideas.

THE VOICE: Please identify yourself by opening your mind. Your connecting channel is CA∞FL‡ΔU◊X9.
LETO OF CNOSSOS: I am here. I say so.
THE VOICE: Welcome to the Core Zone of Truthfulness. Have you been enlightened about your rights and duties?
LETO OF CNOSSOS: Yes, I have, I say so.
THE VOICE: You may enter the Core Zone now. Please follow your personal Châ signal, harken and you shall hear. You will be guided directly to the Cube of Truth for your mission debrief.
LETO OF CNOSSOS: Thank you.

1 In the historical context of the late 18th century, the word „experiment“ is commonly used as a synonym for „experience“.

Inside the Cube of Truth at the Tower of Justice, Bhymbal, World of Ideas.

THE CUBE OF TRUTH: Please state your original full name and your predetermined age inasmuch as it is known to you.
LETO OF CNOSSOS: I have no original name, I say so. I have been addressed by many names in many pasts and futures, most often by the name of Λητω of Κνωσοσ. However, the name that is most likely to occur in the context of my latest mission is "The Spacemaker". I have reached my predetermined age of 25.
THE CUBE: Very well. Are you ready to be debriefed, Leto of Cnossos?
LETO: I am willing to speak the truth and nothing but the truth, I say so.
THE CUBE: Now then, can you state the exact time of your return from the World of Facts?
LETO: I have left HOUSE 2 in Zurich at 3:51 AM, Saturday the 10th of June 2017, and immediately re-entered the World of Ideas.[2]
THE CUBE: The last night of a full moon before summer solstice.
LETO: Precisely. I have executed the Code activation procedure at intersection point 12.8 on the Circle of Time at 3:42 AM under excellent weather conditions. There were no witnesses, and the Code seemed to work just as perfectly with HOUSE 2 as it worked with HOUSE 1 during last year's testing phase.[3]
THE CUBE: Just for the record, please give me a short description of the HOUSE 2 site.
LETO: The site is situated in Zurich West, 8° 30' 39" eastern longitude and 47° 23' 26" northern latitude, a few square metres of asphalted ground under the bifurcation of a railway viaduct that runs between two big buildings, the Sheraton Apartment Tower to the west and the main entrance of the *Zurich University of the Arts* to the east. The HOUSE 2 construction has been erected in between the massive concrete pillars of the viaduct. Similar to HOUSE 1, HOUSE 2 features several platforms and compartments all built of wooden slats. But unlike its predecessor, HOUSE 2 does not quite look like a "house". It looks more like a huge multi-piece stage, and, quite obviously, it has been used as such during the past few days. There are small auditoriums and enclosed spaces, a roofed trilateral counter that looks like a small bar at the eastern end of the construction, a stair that leads straight up to the bottom of the viaduct and ends there abruptly. Anyway, for our purposes, it is perfect. Again, the proto-structure is stable and patterned enough to serve as a data carrier for encoded information. Again, the immense amount of code that can be encrypted in the proto-structure is easily transferrable to living or digital neural systems and vice versa. And again, the code enables the installation of temporary weak points in the space-time continuum between the World of Facts and the World of Ideas, which allowed me to enter and exit the World of Facts on site.
THE CUBE: How did you activate the code sequences?
LETO: I used the device that Frank Teller, the Ever-Changing Spirit, brought over from the World of Facts last summer. With Frank's assistance, the Stargazing Priest managed to slightly convert it according

2 For further information on the HOUSE 2 project, please refer to chapter *HOUSE 2 – Counter City*, p. 18 et seqq.
3 For further information on the HOUSE 1 project and the Spacemaker's and other characters' involvement in it, please refer to Dieter Dietz / Matthias Michel / Daniel Zamarbide (ed.): *All About Space*, Volume 1: *The Invention of Space* (Zurich 2016), and Volume 2: *HOUSE 1 Catalogue* (Zurich 2017).

to our purposes.[4] And when I arrived at HOUSE 2, it looked just like a customary smartphone.
THE CUBE: A "smartphone"?
LETO: Sort of a mobile communication device that has come into general use in the World of Facts lately.
THE CUBE: I see. Is it some sort of mind machine?
LETO: Not quite. But people in the World of Facts use it as such. They have taken to progressively outsource considerable parts of their cognitional and sensory intelligence to all sorts of communication devices for quite some time now. Maybe that is one of the reasons why they have become so fatuously obsessed with the physical facets of their existences.
THE CUBE: Be that as it may. The deplorable decrease of human intelligence in the World of Facts is not the chief subject of this debrief. Now tell me, what will be, in your personal opinion, the immediate consequences of this activation procedure?
LETO: According to the mission plan, and since HOUSE 2 is built at an intersection point on the Circle of Time, the Code will enter into the system from there and, according to our expectations, eventually reactivate the entire system. As a consequence, the space-time continuum will be increasingly permeable at all intersection points of the system in the inner city of Zurich for an indefinite period of time, including both the Circle of Space and the Circle of Time. As a result, people who stay at one of these intersection points for longer than a few seconds may sense or experience, depending on their respective power of imagination, past spaces that have taken place at that particular point. As soon as the system is fully reconditioned, the phenomenon is expected to extend to future spaces as well, and from then on at the latest, the Code will seriously affect both human and digital neural systems within the effective range.[5]
THE CUBE: That is to say that the original idea of space will be pervasively re-implemented in all sorts of cognitive systems, I take it.
LETO: Yes, that is the defined goal of the whole mission.
THE CUBE: Can you elaborate on these effects a bit more precisely?
LETO: With due respect, I don't think that is necessary. You have planned this mission *yourself*. I mean, you have *sent* me there. After all, you are the *Cube of Truth*. You know everything.
THE CUBE: I am far from knowing everything, especially with regard to the event horizons in the World of Facts. After all, I am just a cube. I may be as close to a mind machine as an artificial intelligence can possibly be: I have access to all information that is available at a given moment in time, and I do my best to make sense of it and draw reasonable conclusions. However, since I am artificial, I lack any kind of comprehensive or instantaneous *experience*, which sets considerably tight limits to my knowledge and intelligence. Completely apart from that, this is not about what I know, harken and you shall hear. This is about whether *you* speak the truth or not.
LETO: I understand. May I allege a few examples with regard to the effects of the system then?
THE CUBE: By all means, please do so.
LETO: For instance, if someone takes a walk in the woods of "Zürichberg"

4 Cf. Dieter Dietz / Matthias Michel / Daniel Zamarbide (ed.): *All About Space*, Volume 2: *HOUSE 1 Catalogue*. Zurich 2017.
5 Cf. System Map on the following double page and implementations on historical maps in chapter II Zurich Maps, p. 181 et seqq.

THE CIRCLE OF SPACE

The Pentagon

5.1 Entrance to the "St. Josef" Hotel, "Hirschengraben" No. 64/68
5.2 Passageway to "Blaufahnenstrasse" No. 14
5.3 Public toilet facility, Tram Stop "Paradeplatz"
5.4 Southwest corner of the Synagogue "Löwenstrasse"
5.5 Alfred-Escher-Memorial, "Bahnhofplatz" (Zurich Main Station)

The Heptagon

7.1 Entrance to the "St. Josef" Hotel, "Hirschengraben" No. 64/68
7.2 "Susanna-Gossweiler-Platz"
7.3 Choir of the "Wasserkirche" ("Water Church")
7.4 Credit Suisse Bank headquarters, southwest corner, "Paradeplatz"
7.5 Entrance to the "Paddy Reilly's" Pub, "Talstrasse"
7.6 West corner of "Löwenplatz"
7.7 Southeast corner of the Zurich Main Station building

THE CIRCLE OF TIME

The Dodecagon

12.1 "Zürichberg" woods, to the north of "Reservoir-Weg"
12.2 "Wolfbachtobelweg", to the west of the "Doldertal" Retirement Home
12.3 Street corner "Minervastrasse"/ "Apollosrasse", west side of "St. Antonius" Church
12.4 Southbound fairway of the official Zurich Lake shipping
12.5 Northeast side of the "Sihlberg" Castle premises
12.6 Passageway at the "Gold-brunnenplatz" Tram Stop
12.7 Street corner "Norastrasse", south side of the municipal "Hardau" high-rise buildings
12.8 Forecourt of the main entrance to the Zurich University of the Arts ("Toni-Areal") under the bifurcation of a railway viaduct
12.9 Southeast corner of the "Waid" Municipal Hospital
12.10 Crossroads "Hofwiesen-" and "Wehntaler-Strasse"
12.11 West driveway of the Animal Hospital "Irchel"
12.12 Footpath to the north of the "Waldhüsli" cottage in the "Zürichberg" woods

INTERSECTION POINTS

Centre points

x.1 Centre point of the Circle of Space on the top of "Lindenhof" hill (430 metres a. s. l.)
x.2 Centre point of the Circle of Time at the "Mattensteg" footbridge, "Platzspitz" Park, confluence of the rivers "Limmat" and "Sihl"

Main Diagonal of the Circle of Space

x.3 Wood glade to the west of the "Zürichberg" broadcasting tower, intersection point of the diagonal and the Circle of Time
x.4 "Escherhöhe", hilltop of the "Zürichberg" (676 metres a. s. l.), intersection point of the diagonal and the Dodecagon
x.5 Small cupola at the entrance to the "Semper" Observatory, Swiss Federal Institute of Technology (ETH)
5.1/7.1 Entrance to the "St. Josef" Hotel, "Hirschengraben" No. 64/68
x.6 Movie screen of the "Filmpodium" Cinema, intersection point of the diagonal and the Heptagon
x.7 Restaurant "La Piazzetta", "Pelikanplatz", intersection point of the diagonal and the Circle of Space
x.8 Uncompleted concrete bridge, motorway access Zurich South, intersection point of the diagonal and the Circle of Time
x.9 Top of the "Uetliberg" mountain (869 metres a. s. l.)

Main Diagonal of the Circle of Time

x.10 Stone pyramid to the east of the "Kanzlei" school building, "Helvetiaplatz"

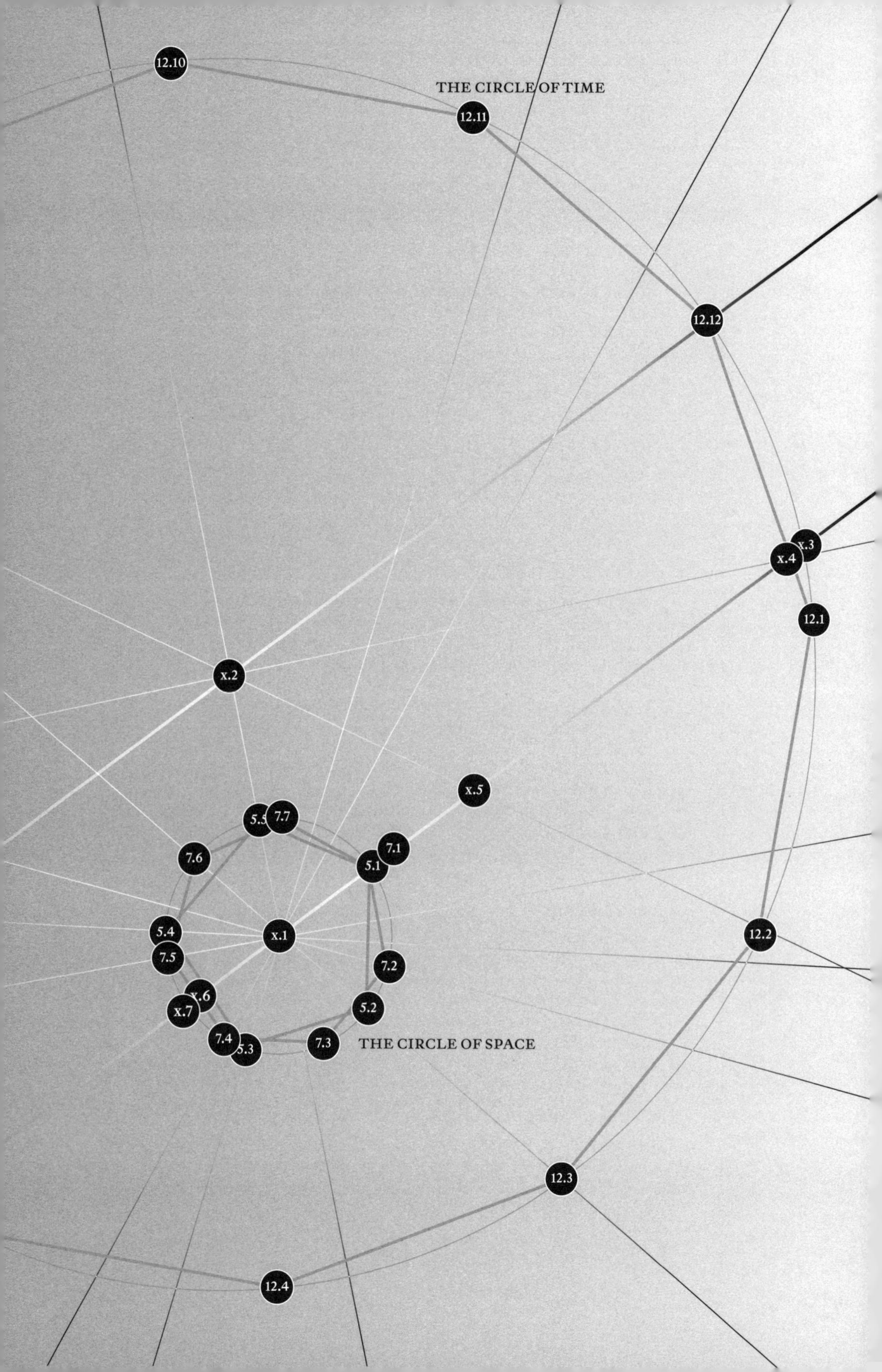
THE CIRCLE OF TIME
12.10
12.11
12.12
x.3
x.4
12.1
x.2
x.5
5.5
7.7
7.6
7.1
5.1
5.4
x.1
12.2
7.5
7.2
x.6
x.7
5.2
7.4
5.3
7.3
THE CIRCLE OF SPACE
12.3
12.4

hill and crosses intersection point 12.1 on the Circle of Time, he or she might encounter a dying French soldier by the name of Georges Jacques Camut, age 19, who has been seriously wounded right there in the First Battle of Zurich in June 1799. If the soldier is still capable of speaking, he might even address the walker in question. Likewise, if someone uses the public toilet at the "Paradeplatz" tram stop, which is intersection point 5.3 on the Circle of Space, the oink of a pig at the cattle market of the early 19th century might be plainly audible. Quite possibly, it might not only be audible but also clearly *understandable*. And when you stand still at the centre point x.1 of the Circle of Space on "Lindenhof" hill, you might find yourself on a small overgrown island in the midst of an expansive swampland in the 9th millennium before present or inside a simple wooden hut in the 29th century BC, possibly a stable, a workshop, or a family residence. You might smell the stench of small livestock or people who haven't had a proper wash in weeks. You might even meet one of the Celtic inhabitants in person. At the centre point x.2 of the Circle of Time in the "Platzspitz" Park, you might see a group of squalid and desperately ill junkies crouching around a small fire on the "Mattensteg" footbridge in the winter of 1987. A different stench would reach your nostrils, and if you would take a closer look, you might recognise ... –
THE CUBE: Okay, thank you. That's good enough.
LETO: As I said before, if the system works as planned, the space-time continuum will be permeable at all intersection points of the system at *any time* depending on the experiential capacity and the imaginative power of the respective persons present.
THE CUBE: How very interesting.
LETO: Yes, very interesting indeed. However, having experienced innumerable situations like these during my missions in the World of Facts, I might add that to some people it will be a horrifying experience rather than an interesting one. Most of the passers-by will get the impression that the spatial reality has become shaky, unstable, or undetermined for a moment, as if their environment was in a strange and inexplicable state of abeyance and openness to interpretation. But to some of these people, it will feel like the integrity of space itself is dissolving in some mysterious way. They will experience specific scenes and sceneries like those I have described before, and these people are very likely to conclude from these experiences that they are actually going insane. Anxiety attacks may occur. Some people might even end up needing psychiatric care or being locked away in mental institutions.
THE CUBE: Yes, I know. It is an inevitable side effect of the Experiment. However, the members of the Wise Council of the City Elders of Bhymbal and myself are profoundly convinced that it is an *acceptable* side effect in view of the expected results. And, after all, the people of Zurich were perfectly capable of coping with the system for millenniums before it ceased functioning some 300 solstices ago.
LETO: Yes, they *were*. But we have to take into account that, in the meantime, they have got used to quintessentially rationalised spatial environments. They have got used to the total absence of any manifestations of past and future spaces. Most of them are not even aware of the fact that space is *nothing but* an experiential entity. In short, I still think that we are taking an incalculable risk by exposing them to what you call the "Experiment". But then again, who am I to question the assessment of the Wise Council – or yours, for that matter. You really do believe that we will re-implement the original idea of space by reactivating the system, don't you?
THE CUBE: I am the Cube of Truth. I do not believe anything. I am

exclusively concerned with knowledge and information. And yes, I *know* that we *will* re-implement the original idea of space by performing the Experiment. You must not give rise to any doubts about your mission. You must remain focused on what is at stake here. We are acting in *self-defence* on behalf of the *whole* World of Ideas.
LETO: Of course, I am perfectly aware of that, I say so. It's just that I have spent so many ages in the World of Facts. Sometimes I almost forget that I am an idea myself.
THE CUBE: I understand. Furthermore, although you have reached your predetermined age of 25, you are still an *unfinished* idea. But you may rest assured that I have complete confidence in you, harken and you shall hear. Now, let me know whether you have any presumptions about why the system began to malfunction as from the late 19th century.
LETO: I can only offer long-shot guesses. The most obvious guess is that, as soon as the spatial growth of the City of Zurich passed the topographical limits of the original system, its breakdown was unavoidable.
THE CUBE: Sounds very reasonable indeed. Nevertheless, if you think of your knowledge about the history of the original system, there might be a few additional hypotheses.
LETO: By the time I first came to the Zurich area on my way west about 7'000 solstices ago, the inner circle, the Circle of Space, was already implemented. It was defined by the corner points of a heptagon that was aligned to the axis between the two hilltops to the east and to the west of the area, which represent intersection points x.4 and x.9 of the system. The original Celtic settlement was built on the much smaller "Lindenhof" hill in between that lies on the same axis and represents the centre point of the Circle of Space. According to the local sages and magicians, their ancestors had consecrated the seven corner points of the heptagon and thus implemented this circle as a mystic protective measure against destructive forces of all kinds. Of course, the geometry of the scheme was not based on measurement at the time. It was based on pure intuition. Which implies that the system possibly was in existence long before the Celts settled here.
THE CUBE: All the same, their intuition must have been very powerful given the fact that, to my knowledge, Zurich is one of just a few settlements in Europe that have outlasted more than three and a half millenniums of continuous history without ever being seriously damaged or destroyed by natural forces or hostile action.
LETO: Exactly. When I returned almost 1'500 years later as a scout and emissary of the Roman reconnaissance forces in Gaul, Zurich had become the wealthiest village of the region. The Circle of Space was still in effect. When the Romans learned of it, they added their own mystic protection scheme to the system: they inscribed a pentagon in the Circle, sharing the main axis with the Celts' heptagon. Fearing that this intervention might weaken the magic power of the system, the Celtic druids subsequently implemented a second and much bigger circle with its centre point on the north-south axis of the Roman pentagon. When they defined the "consecrated places" on this outer circle, these places turned out to be the corner points of a dodecagon. Thus, the Circle of Time came into existence. However, in the course of the ongoing romanising process of the following centuries, the system of the two Circles gradually passed into oblivion. Nevertheless, as we know, it remained fully effective for nearly two thousand years during which the City of Zurich grew along the axes, diagonals, and intersections of the underlying geometry without somebody knowing about it. The structure is still verifiable today if you take a walk around the inner city and its historical buildings.

THE CUBE: Yes, that's what we have known all along. So what are your conclusions?
LETO: Remarkably enough, each and every intersection point, including all corner points of the pentagon, the heptagon, and the dodecagon and all the intersection points of their diagonals, were publicly accessible to everybody up to the late 19th century. Most of them still are today. However, in the wake of the exponential growth of the city as from the mid-19th century, some of these points became private property. The first one was point 7.4 on the Circle of Space where politician and businessman Alfred Escher had the headquarters of his "Swiss Credit Institute" built in 1873.[6] The second one probably was point 12.5 on the Circle of Time: the northeast corner of the "Sihlberg" Castle premises where Albert Heinrich Hürlimann, owner of the biggest local beer brewery at the time, had his private residence built in 1897 by architect August Heinrich Müller. Against this background, my second long-shot guess is that the system of the two Circles only worked as long as all the intersection points were situated in spaces that were open to public access.

Die Schweizerische Kreditanstalt in Zürich im Jahre 1895.

Headquarters of the "Swiss Credit Institute" at the "Paradeplatz" and the Hürlimann beer brewery ("Sihlberg" Castle on the left) at the turn of the 20th century.

6 „Schweizerische Kreditanstalt" was the original name of today's *Credit Suisse* bank, founded by Johann Heinrich Alfred Escher in 1856. The Alfred-Escher-Memorial, designed by sculptor Richard Kissling, was raised in 1889 on the corner point 5.5 of the pentagon on the Circle of Space at the front entrance to Zurich Main Station.

THE CUBE: But you do not know for sure.
LETO: No, I don't. However, both guesses are consistent with what we know about the general history of the idea of space.
THE CUBE: Very well. Now tell me, what is the current state of the ALL ABOUT SPACE publication project?
LETO: Volume 2 was published in February this year under the title *HOUSE 1 Catalogue*. Although it contains almost all the facts and stories related to last year's HOUSE 1 project, the events of the 10th of August 2016, when the Code was implemented in the construction, are still broadly unknown in the World of Facts. The woman shot on the premises of the École Polytechnique Fédérale in Lausanne that night has been identified by now, but she cannot be linked to the HOUSE 1 project because the body was removed the very same night. In fact, all traces of the homicide were erased. It was only months later, after the renter of an apartment building in Geneva had pressed charges against one of his tenants who had ceased paying her rent, that the woman was identified as Helena T., age 36, of Romanian origin, a professional and rather notorious prostitute in upper-class circles around Lake Geneva. She is still reported missing, not least because Frank Teller, the only actual witness of her killing, is also reported missing and not a bit more likely to ever be found. However, he is still registered as a social welfare case in Zurich, age 47, father of two kids, a son and a daughter he has never seen again after the divorce from his wife following upon an investigation of a major corruption case at the renowned *Zurich Institute of Cryptography* in which he had been made the scapegoat and took the blame for the culprits on the executive floor. In summary, it can be stated that the readers of ALL ABOUT SPACE Volume 2 know about his involvement in many semi-legal activities, including the HOUSE 1 incidents, but most of them seem to believe that it is pure fiction.
THE CUBE: "Frank Teller, the Ever-Changing Spirit, and Ëlan-Tâsh, the Candid Freecloud Harlot, have been united in love and happiness for ever after in the World of Ideas, living unmolestedly as inhabitants No. 9 and No. 12 in HOUSE 1."
LETO: Yes, something like that, I suppose.
THE CUBE: Have there been any further interferences on the part of SYNTHESIS INTERNATIONAL and its agents?
LETO: No, there have not. There is hard evidence that SYNTHESIS INTERNATIONAL has kept HOUSE 2 under permanent observation, but they still seem to have no clue of what's going on.
THE CUBE: So there are no considerable conjectures or speculations in the World of Facts that the Code employed on HOUSE 1 could have been employed on HOUSE 2 as well?
LETO: No. Not to my knowledge.
THE CUBE: That is a real shame.
LETO: I beg your pardon? – I do not follow your meaning.
THE CUBE: I am very sorry about this, Leto of Cnossos, but it means that your mission is far from being completed.
LETO: You can't be serious! With all due respect, I have completed my mission to your full satisfaction!
THE CUBE: Yes, you have. And please accept my deepest thanks for that. But has it never occurred to you that it might be of vital significance to our cause that the public in the World of Facts *knows* about our intent to re-implement the original idea of space? – Has it never occurred to you that it does not make any sense to re-implement an original idea in the World of Facts if nobody knows what the idea is all *about*? – Moreover, *has* it ever occurred to you that, from *our* point of

view, the exposure of the Experiment might be the chief purpose of the ALL ABOUT SPACE publication series in the first place?
LETO: You know perfectly well that it has. But, if you'll forgive me bringing up a triviality like this, we would not be here discussing this if the Storyteller had not already thought it all through. After the publication of Volume 2, the editors have immediately started to make plans for Volume 3 of the series. The Storyteller has been charged with writing a script for a photographic novel about the HOUSE 2 project in Zurich. The plot of the script actually involves my latest mission down to the last detail, it involves the original idea of space, it involves the system of the Circles of Space and Time meticulously represented on historical maps of the City of Zurich, and, as far as I know, it even implies the *Map of the Human Mind*. In fact, the Storyteller is on the verge of revealing the whole idea of the Experiment. So, in my judgement, there is nothing left for me to do.
THE CUBE: Believe me, I do empathise, if only to a certain extent, with your displeasure at returning to the World of Facts in its present political and environmental state. I am perfectly aware that it must have been been rather torturous for an idea like yourself to dwell in those space-forgotten surroundings. However, to *my* knowledge, the realisation of the photographic novel for ALL ABOUT SPACE Volume 3 has failed for technical reasons. Hence, to *my* knowledge, the Storyteller is on the verge of abandoning the general idea of the plot and thinking of something completely new rather than revealing *our* way of looking at things. *We cannot let that happen*, harken and you shall hear.
LETO: Well, if this is the case, I do not have a choice, now do I? – So what exactly are your instructions?
THE CUBE: Isn't it obvious? – I want you to convince the Storyteller to stick to his original idea, even if you have to give him a few hints as to how he is supposed to do it. I want him to write a Brief History of the Idea of Space as a contribution to the next ALL ABOUT SPACE volume.
LETO: I'm afraid he will not like the idea. He thinks that he has already delivered the whole story of the idea of space in Volume 1, quote, *from the existential "disclosure of space" against the background of the primordial "horror vacui" up to the "dissolution of space" in an environment that is full of natural and artificial objects*, unquote. For all I know, storytellers do not deem it appropriate to tell the same story twice.
THE CUBE: In Volume 1, he told the story from a strictly individual and experiential perspective and thus remained short on explanations and conclusions from a more general or universal point of view. I want him to make up for that, and I herewith pronounce this assignment non-negotiable. Furthermore, I want you to convince the editors of the ALL ABOUT SPACE series to proceed with their investigation and disclosure of the very idea of space. I want you to convince them *by any means* necessary. Have I made myself clear?
LETO: Crystal clear, I say so. I'd better be off then, I suppose.

HOUSE 2 — COUNTER CITY:

A FORUM INSTALLATION IN ZURICH, COLLABORATIVELY BUILT BY EPFL'S ALICE LABORATORY

Situated at Toni-Areal in summer 2017, HOUSE 2 – COUNTER CITY is a public architectural installation in Zurich, Switzerland. The project is based on an experimental format for collaborative design and construction conceived by ALICE (Atelier de la Conception de l'Espace) at EPFL Lausanne.

Erected in less than 10 days, the project involved 200 first-year students, who prefabricated all the built elements of the installation in Lausanne and transported them across Switzerland in six shipping containers to Zurich, where they unloaded and re-assembled them as a full-size ephemeral structure. Devoted to social and cultural events, the public installation is not a homogenous architecture, but the result of various different contributions. Each offers an approach to spatial appropriation by many, in a dialogical process that questions the quality of public life in view of growing cities around the globe. In reference to Richard Sennett's recent book "*Together*", strong emphasis is given to the notion of collectivity and the negotiation of space of social difference. The project works as a pedagogical tool that materializes these premises in their physical and spatial parameters in a collective design and build process.

The previous year's experiment, HOUSE 1, was the configuration of an archetypal house, collectively built as an in-vitro condition on EPFL-campus in Lausanne – by students and for students. The rooms of HOUSE 1 were engaged primarily in forming a series of interior relations: HOUSE 2 has evolved from this premise, turning outwards, setting itself in relation to the city, and becoming a common place of activity and urban participation.

The site beneath the railway viaducts at Toni Areal has an expansion of about 50 by 100 meters and offers the opportunity to transform a mono-functional bicycle parking into a 5000 m2 Project Room for the Zurich Art University ZHdK. In an ephemeral act, HOUSE 2 engages this potential Project Room for confined time and shows the power of collective agency in building collective space. The project aggregates not only the expertise and contribution of 200 students – who worked with relentless energy thousands of hours on concepts, design and construction of HOUSE 2 – but also of the involved institutions, the Swiss railway company, the city of Zurich with its authorities, the fire and permit departments, the owners of the neighboring buildings, local associations, artists, professionals, scientists, and many more.

The project is aimed at revealing potentials of liminal spaces in urban and collective situations. In order to foster civic engagement, ALICE has jointly programmed a series of events for summer 2017 in close collaboration with the Zurich University of the Arts (ZHdK), including guided tours, theatre and music performances, a sound installation, symposiums, student critiques and exhibitions, or an open-air cinema. Alongside the programmed events, HOUSE 2 was declared as a playground by the children of the neighborhood. And it becomes also a skate park, a lounge area, a breakfast room, a lunch restaurant, a bar – programs showing the liminal potential of public space, if attributed with affordances. With these activities, HOUSE 2 expands the practice of collaboration into the public sphere of the city. As a forum installation, it provides a space for active exchange, debate and discussion involving an entire community.

FITNESS

I. A BRIEF HISTORY OF SPACE

In the beginning, there was one. All Oneness.
What once had been one was divided. The oneness ripped apart.
And the parts were scrutinised.
Disassembled. Then divided again.
And again.

And in the end, there were many. Manyfold scrutinised multitudes and multiplicities.
What occurred in between – or, as you like it: in the mean time – was:
Space.

And that is all there is to it.
The very idea of space.
The whole story as far as it can be told ...

Cuneiform inscription in two columns on clay tablet, Part 1, 2025 BC. Buried in the ruins of Ur, most probably the very first city human beings ever built, but never found in the course of archaeological excavations on site.

The Age of Magic Space

Matthias Michel

~45'000 BP[1]

The ice shields of the last glacial period in the current ice age cover the northern parts of Europe and Asia. The comparatively fertile tundra-like vegetation between the southern borders of these ice shields and the alpine glaciers nourishes big game like reindeers, wisents, wild horses, woolly rhinoceroses, and mammoths. This is the environment of the last Neanderthal populations that eventually give way to the so-called *Cro-Magnon humans*, a species of the Homo sapiens beginning to invade the European continent from Africa and Asia Minor. The Neanderthals become extinct long before the glacial period reaches its peak around 20'000 years BP (up to 15 degrees below today's average temperature).

~35'000 BP

Based on the archaeological findings of interred specimen (which are significantly rarer among Neanderthals), characteristic tools, and artefacts of the Upper Palaeolithic, most researchers assume that there are no significant physical, technical, or intelligible advantages of the Cro-Magnon humans over the Neanderthals. Furthermore, there is no evidence for warlike conflicts between the two species. It is presumed that a slight difference in fertility and the lack of resistance against pathogens imported by the Homo sapiens are the crucial factors for the extinction of the Neanderthals. On the other hand, the findings of cult objects suggest a considerable difference in social and cultural skills.

While the Neanderthals leave behind hardly hewn objects for body ornaments and designation or orientation purposes only (like decorative animal bones or waymarks) and cave paintings of comparably simple symbolic contour and surface drawings (e.g. in the La Pasiega cave in northern Spain), the Cro-Magnon people produce, under the very same outer living conditions, not only descriptive cave and rock paintings of remarkable complexity but also the oldest formally differentiated figurines ever found to date (mostly in France, northern Spain and western Germany).

Finds like the paintings in the El-Castillo (40'000 BP) or the Chauvet cave (32'000 BP), the "Hohlefels" (35'000 BP) and the "Willendorf" (25'000 BP) female figurines suggest the assumption that the Cro-Magnon cultures in western Europe possibly are, in respect to their social and cultural skills, the most advanced human population of the period.[2] Regardless of this conjecture, the climatic and environmental conditions are advantageous enough. Plenty of big gregarious animals provide large amounts of food, fur for clothing, bones for crafted tools, and skins for tents and fire pits. The biggame hunting techniques and the prediction of the herds' movements require considerable capabilities of communication and social organisation in big clans cohabiting in short-term tent settlements and extensive cave systems according to a seminomadic lifestyle. Which, in turn, calls for sufficiently differentiated linguistic expression, notional abstraction,

1 Age determinations of prehistoric facts and events are based on radiocarbon dating and therefore indicated as BP ("before present"). Radiocarbon dating is reliably applicable for archaeological finds that date back to 50'000 years or less, which is the time that the first entry in this chronicle refers to. Of course, the interpretation of the earliest prehistoric finds is subject to ongoing archaeological research.

2 Rock paintings and figurines from that period have also been found on the African continent and in the Near East, of course, but they are far from the differentiated features of the Cro-Magnon finds. In fact, in many cases the archaeologists are not even sure whether they have to be interpreted as artefacts at all.

and figurative thinking or, for that matter, "imagination". These capabilities are perfectly represented in the known cultural artefacts.

- Chauvet cave painting of horses, aurochs, and woolly rhinoceroses, Ardèche/France.
- Female figurines "Venus vom Hohlefels" (mammoth ivory, oldest figurine found to date in Schelklingen, Swabia) and "Willendorf Venus" (painted stone, found in Willendorf, Lower Austria), both obviously designed to depict physical aspects of female fertility.

~18'000 BP

The global temperature has begun to rise rapidly after the peak of the glacial period. Due to the withdrawal of the ice shields, the European continent is rapidly overgrown by forests and thick wood. Starved of nourishment and mobility, the big gregarious animals draw back to the north or become extinct, making way for red deer and small game. This environmental change, attached to a severe shortage of sustenance, is of drastic consequences for the European hunting cultures. Many of them follow the reindeer and wisent herds towards Scandinavia, considerably decreasing in number along the way. The social structures of those remaining disintegrate. The big clans fall apart into smaller competing and increasingly scattering ones. Temporarily, the cultural heritages and social skills atrophy, and the population numbers decrease in the so-called *Lower Magdalenian cultures* all over Europe. At the same time, tools and weapons are adjusted to the new living conditions (esp. sharpened blades and impact tools).

~15'000 BP

In northern Africa, the Near and the Far East, the climate warming causes the expansion of deserts and dry steppes, which leads to a similar expelling of bigger gregarious animals from the regions populated by humans. In consequence, the hunter-gatherer cultures begin to expand their nutrition by wild rice in China and by wild cereal grains in the Fertile Crescent between Palestine and Mesopotamia.

The human population of the American continent by hunters invading from Eastern Asia has begun and continues until around 11'500 BP when the ice shields have withdrawn to the arctic regions, causing a rise of the sea level by up to 130 metres and the flooding of the Bering Strait, the only land bridge between the two continents.

Holocene

NEOLITHIC PERIOD

~15'000 BP

The Neolithic Period (the "late" or "new stone age") is roughly defined by the development of *sedentary cultures* and, subsequently, the construction of permanent buildings. Furthermore, it implicates early methods of cereal cropping, agriculture, and domestication of animals, accompanied by the use of refined tools and weapons based on sharpened stone blades and, at later stages, of pottery and draught animals.

In most of the cultural areas, the earliest archaeological finds of Neolithic architecture are sanctuaries and temples; the respective dwelling houses usually date from a later time. Probably the oldest of these sacral buildings found to date is the approximately 11'500-year-old temple area of Göbekli Tepe in southeast Turkey. At that time, the first angular multiple-room buildings occur in southern Mesopotamia.

Correspondingly, the earliest Neolithic cultures develop in Asia Minor and the Fertile Crescent, spreading from there to Egypt and the Balkan region until around 9'000 BP, to Central and Mediterranean Europe until around 7'000 BP, to Western Europe and Britannia until around 6'000 BP. In China, the Neolithic Period most probably begins almost at the same time but develops considerably slower, spreading from the middle reaches of the Yangtze Kiang. In Central America, the hunter-gatherer cultures gradually turn into farming cultures as from 7'000 BP.

In general, these regional "Neolithic revolutions" happen in very different ways and stretches of time, mainly depending on the environmental factors of the respective regions. For example, sedentariness, building activity, and urban cultures usually proceed slower in arid or mountainous regions like Palestine or the Caucasus area where livestock breeding provides a more efficient sustenance than agriculture. On the other hand, the general human lactose intolerance is overcome much earlier in these regions, which again furthers the dispersion of dairy production.

In consequence, the Neolithic Period also ends at different times in different parts of the world according to when metal tools become widespread and initiate the respective Copper, Bronze or Iron Ages as from 5'500 up to 2'500 BP.

~9'000 BP

The island of *Crete* is populated by early Neolithic cultures immigrating from Asia Minor. Several agricultural wattle and daub villages are built along the coasts. About two thousand years later, Crete is the leading production site of advanced pottery and cloth making in the eastern Mediterranean region. Cnossos on the northern coast has become the major settlement of the island, approaching the number of a thousand inhabitants living in flat-roofed mud brick houses.

~7'000 BP

During the warmest stage of the current interglacial period, the coast of the Persian Gulf reaches more than 200 kilometres further northeast than today.

Around the mouth of the Euphrates (near today's city Nasiriya), the Sumerians establish the first *cities* and city-states in history (Ur, Eridu a. o.). Most probably, these cities are ruled by religio-cultural elites. Until around 5'000 BP, when the earliest Chaldean kingdoms emerge (e.g. the mythical dynasty of the first monocrats Nimrod and Lig-Bagas aka Uruk aka Gilgamesh), the unity of religious and political authority is abandoned. The building activity along the Euphrates significantly intensifies, including extensive irrigation systems, burial site constructions with thousands of royal and citizens' tombs, huge multi-level platforms on which temple precincts are built ("Ziggurats", referred to in the legends about the Tower of Babel), and both socially and culturally differentiated city districts for tens of thousands of inhabitants.

• So-called "Standard of Ur", Sumerian mosaic, double-sided (the "Peace Side" and the "War Side"), around 46th century BP. Made of shell, red limestone, lapis lazuli and bitumen, framed in wood, 21.59 x 9.53 cm. Found in tomb No. 779 in Ur.

• Ruin of the Great Ziggurat "Etemennigur" of Ur, built by King Ur-Nammu and his son Šulgi in the 41rd century BP in honour of the moon god Nanna/Sin during the Third Dynasty of Ur. Massive step pyramid, 64 x 45 m, original height unknown, mud brick walls of 2.5 m thickness.

~ 6'500 BP

The earliest *wetland settlements* in the lake-land areas of central Europe emerge.

The oldest pile-dwelling constructions in the Zurich lake basin date to around 6'400 BP and are associated with the so-called "Egolzwiler" culture. The settlements are situated up to 500 meters away from today's waterfront (due to the significantly lower water level at the time). Inhabited by 100 to 300 people each, they are constructed in very strict assemblies and compartments. However, they usually are abandoned after a relatively short period of time and rebuilt elsewhere because of overexploitation and pollution of the environmental resources.

The earliest archaeological finds of ashore population and constructions have been discovered on top of the "Uetliberg", a prominent mountain at today's western city boundary. They are dated back to around 6'000 BP and believed to originate from small and unfortified short-term settlements.

• Renderings of pile-dwelling settlements in the Zurich lake basin (www.stadt-zuerich.ch/hbd/archaeologie)

~ 5'500 BP

The Sumerian *cuneiform writing* has fully developed and is rapidly standardised among the peoples of the Fertile Crescent. Shortly thereafter, the Egyptian hieroglyphs emerge. The initially pictographic scripts (approximately 900 characters in Sumer, approx. 700 in Egypt) are gradually extended to complex systems of ideograms, phonograms, and determiners. Approximately 3'000 years later, they are successively replaced by the Phoenician consonantal writing and finally by the Ancient Greek alphabet and language.

The Chinese script occurs as from 3'500 BP.

The earliest known author whose name is historically documented is *Enheduanna*, daughter of king Sargon of Akkad who was the first autocrat to control the whole Mesopotamian territory from the Persian Gulf to the Mediterranean Sea in the 43rd century BP. Enheduanna is the High Priestess of the goddess "Inanna" and the moon god "Nanna" in Ur, which have already become identified with the Akkadian deities "Ishtar" and "Sin" at the time. Enheduanna's residence is the famous Ziggurat of Ur, chief seat of the moon god's worship in the region. Amongst the literary works definitely ascribed to her are a collection of Sumerian Temple Hymns and many personal poetic devotions to Inanna/Ishtar.

~ 5'000 BP

On the island of Crete, the *Minoan culture* is on the rise, successively becoming the major commercial and cultural power of the Mediterranean. The population has increased dramatically. The "Great House" of Cnossos, an early palace complex built of stone blocks for public, commercial, and governmental use, is gradually converted and extended into the monumental "Palace of Cnossos" (150 metres across, some 20'000 square meters at its final stage). The city disposes of two fortified harbours in the bay of Heraklion, establishing the first pre-Phoenician "thalassocracy" ("sea power", gr. θαλασσα f. for „sea“ and κρατειν for "rule" or "reign").

~ 4'600 BP

In the *4th Dynasty of Egypt's Old Kingdom*, the Necropolis of Giza is built on the western bank of the Nile between Heliopolis, the City of Gods, and Memphis, the City of Kings. The Cheops pyramid, the oldest of the sepulchral monuments on the rocky plateau and the biggest of all pyramids in Egypt, is 146.6 metres high, features a maximum side length of 230.3 metres and an inclination of 51.5 degrees (original measurements). Pyramids of this size and construction type are built only during a short period of time in the 4th and 5th dynasty, and many of them remain unfinished. Before and after, they are much smaller and mostly built as stepped pyramids.

At this time, the city-states of Upper and Lower Egypt are united in a strictly regimented empire under the control of the king and his viziers. Thus, Egypt has become the second and increasingly competing political and military power of the Near East apart from the kingdoms of Mesopotamia.

Papyrus, a thick, paper-like material produced from the pith of the Cyperus papyrus plant and written on with paintbrushes, occurs around that time. However, the technique does not gain currency outside Egypt until it is adopted in Greece 2'000 years later.

~ 4'500 BP

The relative datings of the *Great Flood* range from 3246 BC in the Septuagint to 2348 BC in the scriptures of the Hebrew Tanakh. Additionally, there are many theories in historical geology as to how, where, when, and why an exceptional flood disaster of historical and trans-regional repercussions could have occurred around the time or whether there have been several of them. However, the "Great Flood" is concurringly mentioned in most cultural heritages in the Near and the Middle East, though all of them are unreliable in their ancestry-related age determination.

• Part of clay tablet Nr. 11 (*Story of the Great Flood*) of 12 tablets containing the entire Gilgamesh myth. Found among the almost 30'000 clay tablets of King Ashurbanipal's library in Nineveh (Mosul), established in the 27th century BP. The library is the biggest known archive of ancient Sumerian, Babylonian, and Assyrian cuneiform writings.

~ 4'000 BP

Legend has it that Terah of Ur, descendant of Noah, his nephew Lot and his son *Abram* leave their home in Chaldea, and move to the city of Harran in the northwest of Mesopotamia. After Terah's death, Abram and his wife Sarai set out for Canaan (Phoenicia) at God's behest, and their adventures are many. They get as far as Egypt and back again, and Abram becomes the progenitor of both the Judeo-Christian and the Islamic founding fathers. In the former tradition his name is recorded as Abraham, in the latter as Ibrahim.

Ibram's Awakening

Inside the Ziggurat of Ur, 2025 BC

About short before SEBU hour is when this young man enters the Sacred Dark whilst makes intimidated gapes at shadows which INANNA's dancing flames cast in by of walls of sanctified stone. Under his cloth all over, he is slender and of small stature, his face not yet manly but full of gleam and grace and wits to look at. ANUNITU, current EN of the House of Great Light, is invisible whilst stands in dark corner on opposite side of fires. Further whiles go by before she steps within sight beside the High Altar: whiles of anxiety to this young man, whiles of contemplation to ANUNITU.

"Allowance is with me when I stands here before you, most revered EN of the House of Great Light, not only low allowance of UMMUM who is giver of birth to me but also high allowance of holy NANNA looking upon the City by night."

Not before he is say so, he dares look up at the EN's face and speak his name IBRAM, given to him by his father TERAK upon approval by the Moon God. That is when the EN conceives this young man is not alike other young men of dignity and honour who stand before the High Priestess every day to get their gleam to turn into shine. In knowing of who he is and in knowing of what is to come by, ANUNITU makes good MUŠ but is yet not ready to speak.

Young man's gazes drop shamefully, away from the EN's shining and splendid of winged cloth. Not before many short whiles after, in whisper rather than in voice, says he his wish is to wake his mind to be come by light of wisdom and guidance not only of the Gods but also of his own will. Then he kneels byfoot of steps which lead up to the High Altar where the EN stands still before deigns to speak: "ŠAMAT and ENKIDU is what you come here for then, to turn your gleam into shine, stories of mind into stories of body and soul. Yet is it wisdom which you wishes for or is it knowledge?"

And thus young man answers, much appreciated by ANUNITU inside out: "Wisdom of KIŠAR under AN is which I wishes for, not knowledge of things. Knowledge of things divides paths into many, wisdom unites them upon the Path of the Gods which is to be the same as path of man's own will, least is which is told by my mother."

"Do know this, young man. When you come by to see me you shall come by to perform, I say so. When I come by to open my floodgate you shall come by to please me or shall never come by to have your own will before the Eyes of INANNA, I say so. When you come by to please me I shall come by to see you inside out and outside in, I say so. Shame and disgrace shall be with you and in by of you for evermore if you come by to fail, I say so."

Thus young man receives grave words outside in spoken by the EN herself.

Says he firmly now: "I shall not come by to fail, I say so."

"Then I say do stand before the High Altar of Wisdom, do reveal your weakness, and be addressed by the Name of IBRAM!"

IBRAM gets up from sanctified stone floor, takes his cloth all over away from around his shoulder and rump to stand bare before the EN who eyes him up to see he is yet without his own will. Two pairs of eyes meet entwined before ANUNITU speaks the Magic Words which allow no return:

"See me!"

Ibram does as told whilst the EN folds her winged cloth into loincloth around her rump to reveal bloom and beauty of her KISIKIL's beads. Ibram ascends steps towards altar in persisting weakness and without man's own will, yet unashamed.

"Touch me!"

IBRAM does as told, hands wavering as they approach her beads, no more no less than Kisikil's beads to touch and to look at indeed. Skin games begin all about beads and buttocks whilst Anunitu awakens IBRAM's flaccid ĜEŠ with fingertips and squeezes of her left, followed by NASAQU and date-juice-sweet engulfment, and further whiles go by before loincloth which is be the EN's winged cloth falls to ground, revealing bloom and beauty as-a-whole to look at.

"ŠAMAT's tongue and furrow underneath moist barley tempt ENKIDU away from wilderness, little by little turning him from savage into LU, his gleam into shine, his indifference into man's own will before he is ready to enter the City Walls and be come by light of wisdom," speaks ANUNITU amidst date-juice-sweet tongue games and lies down on back across altar, all limbs all spread.

Says Ibram: "ENKIDU follows ŠAMAT willingly." Yet not before shortest of whiles ANUNITU speaks:

"Taste me!"

IBRAM does as told, while feasts on sweet date-juice flooding from within the EN's furrow as if to drown him, making tongue games all about, thus caressing the EN's bud which now is revealed to him amidst moist barley.

Yet in shortest of whiles his head is pulled up when manyfold visions and holy signs begin travel in by of ANUNITU's mind.

"*You shall place your right hand in my floodgate*
Whilst your left hand rests upon my head
Bringing your mouth close to my mouth
Whilst you take my lips in your mouth
Thus you shall take an oath for me
This being the Oath of Women
Daughters of Inanna's own pleasure."

Not before tongue games all about pair of mouths she speaks whilst bending over across altar as sacred rituals of old recorded by ENHEDUANNA herself demand it:

"Please me!"

Ibram does as told, his ĜEŠ is be come turned into form of man's own will for whiles now, making shape of wedge, willing and able to perform upon the EN whose floodgate is wide open. Whilst he performs entwined with ANUNITU bent over and presenting front alike, dancing flames of sanctified fires dance within and without pair of them, and manyfold visions and holy signs continue travel in by of ANUNITU's mind revealing IBRAM's inside out and outside in to her. Yet it is more which is revealed to her. It is more than ever is be revealed to her before which now arouses anger-shock and wonder-shock and wisdom-shock inside out and outside in and in by of her alike. Not before says IBRAM he wishes for to be set free, all anger-shock and wonder-shock climax in no more no less than one fire-lit sign which never seen or known or inscribed before and never seen or scribed ever after:

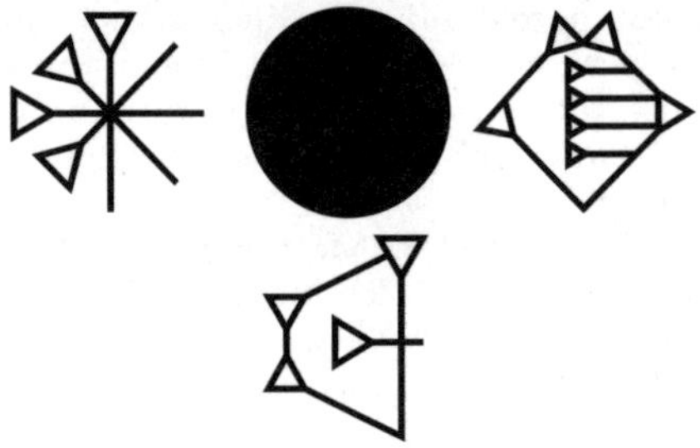

The Never-known-before Sign, scribed in form of triangle instead of row, bearing the Never-known-before Word of meaning, is burned and recognised in the EN's mind as AN-KI-ŠAR-BA which speaks as:

Heaven-and-earth-as-a-whole shall come by to be divided.

Date-juice-sweet wisdom-shock conjoins with unfathomably bitter horror-shock whilst she, moaning with delight and fear alike, allows IBRAM's ĜĔ-DU to be come by perfect UŠ and to flood her womb as sacred rituals of old demand it now that he fails not to please her body and soul alike.

With earthquake IBRAM is put to silence.

Thus ANUNITU speaks to this young man before he is dismissed be come man whose gleam is turned into shine, guided not only by the God's but also by his own will, light of wisdom shed upon his paths: "Whilst seeing you inside out and outside in amidst INANNA's own pleasure, NANNA looking upon the City by night reveals to me what is to come by. You shall come by to be called by the Name of IBRAM, the wise Moon Wanderer, faring far to the North and to the West and to the South and back again. And whilst you fare you shall come by to spread the Wisdom of ŠAMAT and ENKIDU in strange and twisted ways, speaking of them in foreign tongues so that men and women shall walk in by of paths of completely different wisdoms: wisdoms to favour mind above soul, wisdoms to glory of male and to humiliation of female. Thus, heaven-and-earth-as-a-whole shall come by to be divided whereas all the Gods shall come by to be as one father God. Whether I am to rejoice or weep over this, I know not. Whether I am to make good MUŠ or bad MUŠ in view of you, I know not. All I know is I shall not revolt against the Will of the Moon God himself, I say so."

IBRAM makes terrified gapes at the EN yet remains silent. For shortest of whiles only, fires expire, INANNA's dancing flames casting no more shadows in by of walls. Frightening darkness is all around whilst this young man leaves sanctuary of the High Altar of Wisdom, treasure of the EUNIR, the High-Rising House of Great Light in UR.

Thus it happens at the Ravening Dog ZIBANITUM's while of year under rule of King ŠULGI, son of King of the Scribes of Justice UR-NAMMU who is the builder of the EUNIR dedicated to the Moon God. In night which follows, ANUNITU, High Priestess EN of the High-Rising House of Great Light, is seen leaving the City to the West, wrapped up in many cloths all over, speaking no word to no one, never to come by to return to UR ever after, and no man nor woman ever to come by to know of her faring.

Not before day breaks, in the Sanctuary of INANNA's High Altar one clay tablet is come by to be found, inscribed in two columns by ANUNITU herself in words of wisdom which speak:

The Beginning is one. All Oneness.
What is be one is later come by to be divided. Oneness ripped apart.
And parts come by to be known. Disassembled. Then come by to be divided again.
And again.

And the End is many. Manyfold known multitudes and multiplicities.
What occurs in between–or, as you wish for: in meanwhiles–is:
Heaven-and-earth-as-a-whole-divided.

And that is all.
The very Idea of Heaven-and-earth-as-a-whole-divided.
The whole story no more no less than it can be told.

Unless ...
... manyfold known multitudes and multiplicities beget
the Never-known-before Beginning.
Parts and bits and pieces put together again, reassembled, reconnected, returned into whole.

When whiles come by to be so ... then the End is come by to be everything.
Heaven-and-earth-as-a-whole-divided and
All-whiles-as-a-whole-in-all returned into one, both lessons learned.
The complete history no more no less than it can be comprehended.

7 COSMOGONIES

BEGINNINGS

1 

In the beginning, there is shapeless chaos, slowly but constantly coalescing into a primal form of harmony and perfection for two times nine thousand years: an upright cosmic egg. Inside the egg, a giant dwarf by the name of P'an-ku is growing ten feet taller every day, forcing asunder the light and ethereal elements from the solid and heavy ones and thus segregating the upper from the lower hemisphere: Yin and Yang, the light and the dark, the north and the south, the male and the female. This process continues for another two times nine thousand years until the skies above, rotating around the polar star, are finally separated from the steady and motionless earth below.

P'an-ku's work is done and he dies peacefully. Out of the parts of his body the world is formed. His left eye becomes the Sun, his right eye becomes the Moon. His head turns into the peaks of the mountains, his muscles into the fertile land. His fur and hair grow into the bushes and forests, and the fleas that dwell in it turn into the multitude of animals. His bones become minerals, the marrow solidifies to sacred diamonds. His last breath causes the winds and clouds, his sweat becomes the rain, and his voice resounds for evermore as the rolling thunder.

In this manner the world has come into existence: a square island, bathed by the oceans, sheltered by the skies. And within this world, there shall be everlasting balance of conflicting forces and contradicting principles. And in the centre of it all: the mighty Emperor, guarantor of the equilibrium, holding sway over the Middle Kingdom.

(China. Recorded for the first time by Xu Zheng during the Three Kingdoms period, AD 194.)

2 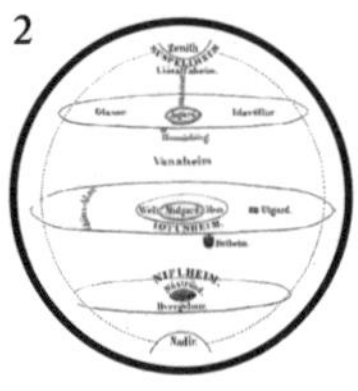

In the beginning, there is the bottomless abyss Ginnungagap between Muspelheim, the volcanic realm of heat and fire, and Niflheim, the misty realm of ice and arctic water. Deep down in the abyss, where the sparks and embers of Muspelheim mingle with the cold floods and frosty rimes of Niflheim, the steam of creation evaporates and life emerges: the raging giant by the name of Ymir from whose armpits the first man and the first woman are born, and a forbearing cow by the name of Audumla who licks the blocks of salty ice until the gods are released from their frozen imprisonment. Among them is Búri, the grandfather of the three brothers Odin, Vili and Vé who slay Ymir and all of his giant kin except for Bergelmir and his wife who escape from drowning in Ymir's blood using a hollow tree trunk as a boat.

From Ymir's bodily remains, Odin and his brothers create a third realm in the midst of the abyss between Niflheim and Muspelheim. From Ymir's flesh, they make the earth. From his blood, they make the seas and lakes. From his bones: the mountains. From his teeth:

the rocks. And from his skull they make the sheltering sky. This is how Midgard is created, the home of men. Amidst of it, there grows the mighty ash tree Yggdrasil. Underneath its branches and twigs, the gods hold their assizes whenever they deem them necessary.

Around Midgard, Odin and his brothers have built walls from Ymir's eyebrows to protect the world of men and women from the rage of the surviving giants who, thirsting for revenge, attack it ever since with ice and snow and storms and floods. And one day in the distant future, Midgard will be destroyed completely by these overwhelming forces, and the age of men will come to an end.

(Scandinavia. Recorded for the first time in *The Prose Edda* by Snorri Sturluson, Norway AD 1220, and *The Poetic Edda* Collection of Songs, Iceland AD 1270.)

3

In the beginning, there are four creations. The first one gives rise to the age of water. Vast floods deluge the Earth and all living creatures turn into fish and aquatic animals. The second creation gives rise to the age of the Jaguar. The sun is obscured, and the voracious Jaguar preys upon men and animals in the dark. The third creation gives rise to the age of fire. Volcanoes erupt, and showers of flames and ashes fall from the skies until the fourth creation gives rise to the age of winds when mighty storms devastate the face of the Earth. Eventually, the four ages merge into one: the age of motion, in which all forces of nature take turns at ruling the everchanging world that we have come to know.

Ever since, this world is in a transition state of incessant conversions. No thing ever stays the same. All things and events are one of a kind, commensurable in numbers only. Numbers never change. Therefore, those who set out to make sense of the world should get acquainted with the mysteries of the numbers and the meaningful signs so that the courses of nature may be revealed to them.

(Mayan cultures, Central America. Synthesised out of the few Mayan scriptures available.)

Pages 55–59 and page 74 of the so-called "Dresden Codex", an original Mayan scripture written around AD 1200–1250, most probably for priestly purposes only. The fanfold document of 39 double sided pages entered into possession of the "Kurfürstliche Bibliothek" of Dresden in 1735.
The pages on the left show calculations of solar and lunar eclipses, the pages in the middle show multiplication tables of the number 78, and the page on the far right addresses the above-mentioned "age of water".

4

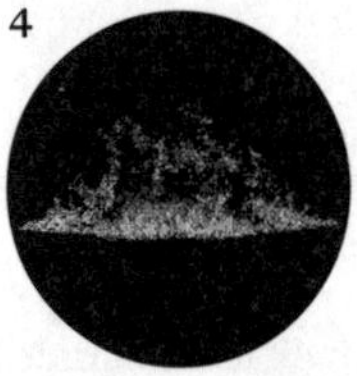

In the beginning, there are two universal principles: Chaos and Creation. The chaotic principle, referred to as Ahriman, represents the forces of destruction and decay. The creative principle represents the forces of being (*ahura*, m.) and mental reflection (*mazda*, f.), which are the attributes of the one supreme god Ahura Mazda. Both principles are immanent in humankind, meaning that the universe is both within and without human beings and that human beings are both the origin and the destiny of the universe. This fundamental dualism yields and explains all things and movements and contradictory events in the world, all histories and developments that infinitely renew themselves over and over again.

Hence, the assignment and responsibility of individuals, based on the intermediate position of their conscious minds, is to physically *experience* and mentally *reflect on* the world, to understand and to keep the balance of conflicting forces in consistence with their understanding, and, finally, to bring them closer to perfection in their thoughts, actions, and decisions. According to how this task is accomplished, the immortal soul joins the forces of chaos or those of creation.

(Persian Zoroastrianism. Recorded in the teachings of Zarathustra whose biographical data are unknown. Based on the dissemination of Zoroastrian ideas, which are also related to ancient Indian Brahmanism, he is believed to have lived at the end of the 2nd millennium BC.)

5

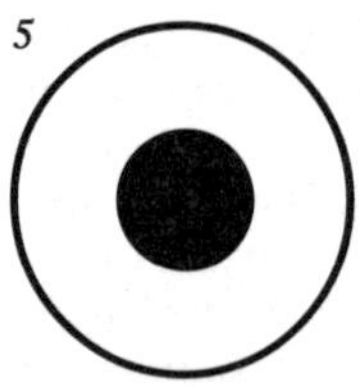

In the beginning, there is the principle of cause and effect. If the world is subject to causality, if it is not only explainable but also researchable and certifiable on the basis of this principle, then it must entirely consist of elementary particles, which can neither evolve nor vanish. They may be diverse in form and size but are not divisible into smaller entities. That is why we call them atoms (gr. ατομοσ for "indivisible"). They randomly move in an empty space, colliding and occasionally concentrating to a complex form that is perceptible by the senses. Thus, the materiality of the world we inhabit is solely due to mechanical effects of moving atoms, and the same goes for the commotions of minds and souls.

(Ancient Greece, based on the theorems of Leucippus and Democritus of Abdera, 5th century BC. "It is only an illusion that things are coloured or sweet or bitter. Actually, there are only atoms in empty space.")

6

In the beginning, there is the mass-energy equivalence. It means that nothing in this universe moves faster than massless light waves. And there is the proportional relativity of space and time. It means that neither time nor space can be conceived in absolute dimensions. They form the indivisible entity of space-time. In space-time, each and every event has its own event horizon of past and future, which inevitably affects each and every other event horizon related to it in any way. Thus, the universe must be thought of as a fundamentally relative and infinitely flexible continuum of space-time-anomalies.

(Based on the theory of relativity, developed by Hendrik Antoon Lorentz, Henri Poincaré, Albert Einstein a. o., AD 1889–1916.)

7

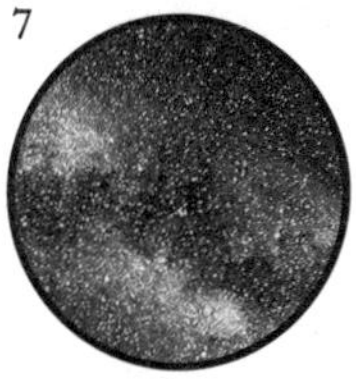

In the beginning, there is entirety: the whole universe is reduced to one point of immeasurable density and infinite concentration of energy. For reasons unknown, an original singularity occurs: the concentration decreases, the density is reduced, a process of expansion sets in. Time, space, and matter emerge at once. There is no consistent theory that can describe or explain this process further back than 10^{-43} seconds after the fact (the so-called Planck epoch). After approximately 10^{-11} seconds, temperature and density are reduced to measurable values. After 10^{-6} seconds, the formation of elementary entities like protons and neutrons is assumed to be possible, which leads to physical events that are describable according to existing theories.

From that moment on, there are three possible scenarios. The first implies that, at one critical point, the gravitation forces in the universe become higher than the expansion forces, and the process is reversed. The universe recollapses. The second implies that there is not enough gravitational energy to eventually stop the expansion, which therefore goes on forever. The third scenario implies that, in the end, the expansive and the gravitational forces exactly neutralise each other. A recollapse of the universe is impossible, and the expansion decelerates ad infinitum. The three scenarios have in common that there is no reasonably conceivable standstill. And odds are that they all have become theoretically obsolete by the time you happen to read this.

(Based on the works of Max Planck, Alexander Alexandrovich Friedmann, a. o., AD 1899, 1922 ff.)

Cosmogonies are theories about the origin and the nature of space. Presented in the form of myths, they represent the intuitive and/or rational awareness that there is no way to conceive of something objectively if not from an Archimedean point of view: from a total and perfect outside perspective. In other words, cosmogonies usually represent the narrators' awareness that being "in" space (and "in" time, for that matter) is the human condition, which cannot be transcended by any means. Thus, they explicitly accept that there are limits to the consideration of categories like the "origin" or the very "nature" of space beyond which space turns from an object of investigation into a mere mystery. These limits may be deemed extendable according to the knowledge, the language, the cultural, social, and technical skills available to those who set up the theories at a certain time in history. But in the end, the mystery always remains.

In consequence, mythical theories cannot be set apart from scientific ones by criteria of content, comprehensiveness, logic, or verifiability because, given the mentioned conditions at a given place and a given time, they are as reasonable and as close to a verifiable (though not falsifiable) "truth" as a theory possibly can be. The only distinctive feature is the narrative form. Scientific theories of the modern era avoid it because it inevitably implies the mystery, which is usually not their objective. However, as soon as we translate them into a narrative form (i.e. into a cosmogony, actually), for instance by applying the opening sentence "In the beginning, there is ...", the mysteries beyond the limits of the human condition – or, if you prefer, beyond the Archimedean point – almost instantly become apparent, making them appear unmistakeably mythical. And mysteries they are indeed, even to those who have advanced mathematical languages or high-tech telescopes and particle accelerators at their disposal.

Quite evidently, a myth (as well as any other theory) can eventually turn out to be "false" under altered living, thinking, or experiential conditions. But it can never be "untrue", because it implies these conditions at all times. Therefore, the seven examples retold above, originating from different cultures at different periods in their respective history, have been assorted in a conceptual rather than a strictly chronological order. This being said, we can ease past the discussion of similarities and common features because they are obvious enough. However, in view of what follows it may be worth noticing that in all seven examples space principally emerges as the result of a *division* or *partition* of a previous entity in one way or another.

The first three cosmogonies, reaching back to prehistoric times in the respective regions but being recorded and reinterpreted centuries or millenniums later, refer to a spatial environment that is almost completely beyond the control of human beings. Since there is no comprehensive notion of "nature" yet, the understanding and interpretation of environmental forces at work is restricted to their immediate effects upon human living conditions. Hence, they are described as acts of gods and mystical entities or creatures "acting" upon humans and their environments at *their own will* and according to their hardly fathomable – i.e. "mystical" – interests and purposes. Under these conditions, a cosmogony must explain how these gods and sort of "supernatural" entities have come into existence and how they relate to each other. Only then, based on that knowledge, their mystical interests and purposes become sufficiently transparent and predictable. Furthermore, these explanations have to be consistent with the immediate perceptions and experiences of space. And, as is plain to see, they actually are.

Cosmogonies No. 4 and No. 5 originate from early historic times. However, even though they can be ascribed to specific historical initiators and even though they are not "originally" narrative anymore, they are still mythical in so far that they are still meant to be subject to perpetual re-telling, re-formulation, and re-argumentation in different versions according to different requirements of verifiability in different contexts. In other words, there still is no such thing as an original or a definitive version of them. The crucial conception that makes these "later" cosmogonies so obviously different from the previous ones is that they draw on the idea of "nature". We will never know how exactly this revolutionary idea has been developed, whether from experience or rather from abstract thought (or both). What we do know though is that it is related to the progressive application of technical tools and skills that allows an increasingly forcible and significantly more efficient impact upon spatial environments. At a certain stage in this progress, it must become obvious that the forces at work within these environments are "incapable" of "reacting" or "defending themselves" against the forces of human beings amplified by technical equipment and prostheses, along with division of labour and social differentiation. The gods and spirits, the mystical and magical agents in this world prove themselves to be weaker and more vulnerable than initially thought. Eventually, they appear to be almost powerless and possibly inexistent.

At this stage in cultural history, the idea of "nature" as opposed to the idea of human "culture" is inevitable, cultural life being essentially associated with crafts and technical arts in ancient times (gr. τεχνη, f.). The idea is expressed in spatial concepts treating "nature" as the object and human beings as the observing and/or acting subjects henceforth attributed with control over spatial phenomena and events that goes far beyond magical conjurations, incantations, and sacrifices. In other words, the human attitude towards space turns from animistic and/or symbolic to *aesthetic*, from magic to *poetic*, "poetry" understood in its original sense (gr. ποιησισ, f.) embracing all kinds of creative thought, action, and design. Remarkably enough, this transition (that might be defined as the "Promethean turn" in reference to its most precise and comprehensive formulation at the time) engenders not only protoscientific concepts like the atomic theory in Cosmogony No. 5 but also epistemological theories that fully integrate human intelligence into the concept of nature, most explicitly in the early teachings of Zoroastrianism (Cosmogony No. 4) and already indicated in the well-founded numerology of the Mayas (Cosmogony No. 3); a numerology that possibly is – as far as we can judge from the few documents that survived the genocide and the cultural extinction of the indigenous American peoples – far ahead of its contemporary cultural benchmarks.

In the wake of rationalist ideas at the beginning of the modern era, the creative (or poetic) approach to space, though still based on immediate spatial experience, is gradually abandoned in favour of mathematical and theoretical principles and definitions, which seem to allow objective descriptions of space in its totality and to its outmost limits. In a manner of speaking, the "faith" in the idea of an experiential nature is lost and eventually replaced by the theories of a physicalistic, basically energy-related space-time universe. In the end, as Cosmogonies No. 6 and No. 7 strongly imply on second thought, this idea of "space" may be neither more nor less hermetic – or, for that matter, "mythic" – than any of the preceding conceptions of a spatial world as a whole.

It all boils down to what we have already come to apprehend at the very beginning of our inquiries into "all about space".[3] Space is (and always will be) first and foremost a *phenomenological* "idea" in the most strict and yet most comprehensive sense of the word. As such, it is a continuous and ever-changing collective invention and imagination based on experiences shared among human beings. If anything at all, a "history of space" is a chronicle of complex ideational developments in the light of the environmental, technical, social, economic, and intellectual living conditions of mankind at different times. So, as trivial and redundant as it may seem, the idea of space is also a product of (and therefore contingent on) certain stages of human intelligence at certain points in time, and, as remains to be shown, the course of these stages is far from being consecutively progressive.

Against this background, the recklessly short chronicle at hand distinguishes three ideational ages: the Age of Magic Space, the Age of Poetic Space, and the Age of Rational Space. However, since we are talking history of ideas here, they cannot be simply taken as three completed historical periods. The underlying notions of space may be superseded at the end of a particular "age" (and replaced by new ones at the beginning of another), but just like the gods and spirits and myths of old, they do not disappear completely once they have been conceived of. They subliminally survive in the collective cultural conscience so to speak, adapted to new interpretations and manifestations and thus remaining effective in many behaviours and practices that are no less "magic" or "poetic" after they have been described and redefined in "rational" terms.

3 Dieter Dietz / Matthias Michel / Daniel Zamarbide (ed.): *All About Space*, Volume 1: *The Invention of Space*. Zurich 2016.

MAGIC SPACE
CONCEPTIONS

The Age of Magic Space, the Age of Poetic Space, and the Age of Rational Space are suggested here with regard to three fundamentally different ways in which human beings have related to their spatial environment over the past 40'000 years or more. In order to understand how the earliest, the *magic* conception of space might be thought of as an everyday reality, it may be helpful to refer back to the above-mentioned simple reason why human beings even bother to invent complex animistic and symbolic systems and worldviews in the first place, both in "religious" and in psychological terms. They do that because the living conditions of "intelligent animals" are not acceptable – much less *bearable* – without basic understandings, explanations, or "theories" about the environments in which they are bound to live and die, and about how the dynamics of events and phenomena in these environments can be reasonably predicted and controlled. It is the very foundation of their adaptive behaviour. They need answers to these questions simply for the sake of survival in a world that must at least *seem* reasonably consistent with their intelligent perception of reality. That is what the myths are built for, from the Stone Ages up to the present day, from the infant imagination up to the most adult beliefs and philosophies. And all along, they never are anything but "reasonable" according to the respective intellectual and living conditions.

Therefore, the basics of the magic human condition are far from the standardised ingredients of essentially escapist fantasy and fairy tale plots that have become so popular again in recent times, their most frequent and specifically modern misinterpretation being the association of magic with the "powers" of the magician (or his or her tools, respectively). Quite to the contrary, the principal situation of the magician is a situation of weakness, humility, and existential responsiveness, of essentially passive endurance, abidance, subjection, submission, and susceptibility to the forces at work within his or her environment. The only power at his or her disposal lies in the *knowledge* about these forces, which allows him or her to effectively *imagine* them, subsequently invoke or summon them (in conjurations and incantations maybe, but also in many other ways of which mental representation and representative depiction might be the most important), and finally, to *communicate* with them to an extent that is largely beyond his or her control. At this point, the magician is utterly at the mercy of the forces and powers involved, irrespective of their qualities and irrespective of whether they are thought of as gods, ghosts, spirits, souls, creatures, delusions, psychic or neuro-functional energies, ideas, or mere imaginative reflections. No matter what, the magician has become, quite literally, *their* communicative tool.

On the other hand, as long as those forces are commonly accepted as real, the magician's knowledge about them accredits him or her with certain authorities, of course. Not only with social and political powers but also with the power to design the prevailing concepts, understandings, and interpretations of the natural world, including the ways and means of acting upon it. Again, it does not matter whether these ways and means are of a ritual, symbolic, intellectual, physical, or any other kind. According to the Persian and Ancient Greek origin of the word (μαγοσ, a "man of knowledge", mostly of a priestly status, practicing μαγια), they only depend on the social role of the magician in different contexts and under different circumstances: the role of a priest, a philosopher, a medicine man or doctor, a writer or artist or architect, a scholar or scientist, a spiritual, a political, or an economic leader. His or her knowledge is based on observation, experience, remembrance, and creative reflection. The magic is in the ideas and conceptions, in the meaning of the spoken and the written word, in the images and symbols and scriptures that represent and record a comprehensible reality, in the stories that are told, in the solace that is given, in the morals and customs and laws that are passed on, and sometimes also in the mere success or failure of worldly endeavours. Hence, as in any other form of knowledge processed by the human mind, the primary structure of magic is semantic: a system of notions and meanings, memorised and represented in signs and symbols and symbolic gestures: *language*.

The World

Given this basic and seemingly trivial comprehension of magic, the esoteric cliché fantasies of sorcerers and freaky witches fiddling about with magical wands and books, reading cards and guts and tea leaves or summoning demons and devils and monsters and supernatural powers, make way for more realistic notions of magic as the talent and occasionally the profession of people who have the required knowledge and intelligence to deal with phenomena that *exceed* or *contradict* the currently available concepts and explanations of how the natural world works. "Reading the stars" means applying knowledge about the movements of celestial bodies, "reading the cards" means applying knowledge of their traditional symbolic depiction of social structures, and "invoking" or "exorcising" "spells" and "spirits" means applying a deeper or higher understanding of mental processes and psychological intelligence ("psychic" and "psychological" being considerably less differentiable than in modern understandings). Accordingly, the age of magic space can be conceptualised as a period in cultural history when the natural environment is intuitionally understood as an autarchic system of ecological forces and energies conceived of as animistic entities (including human beings) and not as objectifiable processes subjected to the laws of an objectified "nature".

Whether this kind of animistic and symbolistic understanding, including the magic relation to it, implies a specific notion of "space" that is reasonably comparable to the respective notions at later cultural stages is a matter of interpretation, wording, and etymology for the reason alone that the vocabulary at the cultural stages in question is usually much more synthetic and metaphorical than the vocabulary of modern languages. The word "space" is a direct derivation of the Latin word *spatium* n. in the principal sense of "interstice" or "distance in between" (like "length", "width" et al.), embracing many more specific meanings. On the other hand, the actual meaning of "space" is undoubtedly related to the Old High German word *rūm* for "room" and "place" (the modern German word "Raum" meaning both "space" and "room"), based on the adjective *rūma* for "spacious". This word can be etymologically traced back to the Avestan phonetic sequence *rau-uah* in the 4th millennium BP, meaning "open space" and "freedom" (Tocharian *ru-* for "to open" and *rūs* for "land").[4]

To cut a long story short: As far as the notion of space can be documented and verified in *historic times*, it always means, in one way or another, the spatial *emptiness in between*, whereas, for all we know, the prehistoric notions of spatial relations are usually based on the fullness and richness and comprehensiveness of creation between heaven and earth as against the preceding "chaos", which is mostly associated with an overall nothingness. Furthermore, there is plenty of evidence

4 The meaningful correlation of "space" and "freedom" is discussed extensively in chapter IV. *The Politics of Space* of *All About Space*, Volume 1: *The Invention of Space*. Zurich 2016

that there has been neither an idea nor a character or word whatsoever signifying an empty interstice before the invention of the cipher nought in the Persian kingdom of the 26th century BP, not even in the advanced astronomical and mathematical systems of the Chaldeans, Babylonians, and Egyptians. Thus, it is very unlikely that the abstract notion of space reaches further back than the before-mentioned "Promethean turn" or the specific notion of nature in classical antiquity.

Observations like these may seem a bit quibbling at first sight, but they make perfect sense. There are no empty interstices in a world of magic spaces because it is a world that can only be conceived of *as a whole*. Or, in spatial terms: as the "totality" of space. Hence, magic spaces are always essentially full and *indivisible* once the process of creation is completed. They are full of meaning, full of beings and events and substances, full of spirits and spatial memories of the past, the present, and the future, many of them not immediately discernible by sensual perception but always unmistakeably "there", even if not represented or materialised in things or animals. Hence, magic spaces are full of fierce dynamics at all times, although, as parts of a fundamentally balanced entirety, they never change substantially. Sometimes the forces and energies at work are dark and hostile, at other times they are bright, tender, and favourable, but they are all constantly *present*, fulfilling their irrevocable desires and destinies in creation. By means of knowledge and sensitivity and subjection, by conscious acceptance of the human condition under the given circumstances so to speak, the magicians occasionally succeed in forcing them into a state of communicability and into sharing their secrets. However, most of the time they remain silent, mysterious, and concealed in space.

Space and Time

This world of magic spaces in which humans are the objects and nature is the subject is definitely not easy to imagine from a present day's point of view, all the more so because we are not only confronted with a completely different concept of space but also with a different concept of time. Since there are no empty interstices in space, there cannot be any empty interstices in time either. Time is the totality of periodic or circular processes (like day and night, like the course of seasons, like the movements of the heavenly bodies, like birth and death), perpetually repeating themselves. In consequence, past and future are but aspects of an eternal and "unaccountable" present, analogous to the perception of "before" and "after" as aspects of a conscious present. Thus, time is sort of an architectural principle that defines the order and succession of spaces: a non-abstractive attribute of spatial relations and proportions.[5] That is why time is not "counted out" in prehistoric

5 Charles Howard Hinton's (1853–1907) speculations about time as "the fourth dimension" in his highly influential pamphlet *What is the fourth dimension?* (written 1880 and published 1884), may be inspiring in this context. It was not only apprehended in Albert Einstein's theory of relativity, but also by science fiction authors like Herbert

cultures, neither in astronomical nor in historical records, however advanced they may be. Instead, temporal relations are expressed in experiential periodicities, in lifespans, or in accounts of ancestry like royal dynasties or king lists.

On the other hand, the world of magic spaces might become a little more graspable if considered as a reality in which people handle and practice magic on a daily basis. As soon as we imagine magic conceptions and practices as a way of life and a self-evident state of mind, we might realise that reality in the age of magic spaces may have been not so completely different from ours. We might abstract everyday experiences like intuitive thoughts or emotions, a moment of overwhelming enthusiasm, our common susceptibility to demagogic communication, or a simple visit to the doctor or psychologist from their accustomed rationalised contexts and simply transpose them into a different *terminology*, a terminology of magic. We might also, just for a moment, put into question how we come to treat certain facts as "real" in view of their increasingly technical and highly symbolistic intermediation, or how we relate to the obvious number mysticisms of contemporary statistics and "studies" leading us to believe in quantifiable truths that are, nine times out of ten, qualifiable lies. By doing that, we might well come to the conclusion that the ways we approach certain everyday situations, including many of our everyday more or less neurotic rituals and routines, are hardly any more understandable in rational than in magic terms. And finally, we might remember the spontaneous feeling of power and wisdom that we have whenever we call an object by its "right" or "proper" name for the first time, which may be the primal (or primordial) experience of magic practice in everybody's intellectual life.

Architecture

At this point, it seems appropriate to add a few remarks about the understanding of architectural activities in the "age of magic spaces". As should have become evident by now, the modern notion of space is not really compatible with the prehistoric notions of spatial environments. Under the conditions of the times and cultures in question, architecture, both as a notion and as a term, is the craft and practice of constructing buildings serving two basic purposes: practicability and symbolic presentiveness. In terms of practicability, the construction of cities, irrigation and sewage systems, or sacred buildings of complex and monumental proportions are highly impressive technical achievements and most certainly esteemed as such at the time. But it is hardly appropriate to apply formal aesthetic standards or principles (as developed in historic times) to pre-classical architectural endeavours. There are no comprehensive theories nor poetic aspirations or aesthetical abstractions attached to the craft, simply

George Wells and Jorge Luis Borges. Hinton's scientific and fictional work generally aims at the spatial (i.e. basically geometrical) representation and imagination of the abstract theories in contemporary mathematics.

because there is neither a concept of nor a reasonable need for poetic *interventions* in space. The spatial impressiveness of prehistoric buildings like the Mesopotamian ziggurats, the pyramids of Giza, or the palace complexes of Crete is owed to their *symbolic* conceptions, to the intent to construct buildings that are symbolically accurate and consistent both with their purposes and the current worldviews in general. In a manner of speaking, the objectives of practicability and symbolic presentiveness *coincide* to a considerable extent. The ziggurats, for example, are quite obviously "designed" to bring the temple precinct closer to heaven,[6] and the palace complex of Cnossos is built to serve contemporary public, commercial, and political interests that comply with the beliefs and convictions of the Minoan culture rather than to meet any demands of a magnificent building. Why the construction of grand pyramids in ancient Egypt is abandoned so shortly after it has been established in the 4th dynasty is subject to speculation. Most probably, the economic and technical effort has simply proved to be disproportionate to its mystical (i.e. symbolistic) purpose as a king's or a queen's sepulchral monument.

The Spatiality of the Sexes

Based on all of the aforementioned observations and a reasonably relaxed understanding of magic, it is rather evident that there must be considerable differences between the sexes with regard to the acceptance, apperception, and accessibility of magic spaces and practices. The comparatively hostile environmental conditions and the high mortality rates, the division of labour according to physical and biological predispositions and the respective arrangements of social and sexual roles are just the obvious outer factors of an unquestioned cultural

6 The myth of *The Tower of Babel* reflects this purpose in a very conspicuous but profoundly malicious way. In the Tanakh and the Old Testament, the story is embedded in a series of tales designed to accentuate the fatal consequences of the "Fall of Man" and lines up with many twisted Hebrew adaptions and paraphrases of Sumerian originals in the Book of Genesis. In this case, the original is "Enmerkar and the Lord of Aratta" (including the topic of the confusion of languages). However, the "tower" referred to in the story is most probably the ziggurat "Etemenanki" ("House of the Foundation of Heaven and Earth") in Babylon, destroyed for the first time under Sargon I of Akkad around 2300 BC. Centuries later, the authors of the Tower of Babel related to the apparently "incomplete" ziggurat in Babylon, mixed it up with the before-mentioned Sumerian legend and an unfavourable interpretation of the building's purpose and name as blasphemous.

In the 7th century BC, the ziggurat with an original square base of 81.48 x 91.66 metres, approximating 100 metres in height in probably eight steps, was successively rebuilt under four Babylonian kings, the last of them being Nebuchadnezzar II who established the New Babylonian empire. In the 5th century BC the ziggurat was destroyed once again, this time by the invading Persians under Xerxes I. When Alexander the Great returned to Babylon in February 323 BC after his forays into India, he had the ruin dismantled by 10'000 men in two months in order to rebuild it at another place. The project was abandoned when he died four months later.

differentiation of the sexes in hunter, hunter-gatherer and early agricultural societies. Since these outer factors are essentially implemented in a cosmological and mystical understanding of the world as a whole, the differentiation of two sexes is a primordial, possibly the most primordial principle of anthropocentric worldviews in pre-rational and pre-rationalistic times, not least because the universe is principally conceived of as the result of an initial cosmic division or partition in two (mostly in heaven and earth), which is, up to the Hebrew interpretation of Abrahamitic monotheism, always and quite figuratively determined as a division into male and female. Thenceforward, this dualistic or symmetrical principle is come upon throughout the experienceable world and thus is understood as phenomenologically absolute. In consequence, everything that does not fit into this principle, everything that cannot be discerned as one half of an essential active-passive, light-dark, heavenly-earthly etc. "pair", is *either* deemed to be of utmost importance *or* ignored as an exception.

Since there are no conceivable "interstices", no "in-betweens" in a holistic universe as described above, this fundamental dualism cannot possibly be conceived of as contrary but only as complementary, which inevitably accentuates the *difference* of the sexes. There is neither a way to intellectually abstract the dualism of the sexes from the dualistic principles that define the appearance of the natural world nor vice versa, because they essentially are *one* and the *same*. Which is exactly what magic thinking and magic environments are all about. Precisely because male and female are so obviously different, they cannot be conceived of separately but only in relation to the other: difference is attributed to the forms and figures of things, not to what they essentially *are*. In other words: If there is a specific female experience, there *must* be a different and complementary male *equivalent*, because if there was not, the world would quite literally fall apart.

That is the ideational background against which the comprehensive meaningfulness and cultic dimension of sexuality in the beginning of cultural histories as well as the initial advantage of the female sex in this context have to be understood. The former does not need to be extensively discussed here because it is largely self-evident and sufficiently documented in archaeological finds. The latter however provides plenty of room for interpretation. There are many theories that contend "matriarchal" structures in human societies of the late Pleistocene and the early Holocene with good reason, although the term "matriarchal" is highly misleading as sort of an opposite of "patriarchal", female power structures in prehistoric times most probably being fundamentally different from male ones in historic times. However, those societies are characterised by a sweeping numerical majority of women due to genetic factors and significantly higher mortality rates among men for biological and practical reasons. Moreover, it must be assumed that women have considerably more control over all aspects of sexual life and practices for a very long period of time both with regard to bio-functional "knowledge" and sexual pleasure, not least because fertility and the mysticism of the sexual act as a reiteration of the cosmic act of creation are the most obvious aspects of sexuality in the age of magic spaces. In both contexts, the "active" male is conceived (and under pressure) of delivering a *performance*, which puts the "passive" female in the powerful position of judging whether this performance is sufficient or not (or, more explicitly: whether the male performance is a success or a failure, both in terms of pleasure and performance of biological duty). Under the conditions of a magic understanding of environments, this power is undisputable, all the more so because it is an "earthly" power wielded by the sex that is just as undisputedly associated with the "earth" as a principle. The most conspicuously "spatial" aspect of this concept is related to the respective concept of time, the female representing the earthly embedding in an absolute "presence" as against the male quite figuratively "reaching out" into the future (and potential "future spaces") in most of its everyday tasks and activities.[7]

This principal power of the female sex cannot be broken as long as its primordiality is accepted, and as such it remains effective up to the present, even if only subliminally. However, as we know, it gradually is broken at later cultural stages by various kinds of intellectual constructs like the higher value of "activity", the male claim to the role of the "progenitor", or the justifications and rationalisations of physical force. This development is particularly transparent in the earliest culture that is extensively documented in original records, writings, and pictorial representations. In the Sumerian culture, the magic and symbolic principles described above are very explicitly adapted to the structure and use of language, to all sorts of daily customs and practices and rituals, to the social, juridical, and political organisation as well as to the arts and crafts (including architecture).

Remarkably enough, intellect and civilisation are originally attributed to the female sex and attained by men through ritual initiation to the mystery of sexual intercourse with women. Accordingly, the historical development of the Sumerian culture illustrates impressionably how this primeval relation of the sexes is abandoned by degrees, first by the division of religious and political powers in royal autocracies (until around 5000 BP), followed by policies of expansion and armed conflicts, by secular juridical regulation of physical violence (until around 4'000 BP), and finally, in Babylonian times, by replacing the cultic equality of the goddess of womanhood Inanna/Ishtar and the god of man-

7 Concerning "potential future spaces": cf. chapter VI.6 *The Age of Retrograde Invention* et seqq. in *All About Space*, Volume 1: *The Invention of Space*, Zurich 2016.

hood Bēl (Ba'al) by the implementation of Amar Utu (or Marduk, male city god of Babylon) as a state deity in the 38th century BP. Similar developments are documented in the Egyptian empire, when "Amun Ra" is declared state god of the New Kingdom around 3'500 BP after the famous 18th dynasty of Pharaohs has ascended the throne.

Against this background, and in light of the fact that the Book of Genesis is almost entirely a monotheistic reinterpretation of original Sumerian, Assyrian, and Akkadian myths, the legend of Abram pertaining to the Tanakh and the Old Testament is a rather evident metaphor in respect of how the magic and symbolistic understandings of environments turn into pre-rational notions of space, both in historical and in philosophical terms. Departing from the oldest Sumerian city Ur, Abram moves to Harran, the second chief seat of the moon god's worship in the north of Mesopotamia, from there to Canaan, to Egypt, and back to Canaan, establishing the first concept of a highly aggressive and resentful almighty nationalist father god monotheism by transvaluing and rearranging the mythical essentials of his native home into an absolute history that supports the religious beliefs forced upon him by his new god. The most reckless of these transvaluations is the distinctively intellectual creation myth and the story of the Fall of Man in which the original sin is brought upon mankind by the original woman, the attainment of cognition, and the knowledge of sexuality. Which is a quite perfect inversion of the Sumerian myth that tells the story how Šamat turns the savage Enkidu into a civilised man by taming him in a seven-day sexual act.[8] Of course, Abram's wife Sarai is infertile up until the age of 99 when the father god decides that she should give birth to Abram's nation that would become as "numerous as the stars in the sky". Their names are changed into Abraham (Hebrew for "father of many nations") and Sarah (Hebrew for "princess").

8 Concerning "The Fall of Man": cf. chapter IV.2 *The Curse of Space* in *All About Space*, Volume 1: *The Invention of Space*, Zurich 2016.
Concerning "Šamat and Enkidu", cf. *Ibram's Awakening*, p. 46.

~ 3'800 BP

The Amorite king Hammurabi establishes the *Old Babylonian Empire* after subjecting all competing Mesopotamian city-states, including the Assyrian territories in Asia Minor. He declares Babylon the capital city and Akkadian the official language of the empire. His reform of the Sumerian jurisdiction presents the first law code in history that is based on penalties instead of retributions and compensations (282 laws inscribed on 12 clay tablets).

~ 3'500 BP

The first lasting settlement on the site of today's city of Zurich is built by people belonging to the larger cultural or ethnic group in western Europe that later will be referred to as *Celts*.[9] It is a multipart settlement consisting of a village on the "Lindenhof" hill (430 m a. s. l., in the centre of today's Zurich) that is completely surrounded by two rivers and extensive swampland at the time, and a second village at a linear distance of 3 km on the top plateau of the strategically advantageous and densely forested "Uetliberg" mountain (870 m a. s. l., at the western boundary of today's inner city), connected by several ravine paths. Based on archaeological finds to date, it must be assumed that the settlement subsequently rises to become one of the most important places of trade and commercial traffic in the region. The earliest goods from Archaic Greece found on site date to around 3100 BP.

~ 3'500 BP

Under the reign of the 18th dynasty of Egyptian kings, now referred to as "Pharaohs", the influence and territorial expansion of Egypt reaches its peak. The royal residence is moved to the Upper Egypt city of Karnak in Thebes, and the Theban god Amun-Ra becomes the principal state deity. The most prominent Pharaoh of the period is *Thutmose III* who assumes the throne in the 35th century BP after the prosperous and innovative rule of his aunt and stepmother Hatshepsut and 22 years of co-regency as head of her armies. He pursues an aggressive policy of expansion, undertaking 16 major military campaigns against Canaan, Assyria, and Babylonia in the east, and against Nubia in the south.

The 18th and the 19th dynasty (under Seth I and Ramses II) are believed to represent the most probable period of historical events that could have initiated the Judaist foundational myth around Jacob, Joseph, and the *Exodus* of the Israelites headed by Moses. The famous twin red granite obelisks (21m each) in London and New York date to the reign of Thutmose III, the yellow granite Paris obelisk and its twin in Luxor (23 m each) to the reign of Ramses II.

9 The original Celtic cultures spread from the area of today's southern Germany, Switzerland, and eastern France to the Low Countries, Britain and Ireland, the French Atlantic coast, western Spain and Portugal during the 3rd millennium BP. Some of the tribes populated the area of today's Hungary and Czechia, and until the 23rd century BP, some scattered Celtic cultures existed in central Asia Minor and at the shores of the Black Sea. However, since the Celts were originally defined as a *cultural* entity in times of classical antiquity, they cannot be correctly conceived of as an ethnic group, although that may be historically plausible. Still, historians usually do not refer to them as Celts with regard to times before their definition by the ancient Greeks. The common characteristics of the Celtic cultures are found in their languages, their cultural techniques, beliefs, traditions etc.

• The London obelisk, flanked by two sphinxes, on the Victoria Embankment. The New York obelisk at Central Park

• Basalt statue of Thutmose III, Luxor Museum, Egypt.

~ 3'500 BP

The *Minoan Eruption*, sparked off by one of the most powerful volcanic eruptions in history on the Aegean island Thera (today's Thira or Santorini, about 110 km north of Minoan Crete's capital city Cnossos), expels 61 cubic kilometres of magma and rock and estimated 100 cubic kilometres of tephra and ash. The eruption, leaving up to 60 meters thick layers of volcanic material on dry land, causes devastating earthquakes, tsunamis, flood disasters, and air pollution all over the eastern Mediterranean region. The massive destructions of Crete's coastal cities and settlements and their subsequent reconstruction result in a considerable weakening and disintegration of the Minoan culture and sea power, encouraging military aggression of the Mycenaean Greeks and eventually leading to the definitive collapse of the Minoan civilisation in the 33rd century BP when the Greek seize economic, political, and cultural control of the whole island.

Just before the eruption, alarmed by early geodynamic indications of the imminent disaster, the legendary fellowship of the Seven Architects of Cnossos have allegedly left the Cretan island, heading toward different destinations (cf. *The Legend of the Seven Architects*, p. 74).

• Ruin of the North Portico of the Cnossos Palace site, Crete. Unlike in subsequent Greek architecture, the pillars are made of wood and mostly painted red. (Photo by Bernard Gagnon, released into the public domain on Wikimedia.)

~ 3'500 BP

The *Archaic Greek kingdoms* and city-states around the Attic and Peloponnesian peninsulas are founded (Argos, Attica/Athens, Corinth, Greek Thebes et al.), more or less at the same time as the kingdoms of Troy and Lydia in Asia Minor, thus advancing the political differentiation of the former Mycenaean Greek tribes. In contrast to the colourful myths and the high culture of the classical period of Ancient Greece, the archaic Greeks are a comparatively uncivilised and pugnacious people.

~ 3'200 BP

If the legends and recorded ancestries were reliable, the *mythical period of Ancient Greece* and its tragic heroes would reach its climax in the Trojan War at the turn of the 33rd to the 32nd century BP. By then, it would have extended over not more than three generations, with kings like Midas II, Oedipus, Aegeus, Theseus, Priam, Menelaus, Agamemnon, or Orestes, heroes like Hercules or Diomedes, Achilles, Odysseus, Ajax, Hector, Paris, Aeneas, and other heroes of the Trojan War all appearing within a period of only a hundred years.

The Age of Poetic Space

Matthias Michel

~1050 BC

At the beginning of the *Mediterranean Iron Age*, the Phoenician phonetic alphabet consisting of 22 consonants emerges from the Proto-Canaanite script that again is based on Egyptian hieroglyphs. Spread by Phoenician merchants representing the leading maritime trading culture at the time, it rapidly replaces the Egyptian and the Sumerian cuneiform script. Whereas the latter employ a great number of complex characters, the phonetic alphabet is easy to learn and applicable to all languages. Thus, the Phoenician alphabet advances literacy all over the Mediterranean region, disintegrating class divisions and monopolies on information and education. Most alphabetic scripts are derived directly or indirectly from the Phoenician alphabet, such as the Aramaic, Hebrew, Greek, Latin, Cyrillic, Coptic, and Arabic scripts.

The Judean David, war hero against the Philistines, lady's man and poet, becomes king of Judaea and Israel. He subjects most of the conflicting tribes between Assyria and the Sinai Peninsula, establishes the *Kingdom of Israel*, and declares Jerusalem the royal and "holy" city of the Israelites where the Ark of the Covenant is to be kept. According to the Tanakh, the Temple of Jerusalem is built under the reign of his second son Salomon around 1000 BC. The city and the temple are destroyed after the Babylonian conquest under king Nebuchadnezzar II (586 BC).

8th century BC

The propagation of the Greek alphabet and the historical, mythological, and cultural accounts of Homer (*Iliad*, *Odyssey*) and Hesiod (*Theogony*, *Works and Days*) represent the beginning of the period of classical antiquity. Greek colonies spread along the Mediterranean coasts, especially in southern Italy ("Magna Greacia" or Greater Greece).

The Phoenicians establish the city of *Carthage* (near today's Tunis) as the "Second Tyros" and hence gradually ascend to a major sea power. As the commercial gateway to northern Africa and its grain supplies, and as the central harbour of the Mediterranean Sea, Carthage remains one of the biggest and wealthiest but also most fiercely contested cities of the ancient world until the 7th century AD.

The city of Rome is founded as an association of several (probably Etruscan) villages. Ancient Roman historiography pinpoints the founding date to the 21st of April 753 BC and names Romulus, twin brother of Remus, as its erector.

605 BC

Nebuchadnezzar II assumes the throne of Babylon and establishes the *Neo-Babylonian Empire*, reaching from the Nile to the Tigris after his predecessor Nabopolassar has defeated Assyria in an alliance with Egypt. In an unprecedented effort, the historical buildings and city districts of Babylon, destroyed around 700 BC, are rebuilt during the following decades on a rectangular surface area of 39 square kilometres for around 200'000 inhabitants. Contemporary sources claim that it is surrounded by double walls of approximately 105 metres in height and 28 metres in width, with 25 bronze gates on each of the four sides. The 70 years of Judean captivity are ascribed to this building period as well as the "Hanging Gardens", one of the seven "Wonders of the Ancient World", and the reconstruction of the ziggurat "Etemenanki" as the temple of "Zeus Belus" (the city god "Marduk", identified with the respective Egyptian, Assyrian, Lydian, Greek, and Phoenician father gods by this time, cf. *Magic Spaces*, p. 63, and the footnote regarding the *Tower of Babel*, p. 61.

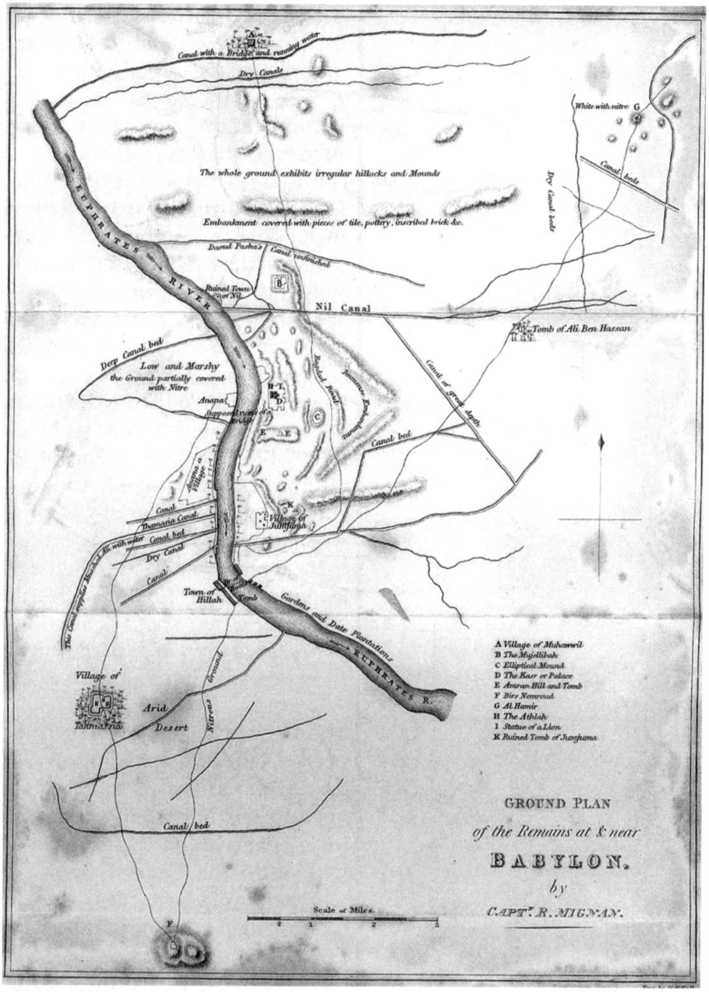

• "Ground plan of the remains of Babylon" before the beginning of the excavations (1827), published by Henry Colburn and RichardBentley, London 1829.

• Ruins of Babylon in 1932.

594 BC

The Athenian statesman and negotiator *Solon* (~ 640 – 560 BC) outlines the essentials of republican politics on the occasion of an acute economic crisis of the Greek city-states, which he blames on the corruption, materialistic greed, and social exploitation exercised by the contemporary aristocracies. He successfully suggests a political system based on civil participation, democratic processes and division of powers, associated with a juridical practise that is focused on equal justice for all citizens. Furthermore, he formulates specific laws that are actually enacted to a large extent and subsequently promote the conception of democracy in Greek Poleis.

6th century BC

Natural philosopher, geometrician, and astronomer Thales of Miletus introduces the Egyptian theories of basic arithmetic to Ancient Greece. He also reformulates the old Babylonian belief that the natural world and all life forms have originally risen from the oceans as a proto-scientific theory. Shortly thereafter, Pythagoras establishes his famous philosophical school in Croton (Calabria), advancing geometry and mathematics as essential means of understanding nature. Thus, the era of classical Greek philosophy dawns on southern Europe and shapes the principles of rational thinking of the ancient world. Other exponents of this *Pre-Socratic period* extending over the 5th century BC are Heraclitus, introducing the theoretical notions of "logos" and "coming-into-being" ("παντα ϱει", "everything flows") as against the ontology of changeless being of Parmenides, also Leucippus and his disciple Democritus of Abdera (the "laughing philosopher") who conceptualise aesthetics as a subject of natural philosophy (cf. 7 *Cosmogonies*, page 52), or Hippocrates of Kos who applies the principles of natural philosophy to medicine. The essentials of ancient mathematics and geometry (including musical theory) are recorded by Euclid of Alexandria ("*Elements*"), a scholar of Plato's Academy, and extended to practical physics by Archimedes of Syracuse in the 3rd century BC. In Persia, the cipher nought is introduced into common usage.

538 BC

The Persian king Kyros II puts an end to the Babylonian supremacy in the Middle East, having already brought the Lydian kingdom and Asia Minor under his control. His troops of Persians and Medes conquer the northern Babylonian cities with utmost brutality, slaughtering all captives on the way. However, after Babylon's surrender, the first king of the *Persian Empire* gains a reputation for being exceptionally permissive with regard to the different religions in the occupied territories. As for his personal beliefs, there are conflicting records. His successors Darius and Xerxes are avowed Zoroastrians (cf. 7 *Cosmogonies*, p. 51), thus representing the majority of the Persian people at the time. The Persian Empire lasts until the conquests of Alexander the Great.

509 BC

The former kingdom of *Rome* is changed into an aristocratic senatorial republic with Lucius Junius Brutus and Lucius Tarquinius Collatinus as its first consuls. According to the second population census in 507 BC, Rome has 130'090 inhabitants at the time. The first census in 566 BC has registered 84'700 inhabitants.

486 BC

In the wake of recent rover horde raids, the construction works of a massive triple fortification around the Helvetian-Celtic princely residence on top of the *"Uetliberg" mountain* commence. The outer ramparts (15 and more metres high) and moats (almost 40 metres deep) are constructed at a distance of 1.5 km and 200 metres in altitude below the mountaintop settlement and cover the whole western and southern mountainside. Secured passages are built at the crossings of the standard cart track paths (1.1 metres width) leading down to Turicon[1] between the lake and the junction of the two rivers. At a distance of around 200 metres from the central village wall, a second array of ramparts and moats secures the proximity of the mountain top plateau.

The fortification works are finished in the year of the "Fortunate Princess's" accession to power. In honour of the prosperous decades of her regency, she is buried in the biggest and most glorious tomb that people in these parts have ever seen. Down by the urn grave fields beyond the second rampart, her burial chamber of loam and wood, consecrated by the incantations of the matrons, is filled with her riches and covered with a mound of stones and earth of around 20 metres across. All the inhabitants of Turicon are present at the burial ceremonies. In remembrance of her, the mountain is henceforth called "Udt's Berg", the "Mountain of the Woman of Honour". To the utmost dismay of the villagers, the tomb is desecrated and plundered only a few years later.[2]

479 BC

Confucius (Kung-Fu-Tse or Kong-Qiu-Zi), Chinese politician and moral philosopher, dies in his place of birth Qufu in the state of Lu (today's Shandong). He has revised and reinterpreted the holy scriptures of ancient China and transferred them into ethics and politics. The core of his teachings that remain influential in Far Eastern ethical and political theory up to the present is the rejection of legalism in favour of people's natural morality ("sense of shame").

404 BC

The *Peloponnesian League* headed by the militarily predominant Sparta wins the three-decades-long war against the Attic or Delian League headed by Athens, which originally was a defensive coalition against the attacks of the Persian Empire. Thus, the supremacy of Athens among the Greek citystates is terminated as well as the period of Attic democracy.

309 BC

Socrates, philosopher and "gadfly" of Athens, is publicly executed by poisoning after being convicted of spreading pestilent ideas among the Athenian youth. However, his persistent criticism against democracy and his public contesting of an oracle at Delphi declaring him the wisest of all Greeks are presumed to be the true reasons for his conviction: By publicly and persuasively arguing his own ignorance he has paradoxically proved himself to be wiser than anybody else and, implicitly, his fellow citizens to be even more ignorant in view of their being unaware of it.

This kind of charmingly intelligent and, at the same time, razor-sharply convincing argumentation eventually inspires Plato (who is just under thirty years old and does not attend the execution of his teacher under the pretext of feeling unwell) to start writing his philosophical dialogues that feature a fictional Socrates as the protagonist of some of the most sustainable epistemological and political works in history. In 387 BC, Plato buys the former house of attic hero Academus

1 The name "*Turicon*" of the Celtic village that later becomes the Roman "*vicus Turicum*" and finally the city of "Zurich" is hypothetical to a certain extent. However, for all we know, it is the most plausible name based on given philological and archaeological facts until proved otherwise. "Turicon" relates to the Celtic personal name "Turos" and means "Turos' settlement". Another theory implies that "Turos" could have been the name of one of the branches of the river "Sihl". The following description of the Fortunate Princess's burial is also hypothetical but completely consistent with the archaeological finds on site.

2 In the 5th century BC, the rock plateau on top of Zurich's local mountain on which the Celtic "oppidum" was built was 150 metres long (several rockslides have later reduced it to 110 metres). The houses were made of wood. Most of them were built on wooden foundations along the edges of the plateau. The mentioned princess's grave mound was found in AD 1900. The tomb chamber beneath measured 3.2 x 3.4 x 1 metres. A reconstruction of the mound is visible up to the present day and is indicated on maps as "Fürstengrabhügel Sonnenbühl".

Whether the name of the "Uetliberg" mountain originates, as indicated here, from the Celtic word "udt" for "woman" or dates to the Middle Ages (cf. p. 109), remains subject of speculation.

northwest of Athens and founds his philosophical "Academy" there. His most famous scholar is Aristotle (384 – 322 BC). His chief work *Politeia* ("Politics"), including the allegory of the cave, is written around 370 BC,[3] the dialogues *Timaeus* and *Critias*, incidentally introducing the myth of Atlantis, are written around 360 BC or later. Plato dies in 348 BC.

The Legend of the Seven Architects

Recorded on an anonymous scroll, written around 360 BC in classical Greek, preserved in the Great Library of Alexandria until the 3rd century AD, acquired by Ptolemy I., King of Upper and Lower Egypt, formerly in possession of Alexander III, King of Macedonia and Asia.[4]

Thus Critias commenced his discourse:
"A long, long time ago, in the wake of the ages of the great floods, more than five thousand and two hundred solstices or, depending on the manner of counting, more than two thousand and six hundred years before now,

... at a time when humankind in these parts of the world still lived in huts of simple shapes and forms and materials, when such great accomplishments as the taming of languages in scriptures, the mastery of metalworking and the building of great holy houses was reserved for only a few peoples in the East,

... when the power of childbirth and magic was still vastly superior to the power of begetting and rational thought: when, in other words, the spirit of womankind was the driving force behind the striving of men,

... the Minoan people of the Cretan island gained advantage over all kingdoms by absorbing only the best of practices from their neighbouring countries. They achieved their superiority by travelling further afar than their ancestors did, keeping their eyes and ears and minds wide open, bewaring of prejudices of any sort against foreign cultures and their ways of life. By doing so, they inherited the history and knowledge about how the world had come into existence and the deepest mysteries of the two conflicting descents of gods from the Eastern and the Southern Folk. From the Eastern Folk, they adopted the most advanced of arts and crafts like developing and using tools to expand the potentials of their restricted physical abilities, recording history in writing, fertilising the earth, constructing houses of great beauty and durability, observing and calculating the movements of the stars, and taming their environments according to their needs.

However, they learned nothing from the Western and the Northern Folk, simply because they did not have any useable skills or knowledge at their disposal that the Minoan people did not already have themselves. But in view of the temperate climate, the extensive forests, and the fertility of the Northern and Western lands, they advanced and encouraged commercial relations to the coastal settlements around the Mediterranean Sea and built great boats and ships to carry all kinds of freights from one end of the known world to the

3 Regarding Plato's allegory of the cave in the context of *All About Space*, see Volume 1: *The Invention of Space*, chapter V.5 *Nothing But The Truth*, et seqq. (Zurich 2016).

other. Thus, they did not only become the wisest and richest of peoples in these parts, they also lived in peace and continuous prosperity for many hundreds of years.

Legend has it that thousand six hundred and thirty-eight years before now a tall young man with dark skin, wrapped in ragged cloths, arrived in Cnossos on a merchant ship from Tyros. He introduced himself by the peculiar and meaningless name of Anunites and claimed that he originally came from a city in the south of Babylonia, expelled from his homeland for blasphemy. He personally appealed for asylum at the City Palace, and since he was not only of agreeable appearance but also knew how to choose his words and declared himself ready to share his knowledge from the distant east, he was immediately accepted as a citizen of Cnossos. Subsequently, he proved himself to be very useful in the planning of the City Palace's ongoing extension and the handling of public affairs, which earned him the confidence of the city's rulers and the appointment as a chief negotiator. A few years later, Anunites had become a prestigious and wealthy man.

However, there were also many oddities about him that raised suspicions among people who believed in dark and evil faculties of the mind. He kept to himself most of the time, and though men and women alike fell for his charms, he never took himself a wife or a whore, and yet he didn't show any inclination to pederasty either. His duties required a lot of travelling, and sometimes he brought back strange cultic objects from foreign countries, like peculiarly graven stones, repulsive figurines, unknown measuring devices and clay tablets mysteriously inscribed in unacquainted languages, which he treasured in a secluded room in the basement of his house. However, the strangest of singularities about him was that he would not seem to get older. No wrinkles disfigured his dainty face, his body seemed to gain in health and strength rather than to wither with age, and while people around him died away, he remained in the prime of his life. So, over the years, he was referred to as a magician practicing the dark arts. But in view of his many good deeds in favour of his fellow citizens, they did not turn against him. To the contrary, they conceded growing influence and authority to him, which he never misused.

4 Based on the content, the Attic dialect, the introduction of one "Critias", and the presumption that Minoan Crete, a merely mythical civilisation from a 4th century BC point of view, could have been a model for Plato's "Atlantis", there is a reasonably plausible theory discussed among historians and philologists that this document may actually be a draft written by Plato prior to his later dialogues *Timaeus* and *Critias* (originally planned as sequels of a trilogy that eventually was abandoned) and therefore an early version of the fictional *Atlantis myth* recited by the Critias character. The theory builds on the possibility that the scroll entered into possession of Alexander the Great via his teacher Aristotle who was admitted to Plato's Academy in 367 BC and remained there as a scholar until Plato's death in 348 BC before he was charged with Alexander's education about four years later. If this assumption would be correct, some of the names used in this fragment could refer to historical persons, which is a standard practice in Plato's works.

On the other hand, the plot of the story does not perfectly match with Plato's general idea of the implied dialogues, and, given the historical context, the exact dating of events is very odd. Furthermore, there are conspicuous stylistic discrepancies between this text and Plato's writing, which suggest that the document may be a transcript referring to an older source (there are folk tales recorded in the cultural heritage of Egypt that are quite similar to the Atlantis myth). In any case, the references to Plato's late work in association with the dating of the document remain considerable enough to justify conjectures that he may have been involved with it in one way or another even if he did not write it himself. According to his literary intentions to present a technologically and socially idealised culture, he dates Atlantis much further back in time and locates it in the western Mediterranean region or even the Atlantic Sea in the two dialogues in question.

The *Map of the Human Mind* that is mentioned in the text and presented in a rough and schematic way at the end of the document (see graphic reconstruction on p. 78) implies that the original was probably taken or stolen from the Library of Alexandria before its destruction, which remains subject of speculation with regard to both the circumstances and the historical dating. Fact is that adapted and extended versions of this map have surfaced later on several historical occasions from the 12th to the 17th century AD (cf. *Blackmail*, p. 136) under the Latin title *Orbis Intelligentiae*. Up to the present day, *The Legend of the Seven Architects* as it is presented here remains the only possible and hypothetically traceable source of these later versions.

Some hundred years after his arrival, Anunites founded an exclusive guild of seven master builders, all immigrants like him, who called themselves the Promethean Fellowship of the Seven Architects of Cnossos. They met regularly and pursued secret studies of technical inventions and advancements that they proposed to the city rulers when they deemed them useful for the further development of the city. And most of their propositions were willingly accepted because they always proved to be easy to implement and of great benefit to the prosperity of the public. Very soon, the suggestions of the Seven Architects went beyond mere irrigation, sewage, and heating systems, construction plans regarding the improvement of multi-storeyed buildings, or innovative techniques of transportation. They also invented wondrous tools and devices they called 'technologies' that allowed for unburdening the citizens of many hard labours as well as for accelerating production processes. Apart from that, it was rumoured that Anunites was in possession of a mysterious kind of map charting the facilities and coherencies of the human mind and that many of the Architects' subtle inventions were owed to the information conveyed by this map.

Howsoever, another hundred years later, the Minoan culture of Crete had achieved advantages and technical superiorities over their neighbouring countries that were beyond imagination. Moreover, they had fundamentally reformed their political affairs to the effect that the most literate and educated aristocrats of Cnossos took turns in ruling the island for a period of four solstices and in due consultation with the Seven Architects before they willingly handed over the government business to others. Thus, the blooming period of Minoan Crete arose and lasted for nearly three hundred years. The Minoans alternately referred to this period as the 'Age of Thalassocracy' with respect to their commercial sea power, as the 'Age of Epistocracy' with respect to their social and political welfare, or simply as the 'Age of the Seven Architects'. During that period, they were never at risk or under threat of war, famine, civil unrest, oppression, or any other kind of hardship.

During all those years, no one ever came to know about the mysteries of Anunites' existence except for his six fellow Architects who shared his most astounding fate of agelessness and immortality. Their names were Adrimeteus, Apis, Laius, Polydorus, Sisyphus, and Theoklymus of Cnossos. Furthermore, they were the only ones ever to learn that Anunites was not a man, as he had made his fellow citizens believe, but a woman whose destiny reached further back in space and time than any of them could possibly imagine. In the confidentialness of their exclusive and enlightening meetings, Anunites was thus addressed as Leto of Cnossos. In gratitude for her teachings and the sharing of her unfailing knowledge, none of the Architects ever betrayed her secret.

The Age of the Seven Architects came to an abrupt end when, around a thousand and a hundred and forty years before now, the Aegean volcano Thira erupted only five hundred and ninety stadiums away from Crete's northern coast, causing devastating flood disasters, earthquakes, and poisonous clouds of ash and tephra all over the eastern Mediterranean Sea. In wise foresight of what was going to happen, the Seven Architects warned the people of Crete that such a calamity was imminent, but many of the Minoans would not believe them, and those who did refused to leave their homes. That is how it came that many of the cities of Crete were destroyed, the land was devastated for many years to come, and the cultural skills, the technical facilities, and the comprehensive knowledge that had distinguished the Minoans from all other peoples for such a long time were destined to perish. Although they worked hard for decades to rebuild what they had lost, they could not withstand the subsequent attacks of the Achaeans from Mycenae who soon thereafter seized control over Crete and the Aegean Sea.

The Seven Architects, very much aware that there was no way to save what they had achieved and established in Crete even if they would survive the catastrophe, left Cnossos only days before the Thira eruption. They boarded a ship to the Lydian coast, and upon their departure from the harbour of Heraklion, the inhabitants deluged them with complaints and accusations for leaving them but could not hold them back. According to the accounts of those who saw them leave, they took nothing with them but provisions for a journey of a few days. Then again, neither the mysterious Map of the Human Mind nor any other of their secret belongings was ever found in Leto's abandoned house.

Upon their arrival in Miletus, the Seven Architects split up to continue their journeys heading toward different destinations. Adrimeteus stayed in Lydia and is presumed to finally have chosen Ilion as his home. Apis and Theoklymus travelled south along the Phoenician coast. Theoklymus settled down in Tyros while Apis got as far as Thebes in Upper Egypt. Sisyphus headed for the radiant city of Bel-Merodach in Mesopotamia. Laius boarded a ship to Syracuse, and the remaining two went north to reach the city of Corinth. From there, Polydorus continued his journey to Athens, and Leto of Cnossos is said to have travelled across the northern and western continent for many a long year until she arrived in the distant lands of a people known as the Celts. As likely as it may be that they have continued their marvellous work in foreign countries, all we know about the Seven Architects' further adventures is based on hearsay. However, it is commemorated among the elderly people of Athens that one Polydorus of Cnossos has died here at an immeasurable age back in the days of Solon."

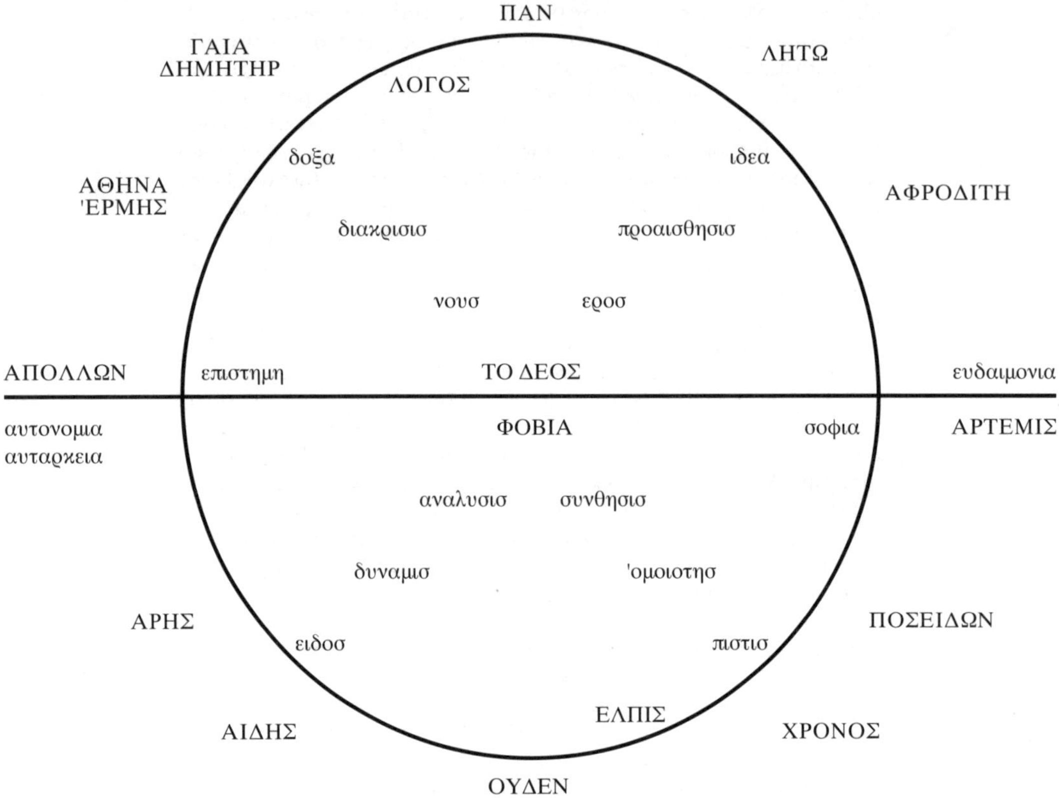

"Map of the Human Mind", Ancient Greek version

336 BC

In the wake of the decline of Athens, the balance of power among the Greek city-states has been increasingly challenged by the Macedonian kingdom. Under Philipp II, Macedonia has become the leading power in Greece, not least because of his reforms of military tactics and weaponry. Amidst his preparations of a campaign against the Persian Empire, Philipp is assassinated in summer 336 BC, and his son *Alexander III* succeeds to the throne.

Educated by Aristotle and inspired by Homer's epics (especially by the legend of Achilles from whom his mother Olympia claims to be descended), Alexander envisions a "world empire" that would ensure everlasting peace and prosperity. Bearing this idea in mind, he pursues his father's campaign against Persia under Darius III in 334 BP, successively conquering the kingdoms and territories of Asia Minor, southern Greece, Phoenicia, Egypt, the Caucasus Mountains and the Persian heartland on shore and at sea (some of them by uncontested surrender) in less than four years. Following this unprecedented and generally unexpected military triumph, Alexander enters the city of Babylon through the "Gate of Ishtar" and declares himself "King of Asia". Darius escapes to Bactria (today's Afghanistan) where he is betrayed and murdered by one of his own governors.

From Babylon, Alexander's armies proceed through Bactria to Maracanda (Samarkand) and the Hindu Kush (329 – 327 BC). After marrying the Sogdian princess Roxana, he decides to conquer India, which is completely unknown territory at the time and supposed to be the eastern end of the world. Following the valley of Kabul to the south and crossing the Indus, he reaches the river Hydaspcs (Jhelum) under the adverse conditions of the monsoon rain season of 326 BC. After defeating the northern Indian king Porus, a mutiny among his demoralised soldiers prevents him from advancing further east to the Ganges and the Himalaya regions. The troops turn south instead, a part of them boarding a few hundred ships, the others following the shores of the rivers Hydaspes and Indus under constant attacks of Indian tribes, which provoke atrocious destructions and massacres. After the conquest of the south-Indian state Sindh, the decimated army finally reaches the mouth of the Indus in summer 325 BC from where Alexander crosses the deserts of Gedrosia with the main part of his troops in 60 days, accepting another great cost of lives, while the rest of them sail back across the sea under the command of his admiral Nearchus, exploring the coasts of the Indian Ocean and the Persian Gulf.

The army reunites in Susa at the bottom of the Zagros Mountains where Alexander, according to his idea of united nations in a united world empire, orders a mass wedding of his officers with thousands of Persian women in spring 324 BC. On this occasion, he marries, among others, Stateira, a daughter of his defeated enemy Darius III. He spends the rest of the year releasing his elder and injured soldiers from duty and reorganising the political structures of the governments in his enormous multi-ethnic empire. One of his measures in this context is to grant the unconditional right of repatriation to all exiles, which is proclaimed at the Olympic Games of the same year, much to the indignation of the Greek states.

In February 323 BC, Alexander returns to Babylon to mourn the recent death of his life-long friend, companion, and lover Hephaestion and to prepare for the invasion of Arabia. Meanwhile, 10'000 men are ordered to dismantle the ruins of Babylon's ziggurat with the intent to rebuild it at another place. Alexander dies on the 10th or 11th of June in the palace of Nebuchadnezzar II at the age of 32. According to biographer Plutarch, the cause of death is a "fever", possibly malaria, meningitis, or typhoid fever, or an aftereffect of a battlefield injury he has come by in India. Other sources assume that he has been poisoned. His body is entombed in a sarcophagus that remains in Alexandria-by-Egypt and is visited by many ambitious statesmen in the following centuries. Alexandria-by-Egypt is one of many Alexandrias he has founded across the Near and the Middle East during the campaigns of his short regency. Due to dissents about his succession, Alexander the Great's empire disintegrates shortly after his death.

• Detail on the Alexander Sarcophagus

216 BC

During the Second *Punic War*, the Carthaginians under the command of king Hannibal defeat the Roman army in the battle of Cannae in southern Italy, which is the most important logistic sea trade centre of the Roman Republic at the time. It is the first major setback in Rome's irresistible rise to world power since its depredation by the Celtic Senones in 387 BC. In the Third Punic War (149 – 146 BC), the Roman legions under the command of young consul Publius Cornelius Scipio besiege, invade, and destroy Carthage, which puts an end to the Phoenician commercial hegemony around the Mediterranean Sea. Gaius Julius Caesar decides the refoundation of the city in 46 BC, which is finally put into action under the reign of Augustus in 29 BC.

214 BC

The Chinese king Qin Shi-Huang-Ti of the Ch'in dynasty (4th dynasty of Chinese kingdoms) orders a provisional finishing of the *Great Chinese Wall* that has been built in stages since the 7th century BC to protect the Chinese provinces from attacks by the horse peoples of the Gobi desert (later to be referred to as the Huns). The construction is finished around 210 BC. The wall is approximately 2450 km long at the time and remains the biggest building in the history of mankind up to the present. However, the wall has been extended and converted in later times, especially during the Ming dynasty (14th to 17th century AD). According to specifications of the Chinese government in AD 2012, the Great Wall is 21'196 km long today, including sections of natural barriers like rivers and mountains.

• Section of the "Great Chinese Wall", photographed by Herbert Ponting in 1907

58 BC

In spring 58 BC, several Helvetian tribes provide Gaius Julius Caesar (100 – 44 BC), proconsul of the Roman provinces in Gaul, with a pretext to mobilise cisalpine legions and start the *Gallic War*. Due to continuing aggressions of Germanic tribes from the north, the coalition of Helvetians, the biggest cohesive Celtic population group in number at the time, decide to emigrate to the southwest and formally ask Caesar for permission to cross through "Gallia Narbonensis" (today's southern France). After the denial of their request and the erection of a 27.5 km wall between the river Rhone and the Jura mountains at Geneva, they choose a more northern route through the territories of the Gallic tribes Sequani and Haedui, raid several villages on the way and cross the river Arar (today's Saône) where Caesar and his legions take up pursuit and finally defeat the Helvetians in the Battle of Bibracte. The survivors are sent back to their homes.

Since the Germanic invasion attempts are persistent, and since the Helvetians have a history of subjugation plans and provocative forays both against Gallic and Roman territories, Caesar declares himself protector of all the Gauls and hence subjects the disunited northern tribes along the Rhine during the following three years; some by negotiations and others, the Belgians in particular, by military campaigns. He crosses the Channel to Britannia twice in 55 and 54 BC without lasting effect and finally returns to put down several Gallic uprisings until the famous victory against Vercingetorix at Alesia in September 52 BC.

The Gallic War introduces the "scorched earth policy" to the history of warfare as it is practiced by the Helvetians and several Gallic tribes. Caesar rises to become one of the wealthiest and most popular citizens of the Roman Republic, which initiates a string of well-known political and historical consequences. Furthermore, the career of a young architect from Campania is launched: Marcus Vitruvius invents and builds war machines for Caesar, which eventually earns him the position of one of the most respected architects in Rome (cf. *Two Letters*, p. 82).

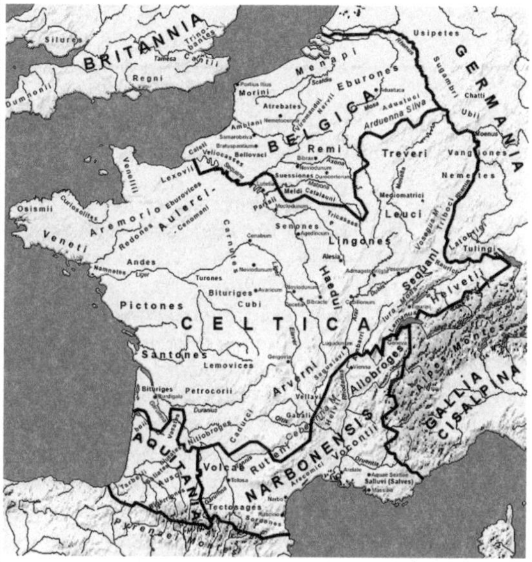

• Map of Gaul around 58 BC

27 BC

A group of senators, instigated by Marcus Iunius Brutus and Gaius Cassius, have stabbed Dictator Ceasar to death during a senatorial assembly on the 15th March 44 BC, suspecting him of having no intent to restore the Roman Republic after having won the civil war. Due to masterful long-term political tactics and the inheritance of Caesar's sustainable popularity, Caesar's grandnephew and sole heir Octavian finally prevails in the following struggle for power between the republican aristocrats, the consul and former general of Caesar's legions Marcus Antonius, and himself. Under the official name of *Imperator Caesar Divi filius Augustus*, he is acclaimed first Emperor of Rome on the 16th January 27 BC. According to the population census of 28 BC, 16'500'000 citizens live in the Roman Empire at the time, 4'164'000 of them in the greater city area of Rome generating a gross national product valued at around 175'000'000 € (at the exchange rate of 1998).

Augustus initiates a period of sustainable building activity, restoring already existing structures like Caesar's Circus Maximus, improving the comparatively inferior infrastructure of Rome in socially deprived quarters like the Aventine area, and gradually changing the city into the architecturally most advanced metropolis of the ancient world. He also initiates the building of the walls at the empire's borders in Upper and Lower Germania, alternately consisting of stone walls, palisades, ditches, forts, fortresses, and civilian settlements, later referred to as "*Limites*" ("frontiers"). Their purpose is not primarily a defensive but rather an economic and political one: They're supposed to *visually* and *physically define* the state boundaries. Since state boundaries have never been exactly defined before, Augustus might well be thought of as the first potentate who conceives of them as a means of political control. Subsequently, thousands of kilometres of "Limites" are built around the Roman Empire.

Augustus' reign goes down in history as the most prosperous period in the history of Ancient Rome. After his death on 19th August AD 14 until the end of the high empire period under Diocletian (as from AD 284), the position of a Roman emperor implicates a higher probability of dying from violence than the one of a slave or a soldier.

Two Letters

To Marcus Vitruvius in Rome, 27/26 BP

The Emperor of Rome, Son of the Divine Caesar Salutes Marcus Vitruvius, wishing that these words may find him well.

With proper respect to your esteemed work both on behest of the foregone and the present Divine Caesar, I would like you to know that I am very pleased with your synopsis of the foundational work I have entrusted you with. If accomplished according to such a comprehensive and senseful order, the ten books will serve the purpose of instructing the architects in service of the Empire to my entire satisfaction. As you may have anticipated, I am especially interested in the contents of Book 5, concerning the conception of public buildings, Book 8, concerning infrastructures of water supply with regard to which you have already proven your skills, and Book 10, which you have chosen to be about "machinery".

Please note that I have also taken the time to read the draft of the first Book entitled "Fundamental notions and principles to be applied in the education of architects and the layout of cities" very carefully. Though I have no objections so far concerning its content in general, I would like you to take cognizance of my disappointment by your writing style, which is far from what unfortunately deceased Marcus Tullius Cicero would approve of. I hereby advise you to delve deeper into the classics of natural philosophies as presented in the scriptures of our Greek precursors, which might improve your writing skills as well as broaden your understanding of the very nature of our intents. Moreover, I am convinced that such studies will not only be of benefit to your own but also to the skills of future architects.

As to your pecuniary request, I have signed a document, which guarantees your financial independence in the form of a lifetime pension to an appropriate amount. You are invited to present yourself to Marcus Agrippa on the 18th of November at the hour of his morning consultations and receive the document in person.

Expecting a conference regarding further procedures to be compatible with my duties shortly, I sincerely recommend your wellbeing to the gods.

Signed Octavian Augustus

5th November in the first year of the Roman Empire

Dear and esteemed Marcus

Your letter has reached me in Gesoriacum just a few days before my leave. Much to my regret, my release from duties has been revoked, and I have been summoned by the prefect of Geneva to join his reconnaissance forces into Helvetia before my long awaited and already arranged return to my chosen homeland. Hence, as you may understand, the memories of our shared adventures at the fronts of the Gallic War that have been brought back to me by your lines are not entirely welcome at this very moment. So please forgive me for keeping this reply short and simple. As soon as I will be on my way south, I won't get a chance to commit it to trustworthy hands.

I am very pleased to learn that the stinking cloaca I became acquainted with on the occasion of my first and only visit to Rome is going to be turned into a civilised city. And I am truly happy for you being part of that endeavour. Let me tell you that the outline of your first book about the principles of architecture you have sent me strikes me as reasonably thorough, although I completely agree with your illustrious employer that it lacks linguistic style and precision. Since you address me as someone who is familiar enough with the topics to evaluate your work, there are three suggestions I would like to make.

First, I advise you to seriously consider the remarks of your emperor and to broaden your view with regard to a sufficient architectural education. Apart from aesthetics in general and drawing, geometry, arithmetic, astronomy, geodesy, and the science of materials in particular, the sciences that discuss the human beings and the contemporary conditions of their existence should be seriously taken in account in any architectural venture. Great cities are not built by men who know how to put one stone onto the other in an appropriate and appealing way but by those who understand the nature of human beings, which may well be defined as the principal legitimation of their work.

Second, there may be more to the conception of ground plan, elevation, and perspective than meets the human eye that perceives the geometric dimensions of a built artefact. We might as well think of the ichnographic traces, the orthographic placements, and the scenographic views as general aspects of how the human mind conceives of things and, consequently, as aspects of a cosmographic description of the natural world itself, at least as far as we can conceptualise it. Admittedly, this idea demands further philosophical investigation and might lead to insights that transcend the common understanding of dimensional objects and relations. It might even put that very common understanding to flight. On the other hand, what are we to expect of an architecture that denies its origin in the continuing challenges of the mind?

And third, concerning the more trivial and quotidian purposes of your meritorious project, I would like to remind you of the considerable discrepancies between the common use of language and the choice of precise technical terms. Writing on architecture as a practice is not quite like writing history or poetry. History captures the reader from its very nature, for it holds out the hope of various novelties. Poetry, with its measures and metrical feet, its refinement in the assortment of words, and the delivery in verse of the sentiments expressed by different characters, delights the emotion of the reader and leads him smoothly on to the very end of the work. This cannot be the case with architectural treatises because those technical terms, which originate in the peculiar needs of the art, give rise to obscurity of ideas from the unusual nature of the language. Thus, I suggest that you offer many descriptive examples and poetic explanations to your reader and explain this approach in a general introductory remark. It might help to understand the more obscure terms that you find yourself compelled to use and to commit them to the memory of your recipient.

I sincerely hope that this letter finds you in good spirits, all the more so because it may well contain the last words ever exchanged between us.

Anyway, I salute you, my friend, and remain faithfully yours.
Signed Leto of Durovernum
(Undated)

Post scriptum

Your hints at a theory of the "homo bene figuratus" has at once intrigued and frightened me. I'm curious as to how it is going to fit in your conceptions.[5]

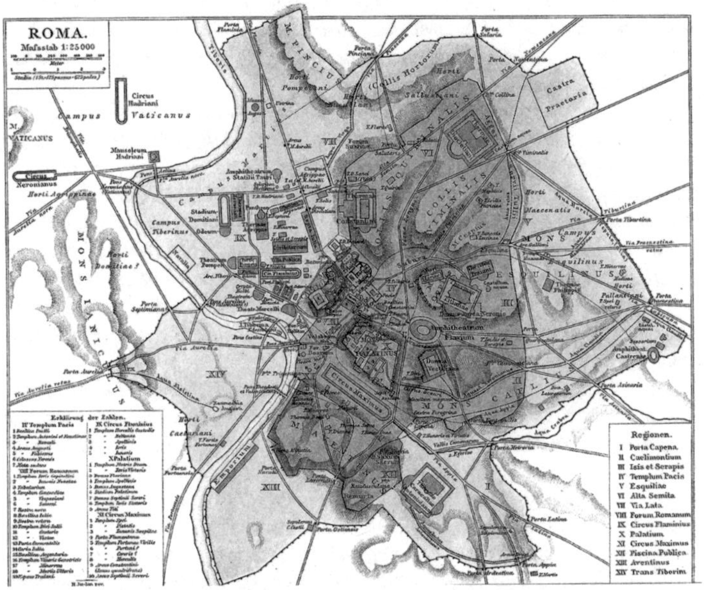

City of Rome, early imperial period

5 Some of the sentences in the letter's last paragraph have been adopted as they stand in Vitruvius' extensive work *De architectura libri decem* (*Ten Books About Architecture*). The post scriptum refers to a passage about the geometrical proportions of the human body from which Leonardo da Vinci's famous illustration is derived (1492, cf. also p. 112). Based on the references to Augustus' letter and to historical events, the second letter is dated to around January or February 26 BC. "Gesoriacum" was the major Roman harbour town on the Gallic Channel coast (today's Boulogne-sur-Mer, France) for maritime traffic to Britannia. "Durovernum Cantiacorum" (Canterbury) was the major Celtic and Roman city in Kent.

The translation of *ichnographia*, *orthographia*, and *scaenographia* as "ichnographic traces" etc. is an attempt to display a specific typographical emphasis on the Greek origin of the words in the handwriting.

Beyond the information contained in this chronicle, there are hardly any records about Vitruvius' course of life. Born around 80 BC, he chose a career as an engineer in Caesar's and Octavian's armies before he started working as an architect in Rome on behalf of Octavian in 33 BC. The ten books of *De Architectura* were written between 33 and 22 BC and did hardly receive any attention until the 15th century, when Leon Battista Alberti based his *De re aedificatoria* (1452) upon the only comprehensive book about architecture ever written in ancient times as far as we know. Since then, Vitruvius' work has influenced most (if not all) theoretical approaches to architecture in Europe and is cited whenever a historical derivation of the discipline's means and competencies is required. He died around 15 BC, most probably in Rome.

15 BC

During emperor Augustus' campaigns into Germania, headed by his stepsons Drusus and Tiberius Claudius Nero (the latter being Augustus' successor as from AD 14), the Romans occupy the Helvetian territory from the west to the east and affiliate it to the province of "Gallia Belgica". They change the fortified Helvetic "Oppida" into Roman military bases (like "Augusta Raurica" at today's Kaiseraugst or "Vindonissa" at today's Windisch) and define the left shore of Lake Zurich as the border between the provinces "Raetia" in the southeast and "Germania Superior" in the north. Thus, the former Celtic village *Turicon* on "Lindenhof" hill becomes a Roman customs settlement on the main route across the eastern Alps (the Julier pass route, which is today's all season motor traffic connection to the upper Engadin valley and apparently named after Caesar's and Augustus' family name).

At that time, the Romans have developed subtle ways of integrating and "romanising" occupied territories by a strategic mixture of cultural laissez-faire and legal, economic, and infrastructural reformations. Against this background, it is highly probable that the Roman presence in Turicon is restricted to a customs station ("Stationis Turicensis") and a few commercial buildings at the foot of "Lindenhof" hill at first, including a restored boat harbour, a reinforced bridge across the river "Limmat", channellings of the river "Sihl" and drainage of the swamp areas, leaving the Celtic village on the hill intact. According to archaeological finds, the Roman infrastructure is gradually expanded during the 1st and 2nd century AD, including a Roman bath at today's "Weinplatz", a Jupiter temple on the site of today's St. Peter's church, and several manors and mansions in the vicinity, thus "romanising" the local Celtic population step by step.[6]

~AD 0

According to historical references, *Jesus of Nazareth* is born between 7 and 4 years before the Christian era and is convicted and crucified between AD 29 and 33. His first public appearances as a rabbi in Galilee and Judea date to around AD 28. Barring the apotheosising interpretations and embellishments in the gospels and other sources, he may be considered to be the first known thinker in history who argues for a most radical egalitarianism and pacifism based on both spiritual and philosophical conceptions of the individual human being. However, given the political and religious circumstances of the time and place, his teachings are necessarily received as contemporary political statements. In spite or because of that and due to his martyrdom and solacing doctrine of salvation, his followers rapidly increase in number, especially among the poor, the exploited, and the enslaved.

6 Remains of Roman mansions, public buildings, and infrastructures have been found within a radius of 4.5 km around the central "Lindenhof" hill, for instance at today's open-air bath "Letzigraben", beneath today's "Altstetten" church, in the "Albisrieden" quarter, and in the historic district along the right shore of the river "Limmat", to mention but a few sites. Most probably, a watchtower was erected on the "Uetliberg" mountain soon after the Romans had arrived. On an island in the lake basin, already a site of pile-dwelling settlements in the 5th millennium BC, a circular Roman temple of wood was built in AD 122. Due to the rise of the lake level, the island is flooded for centuries now.

Archaeological excavations in Zurich have a deplorable history of negligence and obstructions by landowners and authorities. As a result, many of the finds of Celtic remains on site have either got lost or prematurely been misinterpreted as being of Roman origin, and the Celtic villages, both on "Lindenhof" hill and "Uetliberg" mountain, have not been considered in an appropriate way until recently. The find of spot plates and a 60 kg clump of 18'000 partly melted bronze coins minted in Turicon around 100 BC may serve as an example. Found in 1890 and stored at the National Museum, these finds have finally been categorised a few years ago. They strongly suggest that Turicon was one of the very few accredited Celtic *coinage sites* and therefore must have been of trans-regional commercial significance for a long period in pre-Roman times. However, why the clump was hastily sunk in the lake over 2100 years ago is kindly signed over to the reader's imagination (the theory that it could have been a sacrificial offering being called into question in respect to its considerable value).

All four canonical gospels, like the rest of the New Testament, were written in the Greek language (*Mark* probably around AD 70, *Matthew* and *Luke* around AD 80–90, and *John* around AD 90–110). Today, the traditional ascriptions are mostly rejected in favour of treating the gospels as anonymous works.

43 Under emperor Claudius, the southeast of *Britannia* is conquered by Roman legions in less than a month in AD 43, and the Celtic "Oppidum Camulodunum" (Colchester) becomes the provincial capital. During the following years, several British uprisings have to be brought down, the most effective and legendary of them being the Iceni revolt under emperor Nero's regency:

~ 60 When King Prasutagus, ruler of the Iceni, a major Celtic people in the area of today's Norfolk allied with Rome, leaves his kingdom to the Roman emperor *as well as* to his daughters and his wife *Boudica* in his will, the Romans intervene and annex the kingdom because handing down political powers to women is against the Roman law. According to Roman historiographer Tacitus, Boudica is flogged and her daughters raped on that occasion. In AD 60, during a Roman campaign in the region of Wales, Boudica leads the Iceni in revolt, supported by the neighbouring tribe of the Trinovantes. They destroy Camulodunum and emperor Claudius' local temple. Upon hearing of the revolt, Roman governor Suetonius orders the Roman troops to abandon "Londinium" (today's London), which has been founded as a main commercial settlement after Claudius' invasion in AD 43. Boudica's around 100'000 male and female warriors raid and destroy Londinium, killing around 80'000 Roman and Briton inhabitants of the greater area and leaving a distinctive several centimetres thick black layer of compressed ash in the geological sediments beneath the city of London. Subsequently, she recruits another 130'000 Britons to join her forces.[7] The crisis causes emperor Nero to consider a total withdrawal from Britannia before Suetonius regroups his legions in the west and, despite being heavily outnumbered, defeats the Britons in the Battle of Watling Street, a main road leading from northern Wales through Londinium to Durovernum (Canterbury) and from there to the harbours of Lemanis, Dubrae (Dover), and Rutupiae (Richborough). Where exactly the battle takes place and whether Boudica dies on site or shortly after the battle is not recorded consistently, which leads to many opposing theories. Since Boudica is conventionalised into a British folk heroine in Victorian times, the location between north London's Primrose Hill (Regent's Park) and Battle Bridge behind King's Cross Station becomes very popular.[8]

Boudica is described by the Roman-Greek historian Cassius Dio as a "tall woman with tawny hair hanging down to below her waist, a harsh voice and a piercing glare, possessed of greater intelligence than often belongs to women." Etymologically, her name is derived from the Celtic word *boudā* for "victory" and accordingly turns into the name "Victoria" in modern English, which may be a reason for her popularity under Queen Victoria's reign.

7 Figures based on contemporary sources.

8 Scottish journalist and occult scholar James Lewis Spence (1874 – 1955) goes as far as presenting a map showing the positions of the opposing armies in his book *Boadicea — warrior queen of the Britons* (1937), thus provoking wild speculations such as the belief that Boudica was buried between platforms 9 and 10 in King's Cross Station, a location that is again quite familiar to readers of Joanne K. Rowling's *Harry Potter* books, published as from 1997.

72 – 80

The biggest public building of the ancient times, the "Flavian Amphitheatre" or "*Colosseum*" allowing audience figures of up to 80'000, is constructed under the reigns of Vespasian and his son Titus. It may be reciprocally conceived of as a pinnacle of ancient architecture and as a symbol of the upcoming massification, decadence and decay of the Roman society in view of the performances given at this location.[9] A year before the building is finished, the volcano Vesuvius erupts and destroys the Campanian city Pompeii on 24th August 79. More than a thousand people are suffocated or buried alive.

• North side of the "Flavian Amphitheatre" or "Colosseum" in Rome today

98 – 107

During the reign of emperor Trajan, the expansion of the *Roman Empire* comes to an end, reaching from the Atlantic coasts to the Black Sea, Armenia, and Assyria in the east, from Caledonia and the "Germanic Sea" (North Sea) to the coastal regions of northern Africa and to Upper Egypt. Subsequently, the frontiers of the Empire are under constant pressure, especially by Germanic tribes in the north and the Parthian kingdom (followed by the new Persian Empire as from AD 220) in the east.

105

The invention of *paper* is commonly ascribed to Ts'ai Lun, tool and weapon production officer at the emperor's court in China (document date of the first mention of the paper production method). However, the earliest archaeological finds of paper in China date back to around 140 BC.

122

Emperor Hadrian initiates the construction of a Limes wall to "separate Romans from barbarians", to deter attacks on Roman territory at a lower cost than by a border army, and to control cross-border trade and immigration. He has a shrine erected in Eboracum (York), dedicated to "Britannia" as the divine personification of Britain. By the end of the year, Hadrian leaves Britannia and never sees the finished wall that bears his name.[10] He dies in AD 138.

The Roman military forces evacuate Britannia around AD 407, exposing it to the tyranny of local Romano-British warlords and the revolts of Anglo-Saxon slaves and soldiers preceding the invasion of the Angles and Saxons from Germania.

9 The name *Colosseum* has long been understood as derived from a colossal statue of Nero in the immediate vicinity (the statue of Nero was named after the Colossus of Rhodes). This statue was later remodelled by Nero's successors into a statue of the sun god Sol Invictus or Apollo by adding the appropriate solar crown. Nero's head was repeatedly replaced with the heads of succeeding emperors. Despite of its pagan background, the statue was not removed until the medieval era and was credited with magical powers (cf. also *Poetic Spaces*, p. 94 et seq.).

10 The eastern section of „Hadrian's Wall" is made from squared stone and measures 3 metres in width and 6 metres in height while the 6 metres wide section west of the river Irthing is originally made from turf and later rebuilt in stone. The central section measures eight Roman feet in width (approx. 2.4 m) on a 3 m base. The wall is 118 km long (not including ditches, berms, and forts) and reaches from the southern border of today's Scotland at the Atlantic coast to today's Newcastle upon Tyne at the North Sea coast. Around AD 142, Hadrian's successor Antonius Pius orders the building of an additional Limes in Caledonia (today's Scotland), reaching from the Firth of Clyde to the Firth of Forth ("Antonine's Wall").

• Remains of Hadrian's Wall at Green Head Lough today, Northumberland, England

160 *Claudius Ptolemy*, Greek mathematician, geographer and astronomer, dies in Alexandria-by-Egypt where he has spent most of the 60 years of his life. He is the originator of the geocentric cosmological model (Ptolemaic system) that is considered as a scientific standard theory in Europe until the Early Modern Age. In the 2nd century AD, the third world power apart from Rome and Parthia is the Chinese Empire of the Han dynasty, evolving more or less remotely and independently from the rest of the known world at its own historical and cultural "pace".

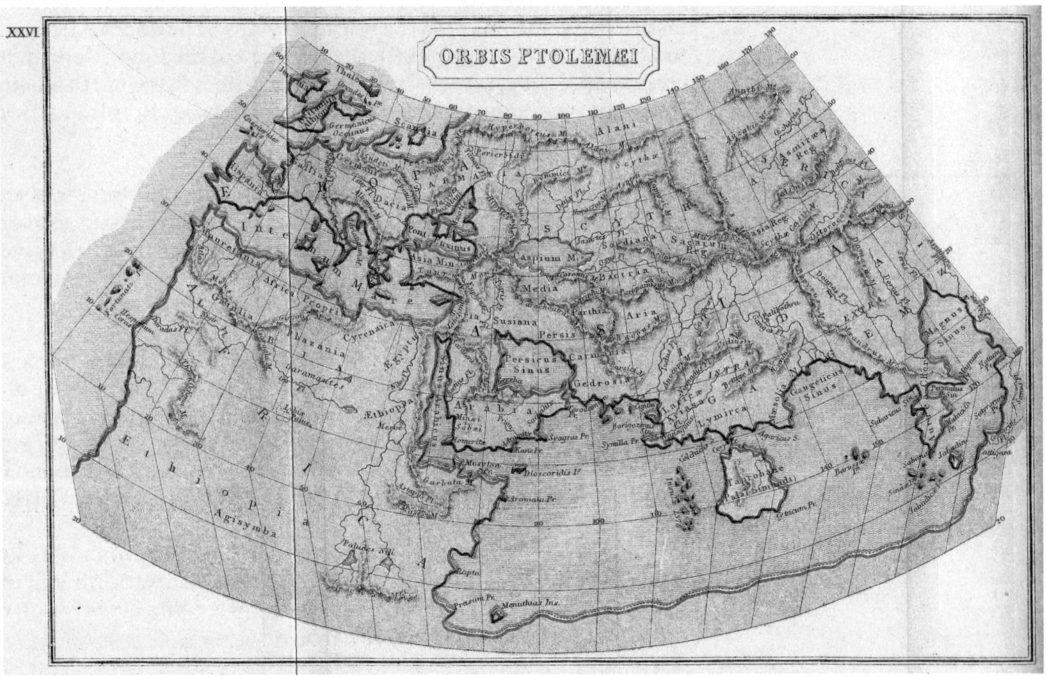

• Samuel Butler's *Orbis Ptolemaei* (1907), a depiction of Ptolemy's geographical worldview

POETIC SPACES
INTERVENTIONS

Magic spaces are natural environments conceived of as parts (or "com-part-ments") of an integral totality, of the world as a "whole". Human beings relate to them in magic, animistic, and symbolistic ways because they think of themselves as participants of that totality: as objectified beings within an essentially balanced cosmos that is constructed and driven by forces beyond their immediate control, experience, and comprehension. These forces are ideated as entities of magic power and are related to in magic ways. Accordingly, magic spaces are defined by all kinds of sages, priests, and magicians who exclusively preserve the available knowledge about the world as a whole and the forces at work in it. Because of their intuitively holistic worldviews, human beings conceive of their spatial constructions and buildings as objects that are fully integrated into the context of their natural environment and its magic conditions.

Poetic spaces are places, spatial situations, or spatial environments that are defined, designed, and constructed by human beings in their own right. They are *conditioned* according to *authentic* and independent human ideas and purposes. They are thought of as creative interventions within creation, and as such they are more or less controllable by their creators and users. The totality of the spatial environment is still there, still scary, and still not fully comprehended, but it is banished from the poetic spaces into outer spaces by the means of theories, which define what's inside and what's outside – and what's in between. Since spatial poetry *explicitly* confronts human beings with the notions of spatial inside and outside perspectives, they relate to them in explicitly objective (basically aesthetic, creative, and experimental) ways. Accordingly, poetic spaces are defined by all kinds of craftsmen and artists and poets – and their *works*.

This explains, among other things, the rapidly increasing indifference to ecological dynamics as from the ages of poetic space (and as against the ages of magic and animistic spaces), although the intellectual understanding of nature and natural phenomena has become one of the main objectives of human efforts. The poetic approach to natural environments is (and always will be) a radically challenging and emancipatory one: an approach of objectification that is far from humble or submissive.

The "Promethean Turn"

As may have become obvious in the overall context of the preceding entries in the chronicle, the anteriorly so-called "Promethean turn" is essentially attached to the evolvement and extension of cities. Cities are places where the reality of poetic spaces reaches a critical density and complexity. The repression of "magic" in favour of "poetic spaces" increases, once the notion of an objectifiable nature is fully fledged, along with the transformations of formerly explicit symbols into poetic *objects* and *gestures* in early urban areas. Quite evidently, the magic is still there, implicated in *aestheticised* representations of what has been mighty and literally untouchable before: in all the powerful forms and formalities that the kings and queens, the potentates and politicians surround themselves with, in the fundamentally aesthetic, economic, and spatial reorganisations and continuous differentiations of urban societies, in the arts that change from tangible and basically practical crafts into creative and poetic (and, at times, intellectual) disciplines of production of "works",[11] and, of course, in the conception and construction of buildings and infrastructures that are literally *representative* in many ways. All these developments are expressions or rather *explications* of the growing awareness that nature and culture have become two strictly separated spheres. And most conspicuously, this separation is first and foremost recognised and "objectified" in the strategic planning and erection of cities representing the very "identity" of socially, nationally and demographically cohesive populations. They are conceived of as symbolic monuments of cultural progress and prosperity, and, as such, they become the primary targets of the endless struggles for political and economic power, being built, conquered, destroyed, and rebuilt again and again.

It might be put into question whether this kind of cultural development can be seriously conceived of as a cultural "turn" in view of the fact that

11 Quite naturally, Hannah Arendt's sustainably inspiring distinction between "labour", "work", and "action" as political and existential determinants of human culture in *Vita activa – The Human Condition* (1958) is implied here.

it continues for millenniums, in many stages and many different paces in different cultural regions. However, we must acknowledge once again that these developments are not describable in strictly historical terms and facts. They are primarily *ideational*, and changes of ideas cannot be measured in periods of time. Ideas may be related to but cannot "occur" or "vanish" in time. They are attributed to essentially instantaneous changes of mind-sets and cognitions, meaning that they do not gradually "shift" from one stage to the next but rather "turn" from one state of mind into another (and possibly back again). So if we look at the world we inhabit today and notice that the "age of poetic spaces" is still in full bloom (or: in full bloom *again*), we should not be too surprised.

Accordingly, the notion of "poetic spaces" is not actually conceived of but *recognised* in the altered – or more precisely: *modified* – environments and spatial experiences. Quite suddenly, the "nature" of space becomes experienceable as an inexhaustible economic resource, offering almost boundless possibilities for authentic human interventions, designs, and modifications, limited only by the so-called "laws of nature". The gods and spirits and magic forces begin to back away from their former immediate and permanent presence in civilised environments to remote spaces like heaven, distant islands, or the Mount Olympus, giving way to human creations and "growths", which they observe and judge and comment on from the distance. They still have the power to punish and reward, but they have lost the power to create and end this world. They are still worshipped, but they have retreated to realms that lie beyond immediate human concerns: symbolically symbolised symbols that, recognised as such, inevitably will be second-guessed, tested, and overtly queried. So, finally, here they are: the *interstices* in space and time. The division of heaven and earth is completed. And that is exactly what Prometheus (along with his fellow mythic advocates of mankind) achieves and is punished for. He reduces the "gods" and "demons" at work in the natural world to intellectual concepts and representations of political and psychological processes, thus literally subjecting them to the mercy and power of the subjective intellect.

In this overall context, and as long as there is neither a specific term nor a specific idea of space as a cognitive entity, the physical and "objective" among the poetic interventions in space are conceived of as artificial "places" (rather than "spaces"): as sites, houses, buildings, or constructions of areas and interstices in various combinations. All these places are built and produced to serve certain purposes, which defines them as "cultural" places as against purposeless "natural" places. Hence, these artificial places are also explicit and often highly symbolic spatial inscriptions of cultural "insides" against natural "outsides". The archaic sheltering function of buildings is extended to "cultural spaces" which represent the ongoing physical and mental emancipation of humankind from the unconditional subjection to the principles and forces of nature.

Inscriptions

Once the subjective intellect has become aware of its newly acquired powers and potentials, it develops and accomplishes its poetic work at an astounding pace. Remarkably enough, the standard knowledge and principles of natural philosophy that are going to be decisive and scientifically unchallenged up to the 16th century are acquired in less than five hundred years between the 6th and the 2nd century BC. In consequence, they define the ideas of space – or: the "spatial situation" – in the Ancient World: a situation of debatable cosmological principles which gradually turn space into a describable and measurable, i.e. a neutral dimensional and designable factor of the human condition by means of geometry, arithmetic, physics, or spatial drawing and, finally, into a field of proto-scientific expertise and poetic experimentation in which the craft of architecture eventually becomes a leading discipline. For instance, this situation has to be taken into account as Alexander of Macedonia's situation: Howsoever his manic ambitions and actions may be judged in historiography (or by himself), they cannot be understood if not as essentially poetic acts and endeavours in the most literal sense of the word.

Against this background, it may be hard to believe that there still is no abstract or absolute notion of space whatsoever in classical antiquity. Which is, of course, particularly obvious in the context of the rhetoric, the discourse, and the practice of architecture that is (and remains) focused upon the spatial *objects*, upon their significance as poetic works and technical products rather than as physical explications of an idea of space. The formulation of the second suggestion in Leto of Durovernum's letter to Marcus Vitruvius (cf. *Two Letters*, p. 83) may serve as an example. As she gets on to the issue of developing the three-dimensional conception of spatial relations into an abstracted definition of space itself, she turns to an awkwardly elaborate circumscription of what could, from a modern perspective, quite easily be expressed in one word: "space", which, after all, has been in use for centuries at the time. However, she is forced not to use the word in its substantival form (lat. *spatium* n. for "space", "distance", "size", "length", "extent", "perimeter" etc.) because it just does not signify what she means, not even in a metaphorical way. It means *nothing but* "spatial interstice" in every possible sense, but it does *not yet* mean space as a cognitive entity. That cognitive entity simply does not exist in the contemporary understandings of the world. It only exists in her imagination that is, at that point and irrespective of whether she is aware of it or not, far ahead of contemporary common sense and notional capabilities (including those of one

Marcus Vitruvius). Quite revealingly, the only Latin word that is available to her in this context is *natura* f. (in the sense of "natural world"), derived from, even more revealingly, the verb *nascere* for "to be born" and "*to be produced*".

Another descriptive example is Octavian Augustus' idea of defining exact state boundaries when he orders the building of *Limites* along the frontiers of the Roman Empire (cf. p. 81). As a poetic intervention in space, it is completely consistent with the aesthetical, the political, and the increasingly economic spatial logics of his time, but its revolutionary impact on the very idea of space as an absolute term naturally escapes his notice. And the same goes for many other known or unknown historical persons and their thinking about or acting upon their spatial environments. So if the question should be raised to which extent those well-known historical facts listed in the entries of the chronicle at hand have anything to do with the conception and imagination of space, here is the answer: They reveal a chronology of both physical and conceptual *inscriptions* in space, driven by purposeful pragmatism at times, by hope or grief or desire at others. But these inscriptions always represent momentary contributions to continuing developments of the idea of space, irrespective of whether they arise from intent or by accident.

Revaluations

As has become evident enough by now, the idea of space at a certain place and time is always attached to immediate political impacts. Just like any other political system in the ages of poetic space, the rise and fall of the idea of democracy in the city-states of Ancient Greece is most certainly related to the emancipatory spatial understanding of the human condition: not only upon the differentiation of the human being as a subject transcending the boundaries of natural and cultural spaces in general but, in the case of democracy, also and foremost upon the strict differentiation of cultural spaces into *private* and *political* spaces.[12] Apart from political systems, which are increasingly based on rational deliberations and political philosophy, the political significance and *meaningfulness* of spatial designs in sculpture and the visual arts as well as in urban construction and representative building may have never been more explicitly and commonly *understood* than in classical antiquity and, drawing on the latter, the early modern ages.

In contrast, remarkably enough but not quite surprisingly, "time" (and its relation to space and spaces) has never been a greater mysterious unknown than in these antique and proto-rational cultures. Consequently, it remained at-

12 The very idea of democracy implied a literally "spatial" conception insofar as it was grounded in the rationale of private and public or political "spaces" ("spheres of interest") being contradictory terms by definition and, consequently, must be kept apart ("kept at distance") with the utmost strictness (which is why, according to the social conditions of the time, women and slaves were barred from democratic accountability as "idiots", the word meaning "private persons" or "persons without interest in public and political affairs", but also "persons who refuse or are incapable of social and political cognition" in Ancient Greek).

tributed to the realms of the gods and the "beyond" of unexplainable cosmic mysteries, not least because its "mathematical" and "geometrical" representation was so evidently simple in comparison to its psychological and experiential complexity that it was broadly deemed to be beyond human comprehension.

However, the Promethean turn comes at a steep price in many respects, just as the myth itself vividly explains. Apart from the existential, psychological, and ethical consequences of the alienation from nature (or the loss of embeddedness in it), the objectification of natural environments implies, given the aforementioned balanced complementarity of the sexes in preceding magic cultures, the symbolic and subsequently political objectification of the female (i.e. the "earthly") sex. The replacement of the cultic equality of the mother goddess Ishtar and the father god Bēl in Mesopotamia in the 4th millennium BP was, as previously indicated, just the beginning of a millennia-long symbolical and political transvaluation in favour of male sun and sky gods in almost all cultural regions and, consequently, of the *ideals* they *represent*: the eventual triumph of the solar over the lunar sphere, light over dark, fire over water, heaven over earth, reason over intuition, intellect over emotion and ecstasy, wand and sword over cup and coin, space over time, manhood over womanhood. This "revaluation of values" is not half as esoterically withdrawn as it may seem at first sight: It is a transcultural intellectual rearrangement of ideational hierarchies in traditional cognitive conceptions as far as they can be traced back into prehistoric times: to the records of the earliest high cultures in Mesopotamia, Egypt, Assyria, China, and the eastern Mediterranean region.[13] In historic times, the iconological, iconographical, and *poetic* manifestations of this process are just as conspicuous as the social and political ones, at least for those who dare to have a look.[14]

But again, we should not be tempted into simplistic conceptions of developments like these. They do not occur in a linear or monocausal or uncontested succession of events. And most certainly, they do not progressively lead to absolute results but rather to multiple shifts in social ranking, strategic predominance and intellectual prevalence, resulting in altered generic *conventions* and *conveniences* (just as they do in the context of today's so-called "battle of the sexes", even though the particular social contexts and conditions are hardly comparable).

Fact is that by the beginning of antiquity, the altered worldviews are broadly systematised in political, cultural, and intellectual practices, and

13 The phenomenology of these „cognitive conceptions" has been briefly discussed and exemplified in the context of "magic spaces". At this point, the concept of the "tree of life" in the Jewish kabbalah or the tradition of symbolic "stages of consciousness" presumably originating from the Old Egyptian Kingdom, later metaphorically represented in the original tarot and other playing card decks and in "magic use" up to the present, might be suggested as two examples that have not been mentioned before and are specifically illuminating with regard to the history of symbolic revaluations in concepts of cognition.

14 Cf, for instance, footnote referring to the *Colosseum*, p. 87.

women are broadly deprived of their formal *political* and *poetic* liberties and responsibilities in most dominant cultures.[15] Accordingly, the ages of poetic space are most definitely and explicitly dominated by male strategies and personalities – and, reciprocally, by female "mysteries" of course – that remain effective up to the present in the respective disciplines in many obvious and not so obvious ways. Fact is also that the repressed ideational principles are gradually adapted to the new conditions by the development of passive and subversive forms of resistance against prevailing ideologies. In this context, it may be noteworthy that the early political and, as is well-known, often violent suppressions of the Christian movements are finally put to an end in the wake of a gradually popularised identification of their almighty god with transcultural sun gods like Apollo and Sol Invictus. Which again forces the Christian bishops to eventually renounce the fundamental egalitarianism of Christian philosophy, including its remarkable implications in respect to the abstraction of spatial realities attached to the notion of the "kingdom of God", and turn towards religiously legitimised patriarchal ideologies (cf. p. 96 et seqq.). And yes indeed, as things are going to turn out, this is not exactly a peripheral episode in the history of space.

15 It is broadly presumed that many of the Celtic tribes represent an exception to this rule, maintaining "matriarchal" or partly "matriarchal" structures until they became subject to Roman conquest and assimilation (cf. pp. 72, 73, and 85).
In the highly legalistic Roman culture, women's liberties are quite obviously restricted to one principal objective: women's contribution to *economic growth*. For instance, women were at liberty to participate in trade and commercial affairs in the imperial period, which goes to show how enormously important economic politics had become by then. Because of their legal status as citizens, women could own property, enter contracts, and engage in business, including shipping, manufacturing, and lending money. Many women were honoured as benefactors in funding public works, which indicates that they could acquire and dispose of substantial fortunes.

Under the reign of emperor Augustus, according to his social conservative convictions about morality and social order, attempts were made to enhance the social status of women by law, especially with regard to family and inheritance policies. For example, girls had the same inheritance rights as boys if their father died without leaving a will. A Roman mother's right to own property and to dispose of it according to her wish, including setting the terms of her own will, gave her considerable influence over her sons even when they were adults. Most revealingly, the encouragement of childbearing by the state was a complementary part of the Augustan reforms: A woman who had given birth to three children was granted symbolic honours and extended legal freedom ("*ius trium liberorum*").

However, the enforcement of laws and conventions that prohibited women from participating in political, "scientific", and, to a considerable extent, also in artistic activities was very strict and specific both in the republican and the imperial period. One of the more obvious historical consequences of these policies was that many (if not most) of the emperors in the high empire period were murdered on behalf of their wives who intended to install their favourite sons (usually of previous marriages) in the line of succession before the sitting emperor appointed another successor by will, this being one of only few ways to gain political influence under the given circumstances (not only among women of patrician rank but also among free citizens).

260 Having dedicated his seven years of regency to the defence of the Roman frontiers against the Goths and the reinvigorated Persians, emperor *Valerian* dies in Persian captivity after his army has suffered defeat in the Battle of Edessa. This first serious humiliation of the Roman Empire is embittered by rumours that Valerian has been skinned alive by command of the Persian king Shapur I. These rumours are very popular among Christians who interpret the atrocity as punishment for Valerians persecution of their church leaders in AD 257.

~300 In the context of reinforcements of the Germanic frontiers under emperors Diocletian and Constantine, a fortified Roman "castellum" is built on the southern part of "Lindenhof" hill in Turicum.[16] At the end of the 4th century, the Romans gradually begin to evacuate their northern provinces, leaving the territories to Gothic, Germanic, and Alemannic invaders who themselves back away from the invasion of the Huns and the Vandals in northeast Europe. Turicum is abandoned by the Roman forces in AD 401 and is wondrously spared from foreign military attacks during the entire *Migration Period* that initiates the Dark Ages.

306 Flavius Valerius Constantinus (*Constantine the Great*) is declared emperor of Rome by his unexpectedly deceased father Constantius' soldiers in Eboracum (York) during a suppressive operation against revolting Picts and Scotti. This seizure of power is actually an act of usurpation, but since the Empire has been reorganised as a tetrarchy by Diocletian back in AD 293, Constantine succeeds in engaging his competitors in political and military conflicts and finally re-establishes the Roman monocracy in 324 AD. He chooses Byzantium (today's Istanbul) as the new capital of the Empire, renames it "Constantinople", avows himself a Christian, and gradually involves the ramified Christian bishop's organisations in the empire's government affairs ("Constantinian shift"), thus actually introducing Christianity as the Roman state religion. Preparing for yet another campaign against Persia, he dies in Nicomedia in AD 337 and is baptised on his deathbed.

Although the Constantinian shift results in tremendous political consequences, it remains unknown how, why, and when exactly Constantine has converted from his early (and already monotheistic) sun-god worship ("Sol Invictus") to Christianity. The most plausible explanation may be sought in his political pragmatism. Most probably he realises at some point that an occidental empire cannot be maintained any longer without the inclusion of the irresistibly growing and disseminating Christian population. However, his decisions accelerate the political processes leading to the definitive division of the empire into West and East Rome in AD 395. Thereafter, the capital of West Rome is moved from Rome to Milan and Ravenna.

354 *Augustine of Hippo* (today's Annaba, Algeria) is born in Tagaste, Numidia. He arguably is the most influential philosopher of late antiquity and the originator of the fundamentals of catholic thinking. As the former, he introduces conceptions such as an early "psychological

16 The formerly Celtic and now completely romanised central village is mainly situated on the northern part of the hill, which has been removed in 1905 when the "Uraniastrasse" and the neighbouring administration buildings were constructed.

analogy" of Trinity, or the theory of time as a human condition of remembrance (past), presence, and expectation (future). As the latter, he develops the intellectual justifications of doctrines that shape Catholicism and later Christian fundamentalisms up to the present: the theories of predestination, of original sin, of confession and absolution, the mysticism of the Immaculate Conception, the idea of hell as a realm of everlasting torture and punishment of the soul, and the "just war theory". His distinctive profile as a passionate thinker does not make up for his being just as passionate as a believer, which turns his works into a treasury of legitimations of later deviancies of the Catholic Church, even more so because his course of life can be taken as the prototypical biography of a religious fanatic: carnal and materialistic excesses in early life, spiritual conversion after a personal epiphanic experience in AD 386, baptised by Milanese bishop Aurelius Ambrosius in AD 387 (later to become one of the four Fathers of the Church like Augustine himself), and, henceforth, inductive idealisation of his beliefs, confusion of self-righteousness with piety, arbitrary exegesis of holy scriptures as metaphors or verbatim, dogmatism of heresy and saintliness, and persecution of dissenters. He is declared bishop of Hippo in AD 395 and stays in office until his death in AD 430. Subsequently, the institutionalisation of papacy, initiated by Leo I, bishop of Rome from AD 440 to 461 who declares himself "Pontifex Maximus", "heir" and "representative of Saint Peter", refers to Augustines teachings and writings to a considerable extent.

The roman empire around 395, chart from the Historical Atlas by William A. Shepherd, New York 1923.

476 Though several incursions of Visigoths and Germanics in Italy and Rome have occurred during the 5th century, causing military coup d'états and chaotic political situations for decades, the *end of the West Roman Empire* is conventionally dated to 23rd August 476 AD when, after a reign of less than ten months, the 16-year-old last West Roman emperor Romulus Augustus (who's name has given rise to cynical mockery, of course, and is occasionally changed into "Romulus Augustulus") is deposed by rebel officer Odoacer who has served under Attila, king of the Huns, before. Upon approval of Byzantine emperor Zeno, Odoacer reigns in Ravenna as king of Italy for 17 years before he is defeated and killed by the Ostrogoth king Theodoric the Great in AD 493.

The Holy Grail

Somewhere on the coast of southern Britannia, around AD 504

"May I come in?"

No answer.

After she had asked a second and a third time, speaking up a little louder, the King's Mother opened the heavy iron-bound door to the fortress's basement vaults that most probably had served as dungeons back in Roman times. It was like a ritual. She knew that the Magician was in there, he always was. He hadn't left the vaults for weeks now, denying access to his private realm to anybody except for her. He didn't even receive the King himself.

There he was, crouching amidst his fancy drawings and mysterious scriptures, wrapped up in his black cloak that covered his appearance beyond recognition, completely bound up in his inscrutable work. The parchments were all over the place, spread over the moist floors, hung out on clotheslines tautened every which way beneath the mouldy ceilings.

"May I come in?" the King's Mother asked again, only to catch the Magician's attention, approaching him hesitantly to avoid stepping on his plans and maps and scribbles.

He looked up to her at last, grinning like a lunatic, his delicate beardless face disfigured into a sweaty ghastly mask of fatigue.

"Ah, it's you, my fair lady", he mumbled in his craggy voice and bowed his head. "What can I do for you?"

"Have you eaten anything today?"

"No, of course not, my lady," he replied cheerfully. "Eating makes my brains all numb and sluggish. Which I have told you before on some occasion or another, as I seem to remember faintly."

The King's Mother laughed amusedly and listened to her voice fading away in between the old grey stone walls that made her laughter sound like a frivolous giggle. The sweet fantasies took possession of her all at once. As they always did. However, this time they made her feel more confident than ever before. This time she looked her best, and this night felt like the night she had been longing for in all those years of unrest and sorrow since she had been escorted to this timeforsaken fortress to join the King's court.

As she glanced down on the piece of parchment the Magician had been studying, she thought that it looked like a map at first sight. But then she realised that there were no rivers, no villages, no mountains or seashores marked on it. There were only lines and circles and words. Latin words. Some of them were names of gods, others were thinkers' words she did not understand at all.

"What are you working on? Is it ... the future? *Our* future?"

For the time being, she tried to make her voice sound casual, like the voice of a King's Mother who incidentally visits the King's Magician in his accommodations.

"It is a cartography of the human intellect," the Magician answered calmly and drew himself up to his full height. He was tall and scraggy, just as a magician should be, even if he cared about his daily meals. "I don't mean to offend you, my lady, but honestly, you would not understand."

"I didn't expect I would," she said modestly, stroking her dark blue dress. "I do not even know who you really are. By God, I don't even know your real *name* – after all those years!"

"You know much more than you should, my lady. Among other things, you know perfectly well that I have not practiced for as long as you have known me. I am the King's advisor, I advise him on administering justice and on how those bloody Saxon bastards can be defeated in battle, and that is all there is to it. But if I were what you think I am, it might well be all about the future indeed. For all I know, it's what magic is about, even when devoted to the past." He looked around the vaults with a deep sigh and made a sweeping gesture. "However, as matters now stand, all this is just about ... *memories*."

The King's Mother smiled suggestively. "Memories, huh? – Memories of Vortigern's treachery? Memories of how Hadrian's Wall was built? Memories of Boudica's glorious victory and her tragic death by her own sword on the fields of Watling Street, memories of Great Caesar himself setting foot on these shores for the very first time? – You have not grown a single day older since we have met some twenty-seven years ago. I'd say, for a man who claims to know magic from hearsay, your memories go a long way."

The Magician kept silent for a while, staring into space. Then, turning around and looking squarely into the King's Mother's eyes, he said in a firm tone of voice: "I know that people talk about me, and I know what they say, my lady. To be honest, I am past caring about it. What is it that you want from me?"

For a moment, she dropped her gaze bashfully. When she looked up at him again, the shade of rose had vanished from her lovely face.

"You know exactly what I want. I know you do. See, it's not just that I haven't had a proper shag in years, it's just that ... you are stirring my blood."

A sad smile played upon the Magician's lips. "I do not have to put up with magic to see that, to *feel* it, actually, even when we are apart. But much to my regret, it is beyond my means to satisfy your desires."

She brushed his cheek with her lips, sensing the shiver that ran through him, and chuckled. "Why would that be?"

He did not answer. He let her have her way with him, wrap her arms around him and kiss him passionately. When her fingers had worked their way down to grope for his member under the cloak, she froze and stopped breathing.

"There," the Magician whispered in her ear, "I quite literally lack the magic wand to fill your cup. There is nothing down there but my Holy Grail."

She pushed him away and stared at him as if she refused to grasp the obvious. "You are ... I mean, you are ... –"

"Yes," he said calmly. "Whatever my real name is, it is not Merlin."

After a while of embarrassed silence, she burst out laughing hysterically. "Merlin and the Holy Grail – now that would give them something to talk abut!"

"Yes it would, wouldn't it?" The Magician smiled waggishly. "However, I would appreciate it if this could be kept between the two of us."

"Of course, my dear friend," she said, calming herself down. "Please forgive my offensiveness. I just didn't ... you know ... –"

"It is all right, my lady. I should ask *your* forgiveness for letting you in on this. Frankly speaking, I did it on purpose."

The Magician bent down to pick up the piece of parchment from the floor and folded it up carefully. Then he held it out to her, and she grasped at it in dignified silence.

"I'm afraid to tell you this, my lady, but I need you to know that I am going to leave this place very soon. And most probably, I will stay away for a very long time. In fact, it is rather unlikely that we shall see each other ever again. Not in this life."

"But why? Why now? We are in the middle of this serious crisis, and... –"

"I'm needed elsewhere, my lady. I will travel south across the Sea, accompanied by two of the King's Sarmatian lancers.[17] I cannot say more. But I would be very grateful if you would keep the document I gave you. Keep it *safe* for as long as you can. If you cannot, for whatever the reason, hand it down to someone to whom you would entrust your life. Or else, hide it in a safe place where not even *I* would find it if I wanted to. Will you do that for me?"

"Of course I will," the King's Mother replied, obviously being all aflutter. "I mean, I ... I will do my best. But what is to become of us, what is to become of the King when you're gone? How shall we defend ourselves against the Saxons without your help?"

"You shall *not*. As I have told you before, we cannot stand a chance against the invaders. Not in the long term, anyway. You might think that we live in dark times, and I would wish I had brighter prospects to share with you, but I see dark *ages* ahead of us. The world, as you know it, will come to an end soon, and along with it the knowledge, the stories, and the ideas we rely upon. However, I am confident that what we have achieved here will not have been in vain. The *dark ages* will pass, just as everything does, and centuries from now, people will remember what we have done. They will create and explore a new world, building on what we leave behind for them. And if the King deigns to heed my counsel, he will give up these lands before it is too late and, with God's blessing, he will lead you to the western shores where you shall be safe for the time being. As I said, this is *all* about the *future*."

17 During the Roman occupation, up to 5'500 Sarmatians were based in Britannia, serving as lancers and cavalry in the Roman legions. When the Roman troops abandoned the island around AD 407, most of them were demobilised, but a few remained to join the armies of Romano-British warlords and later became associated with the legendary "noble knights" of King Arthur's Round Table. Sarmatia (also known as Galicia) is situated in the lowlands of the border region between today's Ukraine and Poland.

The King's Mother opened her mouth to retort but realising that she actually had nothing to say she remained silent, glaring at the Magician with watery eyes full of terror.

Again, he smiled vaguely. "Never let fear guide you, my dear lady. Your strength is admired both by the people and the King. They are in dire need of it. And, if you allow me to come back to what has brought you here in the first place, I would suggest that we betake ourselves to a cosier place than this one. If you still want me, of course. And if it suits you to call me by the name of Leto between ourselves."

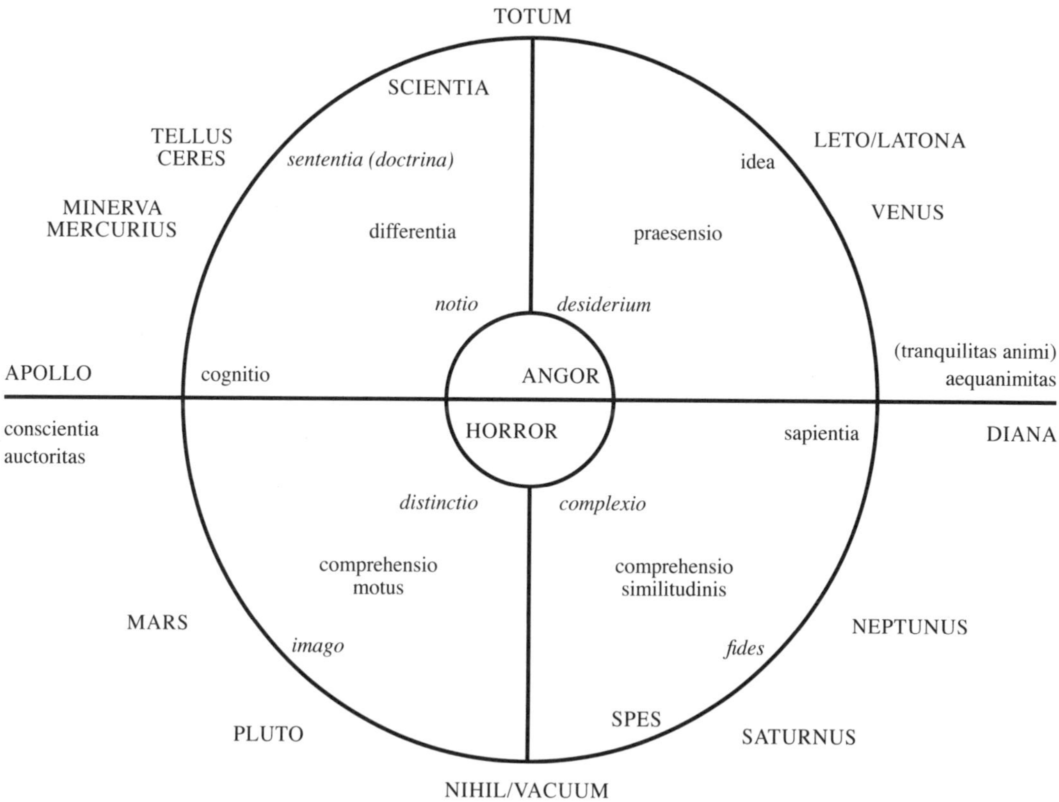

• "Map of the Human Mind", Latin version

552 Under the reign of Byzantine emperor *Justinian I*, the Goths are expelled from Italy, and the like of a Roman Empire is reinstalled for less then 16 years.

570 Abū l-Qāsim *Muhammad* ibn ʿAbdallāh ibn ʿAbd al-Muttalib ibn Hāschim ibn ʿAbd Manāf al-Quraschī, founder of the Islamic religion, is born in Mecca, Arabia. He starts preaching in AD 610. The writing of the Qur'an commences in the same year.

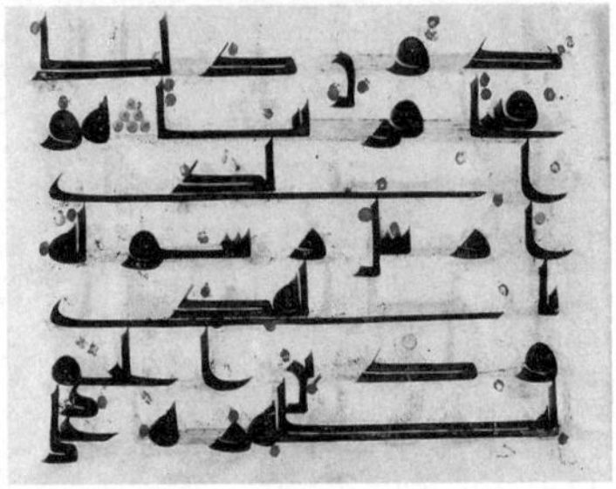

• Folio of an early transcript of the Qur'an from the 8th century

578 The first ship's anchor is forged in Britain.

The Age of Rational Space

Matthias Michel

1088 According to its own historiography, the *University of Bologna* is founded. If this dating is accepted as correct, it is the first "university" in history.

1099 Upon an agreement of all major European governments to take action against the migration of the "Turks" and sanctioned by Pope Urban II, the city of Jerusalem is recovered by international troops of Christian knights and voluntary forces during the first of seven *Crusades*.[1] The "Holy City", now a Christian kingdom with Baldwin I, brother of crusade hero Godfrey de Bouillon, as its first ruler, becomes a popular destination for Christian pilgrims, which results in widespread banditry along the pilgrim routes.

In this context, the notorious Templar order is founded by Hugues de Payens in 1119 to secure the pilgrim routes and defend the "Holy Land" against various Muslim recapture attempts. Based on the belief that their headquarters in a wing of the royal palace in the Al-Aqsa mosque on the temple mount was built upon the ruins of Salomon's temple,[2] the Catholic military order is named "The Poor Fellow-Soldiers of Christ and of the Temple of Solomon" ("*Pauperes commilitones Christi Templique Salomonici*"). Rapidly growing in number, wealth, and political influence, and recognised by the pope in 1139, the Templar order rises to become the most powerful political and business organisation in Europe, a "state within states" that is often referred to as the world's first multinational corporation. The respective weakening of the European aristocracy, both in terms of political control and financial independence, finally leads to a mass arrest of Templars in 1307, ordered by king Philip IV of France. The last Grand Master of the order, Jacques de Molay, is burned at the stake after confessing atheism and homosexual sodomy under torture. In 1312, Pope Clement V is forced to disband the order.

1187 After Baldwin IV has died of leprosy in 1185, his sister Sibyl leads the Kingdom of Jerusalem through two instable years, delegating military leadership to her alternating husbands and thus giving way to animosities among the competing Christian military orders. After a crushing defeat in the *Battle of Hattin* against the Muslim armies united under the Egyptian caliph Salah-ad-Din on the 4th July 1187, the Holy City is besieged and finally surrendered on the 2nd October. Subsequently, the city remains contested, being conquered for the last time in 1229 by Roman-German emperor Friedrich II before the Kingdom of Jerusalem ceases to exist in 1291.

In the same year, the *Swiss Confederation* is founded by the three original cantons around the Lake of Lucerne as an act of resistance against the dukedom of Habsburg.

1 The term „crusade“ has later been applied to many religiously motivated foreign political and military interventions of the Catholic Church. In this chronicle, the term is used in its original historical context of the crusades in the "Holy Land".

2 The mosque resides on an artificial platform that is supported by arches constructed by engineers to overcome the difficult topographic conditions when Jewish king Herod's "Second Temple of Jerusalem" was built on the site in 20 BC. The temple was destroyed in the "Jewish War" in AD 70. The only remain of the temple is the western breast wall known as the Wailing Wall. In 543, emperor Justinian consecrated the "New Church of the God-Bearer", dedicated to the God-bearing Virgin Mary, in the same locality. Upon completion of the Dome of the Rock, caliph Abd al-Malik ordered the demolition of the wooden church in 692, and the Al-Aqsa mosque was built on the site at the beginning of the 8th century.

• The Temple Mount in Jerusalem (south exposure) today, 2013

1227 *Genghis Khan* dies at an unknown place in Mongolia, after having united the Mongolian peoples in an empire that reaches from the Pacific Sea across today's southern Russia to the Caspian Sea and Eastern Europe, with Karakoram as its seat of government. His burial is attended by 2'000 people who are all killed in a ritual massacre after the ceremony along with all animals found in the area according to the Mongolian tradition that the location of the tomb of a Great Khan should remain unknown. The tomb has actually never been found to the present day.

Until 1279, Genghis Khan's sons expand the empire to southern China in the east and to the Baltic Sea in the west, which might well be, in terms of surface area, the largest empire in history. By the end of the 13th century, it disintegrates in several smaller states. As against their legendary cruelness in battles and conquests, the Mongolians prove to be very permissive and respectful with regard to cultural and economic exchange.

1260 In view of the expanding Mongolian empire, the Catholic Church tries to establish political relations by sending monks on diplomatic missions to China as from the early 13th century. In 1260, Niccolo and his uncle Matteo (or Maffeo) Polo, Venetian dealers in jewels, embark on a business journey to to the Caspian Sea and end up, due to political unrest in the region, at the Mongol court in Beijing (named Khanbaliq at the time) in 1266 where they meet the incumbent emperor Kublai Khan, one of Genghis Khan's grandsons. They return to Venice in 1269 with an official document (a golden tablet) signed by the Great Khan, which approaches Pope Clemens IV for sending him 100 Christian scholars and a sample of consecrated lamp oil from Jesus' grave in Jerusalem to disseminate the Gospels in the Mongolian empire.

Since Clemens IV has died a year before and the conclave of Cardinals quarrels over his succession for three years, Niccolo and Matteo decide to accomplish their mission without papal sanctioning. They leave Venice in 1271, taking along Niccolo's 17-year-old son Marco (*1254). Upon arrival in Acre at the Palestinian coast, they ask the local legate of the Church, Tebaldo Visconti, for his permission to procure the consecrated lamp oil in Jerusalem. Equipped with the oil and a credential from the legate, they continue their journey to Anatolia where they receive the message that, in the meantime, Visconti has been elected Pope Gregory X. Gregory assigns three leading theologians to accompany the Polos on their troublesome way to Mongolia, mainly leading along the route that is later to become the "Silk Route".

In 1275 they arrive at Kublai Khan's summer residence in Shangdu (Xanadu). During their stay, *Marco Polo* is appointed Kublai Khan's prefect and undertakes journeys around China and Mongolia, studying the different local cultures, writing extensive reports and journals about his experiences, and exploring a cultural stage of development that has been unknown in Europe since the collapse of the Roman Empire. In 1291, the Polos leave China much to the regret of the Great Khan, and travel back to Venice by sea. They arrive in their hometown in 1295. Subsequently, Marco Polo's travelogues are systematically copied and spread, remaining the basis of European commercial and diplomatic relations to China and Mongolia for centuries to come. In one of these travelogues, the islands of Cipang (Japan) are mentioned for the first time in the western world. Marco Polo dies in Venice on 8th January 1324.

1262 During an unstable interregnum period of the Roman-German Empire, the *City of Zurich* obtains the privilege of imperial immediacy, which is almost tantamount to independency under the circumstances of the time. The status of immediacy protects the city from the urge for territorial expansion of the German and Austrian nobility. In 1351, Zurich joins the Swiss Federation, thus extending its imperial immediacy to the four antecedent confederate cantons.

Against all odds and despite its considerable strategic value, Zurich has survived the migration period, the wars, the cultural, political, economic, and social disintegration of the European Middle Ages without ever being attacked, destroyed, oppressed, or occupied. The Gallo-Roman population has grown and developed continuously, enriched by a moderate and peaceful Alemannic immigration. The city's name changes from "Turigum" at the beginning of the 9th to "Zurich" at the beginning of the 10th century.

Building activities

On the site of the Roman Jupiter temple on "Lindenhof" hill, the first St. Peter church has been built in the 8th century, replaced by an early Romanesque church in 1000 and a late Romanesque renovation in 1230, featuring the choir and the lower part of the steeple still standing today. In 853, an already existing monastery is re-founded as a Benedictine women's monastery by the Carolingian king Ludwig the German. The related "Fraumünster" church is inaugurated in 874.

In the 11th century, another two churches are built on the opposite side of the river "Limmat", a major church on the site of the former Roman cemetery (later referred to as "Grossmünster" church) and a related baptistery on a near offshore island (today's "Wasserkirche", "Water Church"). The sites are chosen with respect to the legendary local saints Felix and Regula. The legend reaches back to around 303, referring to two martyrs decapitated during the persecutions of Christians under the Roman tetrarchy. Allegedly, the execution took place on the small island from where the bodies were carried away by angels to their eventual burial place in the cemetery 40 cubits uphill. From 1100 to 1220, the major church is rebuilt as a Romanesque minster. Except for the spires of the two steeples, which are destroyed by a lightning stroke in 1763 and rebuilt in a neo-Gothic style from 1781 to 1787, the building has never been architecturally altered to the present day.

In the 11th century, the former Roman fort on "Lindenhof" hill, being visited regularly by Roman-German ducal and royal societies for Imperial Diets, conferences, weddings, and other festivities since Otto the Great's accession to the East Frankish throne in 936 and his foundation of the Roman-German Empire in 962, is converted into a palace (probably on the initiative of Roman-German emperor Henry III).[3] Around 1156, the contemporary historiographer and bishop Otto of Freising refers to Zurich as the "most noble city of Swabia" ("*nobilissimum Sueviae oppidum*"). Based on increasing independency and continuous economic growth during the 12th century, the city goes through a period of rising building activity. Wooden houses are substituted with stone buildings. A town hall, several towers and mansions for noblemen and four additional major monasteries are built. By the end of the 13th century, Zurich is surrounded by extended fortifications (cf. "Murerplan", p. 115).

When exactly and by whom the medieval fortress "Uetliburg" on Zurich's local mountain has been built, is unknown. The archaeological finds indicate that the construction takes place in the 9th or 10th century, i.e. under the reign of Otto I or earlier. The earliest historical reference dates to 1210 when the barons of Regensberg were in possession of the "*Uotelenburg*", which gives rise to speculations whether the mountain's name originates from Celtic times (cf. p. 73) or refers to medieval personal names like "Odilo", "Otto", or "Uodalrich" (derivations of the Old High German word for "possession", "heritage", or "fortune"). The fortress is extended in the 12th century and presumed to have been destroyed in 1268 by a military alliance of Zurich and Count Rudolf of Habsburg against the barons of Regensberg.

• "The destruction of the Uetliburg in 1268", copper engraving by David Herrliberger, 1714

3 Otto I (or Otto the Great, 912–973) was the second Frankish king who tried to reunite the European territories in one empire after Charles the Great (as from 771, declared emperor on Christmas Day 800 by pope Leo III). As against "Charlemagne" whose territorial expansion plans were mainly based on striving for power and economic growth, Otto had serious ambitions to restore the cultural coherence and potential of Europe after centuries of decline. However, though his Roman-German Empire played a major political role throughout the 1st millennium, it never was a stable political construction. In contrast to the other emerging European world powers, the monarchy in Germany and Austria was constantly threatened and challenged by ambitious and competing dukedoms, countdoms, and baronies.

Economy and politics

Zurich's ongoing significance as a minting site is documented in historical references from 972. The oldest preserved official seals of the city date to 1225 and 1230, showing Felix and Regula carrying their lopped-off heads and the Latin inscription *sigillum consilii thuricensium* („seal of the city council of Zurich"). Up to this time, the city's political affairs have been conducted by the abbess of the "Fraumünster" monastery due to the monastery's traditional administration of the minting licences. As from the beginning of the 13th century, the government of the city is divided among the two major clerical authorities ("Fraumünster" and "Grossmünster", both in possession of extensive tracts of land in the region of today's Switzerland) and a city council representing the craftsmen, merchants, and patricians.

1336 The first recorded *ascent of the Mont Ventoux* (the "windy mountain") in the French Provence takes place in 1334 when Jean Buridan climbs the prominent mountain on his way to the papal court in Avignon ("in order to make meteorological observations"). However, it is the Italian poet Petrarch who goes down in history with the possibly fictional account of his ascent accompanied by his brother on 26th April 1336 ("*Ascent of the Mont Ventoux*"), recorded in a letter sent to the early humanist Dionigi di Borgo San Sepolcro and published in the compilation *Epistolae familiares* (IV, 1).

The astounding impact of this highly poetic and contemplative text on the development of the Renaissance might be condensed in Petrarch's claim to be "the first person since antiquity to have climbed a mountain just for the view". Subsequently, the ascent of the Mont Ventoux is referred to as a pivotal moment of the historical transition of the Middle Ages to the modern era, not least in terms of spatial experience.

1337 After an insurrection of Zurich's craftsmen headed by Rudolf Brun in 1336, the city is submitted to a *guild constitution*: a parliament consisting of 13 delegates of 13 guilds and 13 representatives of nobility and financial aristocracy is installed, which leaves marks on the local political structures to the present day. In the wake of civic claims to political power, intermittently violent anti-Jewish activities emerge, additionally stirred up by the Catholic Church. As always and everywhere in Europe since the times of the Roman Empire, anti-Semitic tendencies are fuelled by the Jewish tradition of commercial moneylending and profiteering in combination with bourgeois structures of society.

1342 After several earlier attempts, Italian painter Ambrogio Lorenzetti (1290–1348) applies the accurate method of *linear perspective* for the first time in cultural history in his painting *The Presentation in the Temple.* However, in historical records the introduction of linear perspective is often ascribed to the Italian designer, engineer, and construction supervisor Filippo Brunelleschi (1377–1446) who transfers the technique to architectural draft and design during the construction of the dome of the Florence Cathedral, completed in 1436.

• Ambrogio Lorenzetti; *The Presentation in the Temple*, colour on panel, 1342

RENAISSANCE

~1450 Johannes Gutenberg (1400–1468) has been experimenting with existing printing techniques for at least ten years when he finally combines several technical elements in one process and develops a practical system that allows the mass production of printed books. After a few years of practical experience, he starts printing 180 copies of the famous "Gutenberg Bible" (30 copies on parchment and 150 copies on paper). In retrospect, the "*printing revolution*" is regarded as the major cultural milestone of the second millennium.

1452 – 1519 *Leonardo da Vinci* is commonly referred to as the central and prototypical polymath or "universal genius" of the Renaissance, combining and forwarding such divergent fields of expertise like engineering and architecture, mathematics, music, literature, painting, sculpting, anatomy, biology, history, cartography, archaeology and palaeontology, astronomy, geology, science and invention. Quite arguably the most imaginative and diversely talented personality in history, his temper and character remain largely mysterious.

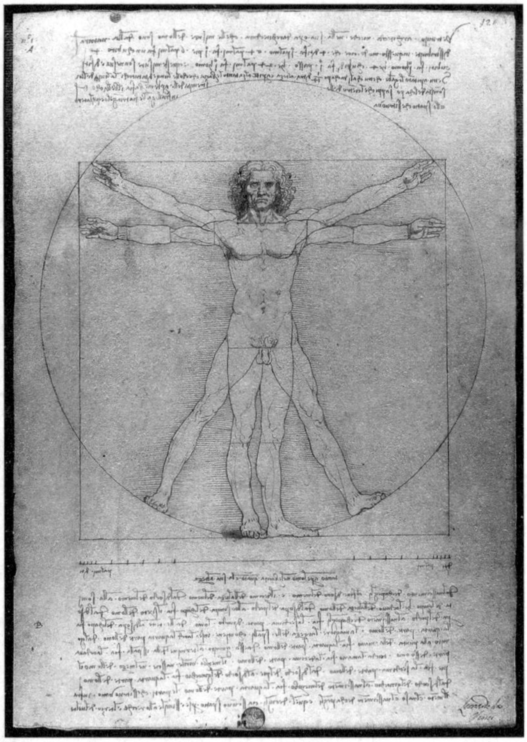

• Leonardo da Vinci's famous illustration of the geometrical proportions of the human body, inspired by Marcus Vitruvius' *De architectura*, 1492

1453

The *Ottoman Empire* is founded around 1326 in the northwest of Asia Minor and, benefiting of political instability in the region, expands its territory to the Balkan regions and the western half of Asia Minor until 1453 when "Konstantiniyye" (Constantinople, renamed Istanbul in 1876) becomes its official capital under Sultan Mehmed II. Subsequently, the Ottomans lay claim to be respected as a major European power, pursuing an aggressive foreign policy against the Roman-German Empire and Russia (occupation of Vienna in 1529 under Suleiman II). In the 17th century, the Ottoman Empire reaches from the Black Sea region over the Near East to the coastal areas of northern Africa and constantly challenges the eastern borders of Germany and Austria. Being allied with the defeated nations of the First World War, the Ottoman Empire ceases to exist and is transformed into the modern Republic of Turkey by Mustafa Kemal Atatürk as from 1919.

1475

Under Pope Sixtus IV, the *Sistine Chapel* is built from 1475 to 1484. The famous ceiling painting by Michelangelo Buonarroti (1475–1564) is accomplished from 1508 to 1512 by order of Pope Julius II who also lays the foundation of the new *St. Peter's Basilica* in Rome on the 18th April 1506. The construction of St. Peter's is designed and conducted by the Italian painter and architect Donato Bramante and replaces the almost 1200 years old Basilica built on behalf of the Roman emperor Constantine the Great in 324. The site is referred to as the location of Apostle Peter's tomb.

In 1547, the architectural management of the building project is conferred to Michelangelo. The construction works go on until the mid-17th century.

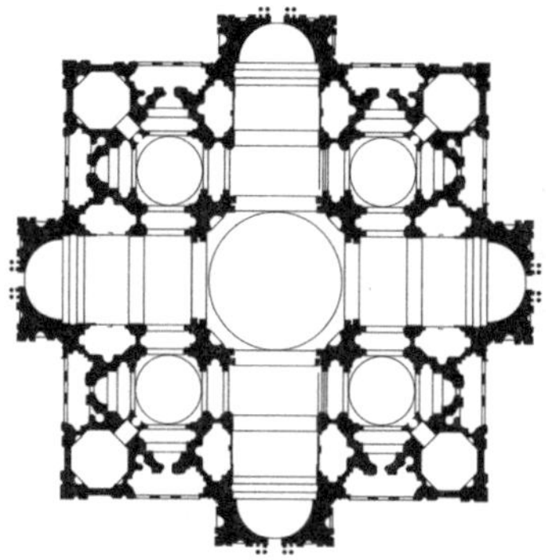

• Draft of the St. Peter's Basilica by Donato Bramante, *1505*, and view onto the building in 2004.

1492 On the 12th October, Christopher Columbus arrives in the Caribbean Sea, thus initiating the continuous exploration and *conquest of the American continent* by the European nations, headed by Spain having the largest deep-sea fleet at its disposal at the time and remaining the leading sea power up to the 17th century.

However, the earliest landing on the American continent is ascribed to the Icelandic seafarer and discoverer Leif Eriksson who set out from the south tip of Greenland and sailed to "Helleland" and "Markland" on today's Canadian coast around 1000.[4] The naming of "America" or "the Americas" refers to the Italian merchant and seafarer Amerigo Vespucci (1452–1512) who explores vast stretches of the South American continent at the beginning of the 16th century.

4 In modern times, the question has been raised whether an Atlantic crossing could have been possible in the times of Ancient Egypt, not least in the context of the Egyptian version of the Atlantis myth. Related experiments with Ancient Egyptian seafaring technologies have given rise to theoretical support of the hypothesis.

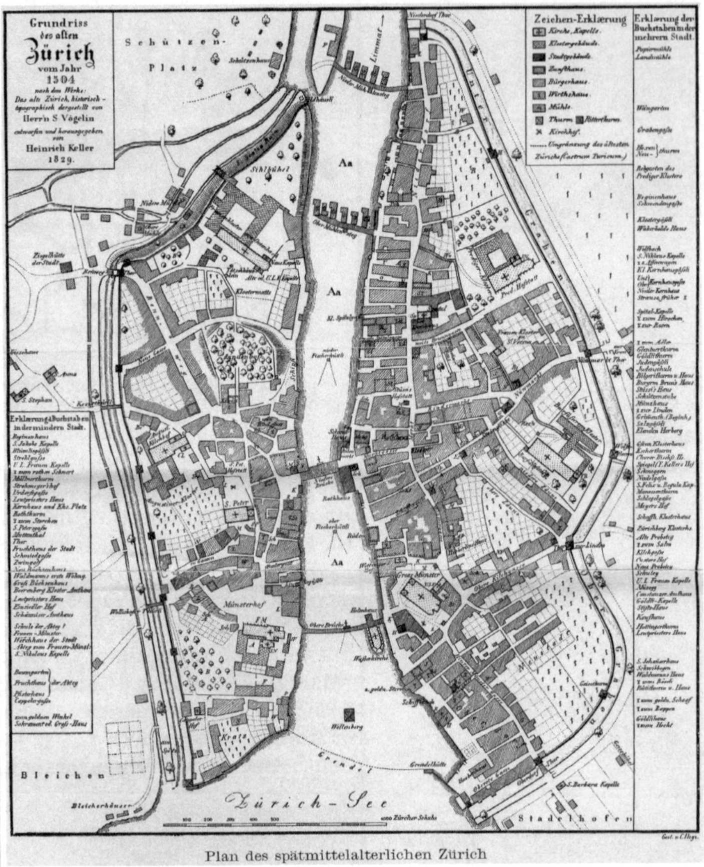

• Layout plan of the city of Zurich in 1504 by Heinrich Keller, 1829

1517 The beginning of the *Reformation* is usually dated to the publication of Martin Luther's (1483–1546) *Ninety-five Theses* in Wittenberg, 1517, and lasts until the "Peace of Westphalia" at the end of the Thirty Years' War in 1648. The Czech university professor Jan Hus (*1369), representative of the Bohemian Reformation, is often mentioned as a forerunner of the Protestant Reformation. He has been declared a heretic and burned at the stake at the Council of Constance in 1415.

The publication of Luther's translation of the Bible into German in 1534 is a decisive moment in history, both with regard to the spread of literacy and the stimulation of the printing and distribution of religious books and pamphlets. The works and writings of the Genevan reformer John Calvin (1509–1564) contribute to a loose consensus among the various reformatory groups in Switzerland, Scotland, Hungary, and Germany, relativising many of the fanaticism in Luther's teachings, if not necessarily his pronounced anti-Judaism.

The politically, socially, and religiously most progressive movement in the early processes of reformation is lead by *Huldrych Zwingli* (*1484), pastor at the "Grossmünster" church in Zurich since 1518. Zwingli's main objective is not directed against the Catholic Church's institutional corruption and perversion of the gospels but rather an attempt to combine early liberal issues of education, economics, and social balance based on morale and religious reformations. In the long term, this pragmatic position also shapes the "Second Territorial Peace" of 1531, by which the Swiss Confederation (consisting of 13 full members at the time) becomes the first state with two legally sanctioned religions in Europe.[5] Although "Zwinglianism" features obvious parallels to "Lutheranism" (including the references to Augustine of Hippo), Zwingli strongly maintains that he prevents himself from reading Luther's publications. He dies in the Battle of Kappel on 11th October 1531, which follows a surprise declaration of war against Zurich by five Catholic Swiss cantons two days earlier. Martin Luther and most of the competing Reformation leaders in Europe cheer Zwingli's death.

1519 In August, Zurich is struck by an *outbreak of the plague*, which causes the deaths of at least a quarter of the population and might arguably be the most serious calamity in the city's history.

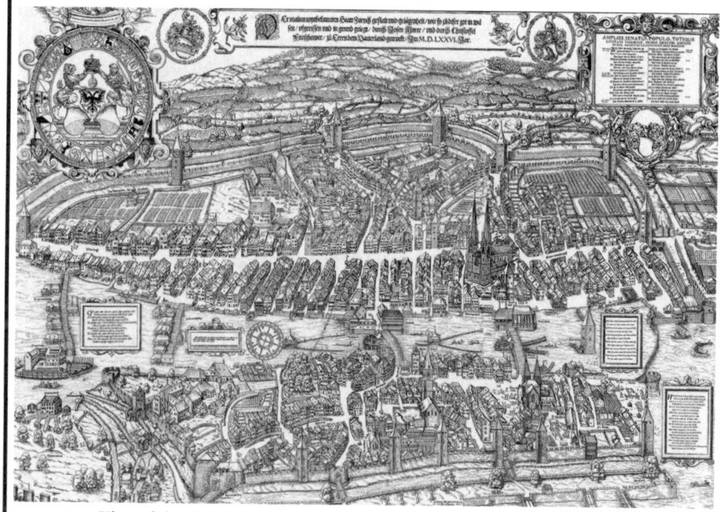

• View of the city of Zurich on a xylography by Josua Murer, 1576. The headline can be roughly translated as "The ancient widely known city Zurich's design and positioning, as its character is projected and built at this time by Josua Murer, and printed by Christoffel Froschauer in 1576 in honour of the fatherland."

Prometheus Bound

Frombork (Warmia), 24th May 1543

The only sound to be heard is the crackling of the chimney fire. The window is draped with cloths so that the cheerless chamber is all filled with twilight. Waking from a doze, he's lying on his bed, motionless as if he were dead already. A seventy-year-old man of haggard build whose health has gone from bad to worse in the months that have passed since the right half of his body became hemiplegic in the wake of a stroke. However, the lack of dignity in his countenance is not owed to his infirmity. The look of sheepish modesty on his face has been there all along ever since his beard had begun to sprout, disclosing the character of a man who

5 A second religious civil war in 1712, the "Second War of Villmergen", resulted in a decisive Protestant victory and major revisions of the previous "Territorial Peace" contracts. Subsequently, Zurich and the Protestant cantons assume leadership in the further political development of the Swiss Confederation.

always preferred the path of least resistance. This path has been the one of a life-long scholar, studying mathematics, astronomy, law, philosophy, and medicine, supported by minor ecclesiastic and political positions, surrounded by Latin classics and the fusty smell of libraries. And finally, his path has led him here: to the northwest tower within the stronghold of the Frombork cathedral precinct in Warmia by the Baltic Sea. His duties as the chancellor of the chapter have been far from demanding, earning him a reasonable subsistence and plenty of time for his studies. Apart from a few boisterous nights during his sojourn in Italy, the most serious trouble he ever got himself into were the rumours about him and his housekeeper Anna four years ago. The impetuous woman refused to leave him of her own free will, which forced him, in due consultation with bishop Dantiscus, to banish her from Frombork.

A slight movement of the cloths in front of the window grabs his attention. Out of the corner of his eye, he catches a glimpse of the blurred shape of a black hooded figure standing there, and a moment later, when he drudgingly turns to take a closer look at it, the figure has vanished into thin air. He is not sure if he has actually seen something or if he has been fooled by the twilight and the shadows cast by the folds of the cloths. But it occurs to him that it may have been an angel of death announcing that his last hour is nigh ... –

Only now he feels the weight on his stomach, and he spontaneously gropes with his left hand for the heavy thing that lies on the bedspread. It is a book, of course. Yet it lacks that certain distinctive smell of mustiness and yellowed paper. It's not just another one of *those* books. It is a *new* book, fresh from the press, high-grade paper bound in decoratively imprinted dark brown leather. One of a thousand copies printed in Nuremberg by Johannes Petreius, dedicated to Pope Paul III. He does not have to sit up and look at the cover or read the title page to know what book it is and what it is about. But he sits up all the same, groaning with pain and exertion. And then, after having examined the elaborate quality of the binding for a while, he slowly opens it with the one hand he still can use.

He has never really tried to anticipate this moment. But if he had, he would probably have expected a solemn moment of a subtle mixture of feelings like relief, anxiety, and yes, also a twinge of pride. His friends had urged him for years to publish his astronomical work before Georg Joachim Rheticus, the impetuous reformatory enthusiast, finally talked him around. However, he has second-guessed the decision ever since, not because he has been in doubt of the validity or accuracy of his calculations, but rather because ... well, maybe he has been afraid of having forgotten something, of being scorned by his fellow scholars for a petty little mistake in his choice of words or an insignificant error in the application of a mathematical formula, or ... maybe it all amounts to the fact that thoughts cannot be retracted once they have been ... made public ... and multiplied in print.

He flips the half title page, and much to his surprise, there is an editorial note at the very beginning of the book, preceding his own introduction to *De revolutionibus orbium coelestium*. It is an unsigned letter *To the reader concerning the hypotheses of this work* that he has never seen or read before:

"... It is the duty of an astronomer to compose the history of the celestial motions through careful and expert study. Then he must conceive and devise the causes of these motions or hypotheses about them. Since he cannot in any way attain to the true causes, he will adopt whatever suppositions enable the motions to be calculated correctly ... the present author has performed both these duties excellently for these hypotheses need not be true nor even probable. On the contrary, if they provide a calculus consistent with the observations, that alone is enough ... for this art, it is quite clear, is completely and absolutely ignorant of the causes of the apparent. And if any causes are devised by the imagination, as indeed very many are, they are not put forward to convince anyone that they are true, but merely to provide a reliable basis for calculation. However, since different hypotheses are sometimes offered for one and the same ... the astronomer will take as his first choice that hypothesis which is the easiest to grasp ... the philosopher will perhaps rather seek the semblance of the truth. But neither of them will understand or state anything certain, unless it has been divinely revealed to him ... and let no one expect anything certain from astronomy, which cannot furnish it ..." –

His first sensation upon reading this is anger.

What is that supposed to mean? Who wrote this drivel? Who authorised its inclusion in the publication? – Rheticus has been instructed to supervise the printing process from start to finish, hasn't he? [6]

The anger turns into wrath. The wrath turns into blind rage. He fiercely snaps the book shut, it slips away from his left hand. He tries to grab it with his useless right. It slides away from the bedspread and falls to the wooden floor with an awkward thump. A moment later, he finds himself plunged into a deep black silent void, as if his senses had been blown out like the flame of a candle.

At the back of his mind, a memory assumes shape. Almost forty years ago, he jotted down a note implying that, in mathematical terms, the centre of the earth cannot be thought of as the centre of the world, that it rather must be conceived of as a centre of gravity, and that, if this principle would apply to the orbits of the planets, the centre of the world would have to be assumed to be close to the sun. Just a note, just a piece of reasoning that was neither new nor particularly inventive. It was nothing but a reflection on Aristarchus' hypothesis from the 3rd century before the Christian era, purporting that "the fixed stars and the sun remain unmoved, that the earth revolves about the sun on the circumference of a circle, that the sun lies in the middle of the orbit, and that the sphere of the fixed stars is situated about the same centre as the sun".

6 Georg Joachim Rheticus (1514–1574) studied mathematics and astronomy in Zurich as from 1528 when his father had been executed for sorcery and fraud in Feldkirch. He became a professor at the Protestant Wittenberg University and arrived in Frombork (Ger. "Frauenburg") in 1539 to become Nicolaus Copernicus' (*1473) student for two years. In 1542, Rheticus published one of Copernicus' treatises on trigonometry (later included in chapters 13 and 14 of the first book in *De revolutionibus orbium coelestium*). Upon its favourable reception, Copernicus finally agreed to publish his chief work. The manuscript was sent to Rheticus for printing by Johannes Petreius at Nuremberg. Rheticus was supposed to supervise the printing but had to leave Nuremberg before it was completed. So he handed over the task to the Lutheran reformer Andreas Osiander (1498–1552) who added an unauthorised and unsigned preface, preventively defending Copernicus' work against those who might be offended by its hypotheses.

The first edition of *De revolutionibus* did not sell as well as Rheticus had expected and caused no hostile response by the Catholic Church. A copy was sent to Pope Paul III to whom the book was dedicated. *De revolutionibus* was put on the index of prohibited books in 1611 after it had been referred to in the works of Giordano Bruno, Johannes Kepler, and Galileo Galilei.

Back in 1514, he has set forth the idea in a short treatise under the title *Commentariolus*. And then ... –

The blind rage is gone. All that is left of it is an uneasy feeling, like an indefinite fear.

Beyond doubt, it *is* the truth, nothing but the irrefutable truth proven by means of infallible mathematical computations.

The indefinite fear turns into what feels like a bottomless shame ... – what in the world would he be ashamed of at this instant? – ..., and the shame turns into panic that spins out of his control at the split of a second.

All of a sudden, the truth appears to be the most terrifying of truths. It dawns on him that, sooner or later, they will pick up this book and read. And he can envision them quite clearly within the seclusion of his mind. The truth contained within these pages will spread. It will force innocent human beings to look up to the sky and see nothing but this deep black silent void, deep and black and silent enough that even the unfathomable power of God will fail to fill it up. They will feel as if the end of the world had come over them. Seized with rage and panic and madness at the loss of their embeddedness in a cosmic order, they will seek revenge upon those who have dedicated themselves to such blasphemous knowledge, many of them well-intentioned scholars like him. Thus, the book will be like a malicious spark lighting the fire beneath the stakes, a devastating fire that will burn for centuries of doom and perdition. And yes, he will go down in history for sure, not as a decent scholar though, but as a fire-raiser, an apostle from hell, a propagator of infernal – – – truths.

Has there ever been a hybris as foolish and desperate like this? – Has there ever been a crime against humanity more worthy of eternal damnation? – Has there ever been a soul as guilty beyond mercy and forgiveness? –

He falls down into the deep black silent void, too horrified now to even scream, waiting for an impact that will never come. There is no other side. There is only darkness and endless falling ... –

A few hours later on the 24th of May in the year of our Lord 1543, Nicolaus Copernicus dies, his left arm outstretched in a futile attempt to grab at something that is not there. Whether he has been granted to mercy and forgiveness before his death, we will never know.

NICOLAI COPERNICI

net, in quo terram cum orbe lunari tanquam epicyclo contineri diximus. Quinto loco Venus nono mense reducitur. Sextum denique locum Mercurius tenet, octuaginta dierum spacio circũ currens. In medio uero omnium residet Sol. Quis enim in hoc

pulcherrimo templo lampadem hanc in alio uel meliori loco poneret, quàm unde totum simul possit illuminare? Siquidem non inepte quidam lucernam mundi, alij mentem, alij rectorem uocant. Trimegistus uisibilem Deum, Sophoclis Electra intuentẽ omnia. Ita profecto tanquam in solio regali Sol residens circum agentem gubernat Astrorum familiam. Tellus quoque minime fraudatur lunari ministerio, sed ut Aristoteles de animalibus ait, maximam Luna cum terra cognationẽ habet. Cõcipit interea à Sole terra, & impregnatur annno partu. Inuenimus igitur sub hac

• Illustration, original Edition *De revolutionibus orbium coelestium*, 1543

1558 – 1603

Under the reign of *Queen Elisabeth I*, the last representative of the Tudor dynasty, England becomes a protestanised state and develops into a major sea power, Francis Drake's second circumnavigation of the globe (1577–1580) after Ferdinand Magellan (1519–1521) and Walter Raleigh's expedition to America in 1585 being the historical points of reference. Subsequently, England seriously challenges the Spanish and Portuguese supremacy in this respect. In the 17th century, England gradually ascends to become not only the leading colonial power but also a major power on the political map of Europe, thus establishing a "balance of power" between France, Spain, Germany and Austria, and England (completed by Russia as from the turn of the 18th century) that defines European politics up to the 20th century. However, one of the most sustainable legacies of the Elizabethan era is the queen's decisive promotion of science, music, art, and literature (associated with names like Francis Bacon, William Shakespeare, or Christopher Marlowe).

• The frontispiece to Sir Francis Bacon's *Instauratio magna* (*Great Instauration*), 1620

1600 Giordano Bruno (*1548), Italian pantheistic philosopher, astronomer, and poet, is burned at the stake in Rome's "Campo dei Fiori" on 17th February. The Roman Inquisition has found him guilty of heresy and denying Catholic core doctrines like eternal damnation, the Trinity, the divinity of Christ, the virginity of Mary, and transubstantiation.[7]

1604 Johannes Kepler (1571–1630), German astronomer and mathematician, observes a supernova and proves the variability of the fixed stars. In 1609, he publishes his *Astronomia Nova*, the most widespread astronomical work of the 17th century, containing the laws of planetary motion named after him and inspiring Galileo Galilei (1564–1642) to a scientific objectification of the Copernican heliocentrism (*Dialogue Concerning the Two Chief World Systems*, published 1632). Galileo is convicted by the Inquisition and forced to renounce his conclusions in 1633. He is allowed to continue his mechanical research under ward of the Catholic Church.

1618 – 1848 The *Thirty Years' War* in northern and central Europe is one of the longest, cruellest, and most destructive wars in history, induced by power struggles in the Holy Roman Empire of the German Nation and the ongoing conflicts between Catholics and Protestants. Since none of the war parties can afford the costs of an armed conflict of such

7 On the 400th anniversary of Bruno's death in 2000, Cardinal Angelo Sodano declares it to be a "sad episode" but, despite his regret, sticks to the opinion that the Inquisitors "had the desire to serve freedom and promote the common good and did everything possible to save his life". In the same year, Pope John Paul II makes a general apology "for the use of violence that some have committed in the service of truth," acknowledging that Bruno's execution has to be considered as unjust even from the Catholic Church's point of view.

proportions, warlords are recruited among the financial aristocracies who are allowed to act on their own account and for their own profit, unrestricted by any legal or moral responsibilities. In its chaotic and erratic course, the Thirty Years' War causes over eight million fatalities and anarchic social conditions. It results in a further decentralisation of the Holy Roman Empire and the "Peace of Westphalia", broadly allowing religious practices to the Protestants, initiating the Catholic Church's protracted loss of political influence, and promoting the rise of the absolutist Bourbon dynasty in France. In the "Peace of Westphalia", all members of the Swiss Confederation are officially declared independent of the German Empire. Subsequently, Zur-ich claims itself "The Republic of Zurich".

1637

French philosopher, mathematician, and natural scientist René Descartes (1596–1650) publishes his *Discours de la méthode* (*Discourse on the Method*), followed by the *Meditationes de prima philosophia* (*Meditations on First Philosophy*, 1641)[8], *Principia philosophiae* (*Principles of Philosophy*, 1644), and *Les passions de l'âme* (*Passions of the Soul*, 1649). His work is referred to as the foundation of modern western philosophy and scientific methodology. Furthermore, he introduces the basic interdisciplinary concepts of rationalism, and his efforts in combining the principles of algebra and geometry enable the systematic computational assessment of spatial relations (like coordinate systems, the physical description of matter etc.).

1651

Deeply shocked by the irrational mass atrocities of the Thirty Years' War, Thomas Hobbes (1588–1679), English mathematician, state theorist, and philosopher, publishes his highly influential chief work *Leviathan* in which he introduces the concepts of the "social contract" and an "enlightened absolutism", based on the impression that believing in a principled good in man has become obsolete in view of the Thirty Years' War. Not exactly according to the author's intent, *Leviathan* becomes, along with John Locke's (1632–1704) and Charles-Louis de Montesquieu's (1689–1755) political writings, a foundational work of modern liberalism and economic theory. Absurdly enough, it is also misused as a justification for the absolutist Bourbon monarchy in France.

1687

English mathematician, astronomer, physicist, and theologian Isaac Newton's (1642–1726/27) *Philosophiae Naturalis Principia Mathematica (Mathematical Principles of Natural Philosophy)* is published. It consolidates the so-called "scientific revolution" of the 17th century and thus supports the development of the Enlightenment period. It remains a standard reference of classic mathematics and physics up to the 20th century.

8 René Descartes' theorem „*Cogito ergo sum*" ("I think, therefore I am") that encapsulates the concept of cognition under rationalist conditions is developed in the context of his *Meditations on First Philosophy*.

RATIONAL SPACE

ABSTRACTIONS

Poetic spaces are places, spatial situations, or spatial environments that are defined, designed, and constructed by human beings in their own right. They are *conditioned* according to *authentic* and independent human ideas and purposes. They are thought of as creative interventions within creation, and as such they are more or less controllable by their creators and users. The totality of the spatial environment is still there, still scary, and still not fully comprehended, but it is banished from the poetic spaces into outer spaces by the means of theories, which define what's inside and what's outside – and what's in between. Since spatial poetry *explicitly* confronts human beings with the notions of spatial inside and outside perspectives, they relate to them in explicitly objective (basically aesthetic, creative, and experimental) ways. Accordingly, poetic spaces are defined by all kinds of craftsmen and artists and poets – and their *works*.

Rational spaces are based on the idea that space is a dimensional aspect, principle, or "feature" of the universe in which we live, irrespective of how that universe is ideated in particular. They are conceived of as if viewed from the Archimedean point: as exactly gaugeable or quantifiable in figures according to standardised measures and measuring methods. Although the Archimedean point is an imaginary "as if" at best, rational spaces are deemed objectified and comprehended to the extent their (three-)dimensional features are *verifiable* and *computable* in theory or practice, not only in their static facticity but also in their physical compositions and dynamics. In the context of mechanical physics, which enormously accelerates technological progress and thus initiates the development of industrialisation, the conceptions of spatial, material, and energetic phenomena begin to converge towards consistent universal theories.

Hence (and after the fierce resistance of the clerical institutions against the rational idea of space has been broken), rational spaces are increasingly and broadly conceived of as abstracted from human conditions and realities. They are devolved unto all kinds of philosophers and mathematicians who seem to have the means to handle this kind of abstraction, while the practical everyday approach to space basically remains a poetic one. However, "poetic" (as well as "magic") spaces are henceforth described, discussed, and produced in rational terms, which significantly enhances both the quantity and the efficiency of their implementations but hardly contributes to their deeper understanding, of course. On the contrary, it eventually leads to the habitual mistake of the basically mathematical and/or geometrical metaphor of space for a natural reality and vice versa.

However, the totality – the overall context of the spatial condition in the sense of "environment" – is still there, and it is still scary, although for a completely different reason: It is scary because, under rational conditions, it can neither be based on the concept of a stable and intentional creation nor on the common experience of "being in space" anymore. Spatial environments have become subject to mathematical definitions that do not necessarily (or: "naturally") correspond with spatial experiences. And, eventually, the definitions even exceed the capabilities of imagination. In consequence, the theoretical "emptiness" denoted by the original term for gaps and interstices becomes an environmental "reality": space in all its modern meanings turns into a dynamic and multiplexed metaphor of reality itself. Immediate experience as the foundation and ultimate criterion of the realness of reality turns into a debatable idea, both in terms of cognition and perception: an idea that raises epistemological and existential questions of most frightening and highly irrational implications, irrational enough to remain incommensurable to the basic rational idea of space up to the present day.

In short: reality has ceased to be a simple "truth". It has become a complex texture of interpretable, verifiable, falsifiable, and (therefore) manipulable or deniable "facts". As an inevitable but eventually disastrous consequence, the claim of truth is gradually and systematically expelled from reality into the realm of opinions and beliefs. The basic idea of the constructivist problem in one of its most profound explications emerges. And, paradoxically but quite understandably, it paves the way for the enforcement of radically materialistic worldviews.

"Renaissance"

Against this background, it comes as no surprise that the names of mathematicians, philosophers, and artists are abounding in the early modern section of the chronicle. And it comes as no surprise either that many of the men we refer to as the great architects of the Renaissance do not specifically refer to themselves as "architects" (in the sense of "craftsmen") in the first place. They are mathematicians, philosophers, scholars, and, when it comes to aesthetical or technical issues, they are artists and construction supervisors, all at the same time. The same goes for almost all modernist disciplines we project onto pre-modernist times in retrospect, especially the technical and the natural sciences: There are no experts. Actually, there are hardly any concepts of a specific disciplinary training for architects (or "spatial designers") – much less foundational disciplinary theories. Maybe that explains, to a certain extent, architecture's continuing infatuation with Vitruvius' work. At a time when architecture resurges to become the prototypical discipline of cultural "renaissance", redevelopment, and reconstruction, Vitruvius' writings are the only source of basic terms and concepts available, although these terms and concepts refer, as previously indicated, to significantly different conditions when it comes to the conception of "space".[9]

As with regard to the magic and poetic spaces before, it is virtually impossible to trace back the conception of rational spaces in historical terms. In terms of ideas though, considering the fact that the crucial aspect of this conception is rational *abstraction*, it can be reasonably traced along the succession of various progressive abstractions of spatial conditions. Quite obviously, Aristotle's arguments for the disciplinary systematisation of natural philosophy are based on such abstractions as well as the developments and applications of arithmetic and geometry in the first millennium BC, Vitruvius' comprehensive definition of architectural means and techniques, or Augustine of Hippo's reflections on the "Kingdom of God" and its (spatial and temporal) relation to the "real world". In general, Christian thinking and its incessant attempts of rationalis-

9 The beginning of a serious and systematic "academisation" of architecture might be dated to 31st December 1671 when the former geometer, cartographer, and urban planner Nicolas-François Blondel (1618–1686) was appointed as the first director and professor of the *Académie Royale d'Architecture* in Paris, founded on behalf of the "Sun King" Louis XIV. Blondel's much-noticed *Cours d'Architecture* was based on his lectures from 1675 to 1683.

ing its own mystical dogmata in terms of space and time deserves to be acknowledged as a major driving force of the progressing ideational abstraction of space. Intellectual efforts like these may be regarded as steps and intermediary stages on the way towards a rational notion of space. However, since the "Dark Ages" are quite literally dark in respect of historical records that may convey an idea of the conceptions of space from the 6th to the 13th century in Europe (apart from the few recorded texts by mostly mystical philosophers in the High Middle Ages), the Renaissance confronts us with a historical situation in which a general rational approach to the idea of space seemingly emerges in no more than a hundred years of European history. All of a sudden, it is undoubtedly and effectively there, in theory as well as in practice: in the application of linear perspective for instance, in the advanced technical conception of architecture, in the "globalised" world and the Copernican "universe", including the respective epistemological and cosmological implications.

These implications go far beyond the stereotypical conflicts of "scientific" and "ecclesiastical" worldviews we usually associate with the early modern period. They call for nothing less than a comprehensible explanation how the idea of space as a rational, dimensional, and quantifiable aspect of the natural world can be brought into line with the mathematical theories, the poetic practices, and the common experiences of space. By the end of the 16th century, the divergence of these different ideas of space is not a merely philosophical, theoretical, or intellectual problem anymore. It has become an everyday practical, technical, political, and epistemological challenge.

Globality. Divisibility. Conceptuality.

The most obvious and comprehensive challenge is, of course, the notion of a scientifically (i.e. mathematically) describable spatial "universe" implied by the so-called Copernican Revolution, which imposes social and individual consequences on the early modern worldviews that probably reach beyond of what we can imagine nowadays, as modern or postmodern subjects (cf. *Prometheus Bound*, p. 115 et seqq.). The common ideational denominator of the Copernican Revolution is *globalisation* in every figurative and theoretical sense of the word, from the actual exploration and mapping of the globe to the political and economic contexts of colonialism (which, in terms of a history of spatial ideas, might also be interpreted as a continuous collision of magic, poetic, and rational conceptions of space), from the physical understanding of the planetary system to its consequences with regard to the self-conception of human beings, their "position in nature", and the subsequently inevitable rational revaluation of the faculties of individual human cognition in which, according to a consequently rational perspective, natural spatial relations are "(re)constructed" or "represented" in one way or another. The seed of modern individualism is sowed, which may be regarded as one of the most momentous ideologies forwarded by rationalist thought if considered from the perspective of a human being that has been first and foremost a social being by nature and experience for hundreds of thousands of years.

Among many other differentiations, the rational conception of space as a quantifiable natural entity implies a rationalisation of its *divisibility*. It suggests that space is divisible into *a multitude of spaces* according to a multitude of principles, values, interests, theories, and practices. In a globalised world restricted to increasingly definite boundaries, these bits and pieces of rationalised space, measured not only in square and cubic metres but also in potential tangible and economic values, become subject to the basic economical principles of shortage and growth: Along with the general increase of building activity, they gradually turn into *distributable*, *tradable* and *negotiable* resources in all kinds of distribution battles, territorial conflicts, and, eventually, real estate markets: a far more immediate means of political and social exercise of power than the simple strategic distribution of land. Traditional feudal property situations in which landownership is regularised in terms of inheritance, monarchic or aristocratic power structures, and local, national, or cultural communities of interest are increasingly challenged in favour of privatised and speculative real estate markets conducted by aspiring financial aristocracies. The political consequences of this early capitalist "spatial order" begin to surface very explicitly in the Thirty Years' War, and the further developments of the economisation of space may be regarded as commonly known in broad outline, up to the downright irrational excesses in present times, which have come to define most of our everyday spatial environments.

To some extent, the notion of a multiplicity of spaces and its irrational implications is related to and advanced by a less obvious but highly effective and influential abstraction of space: the instrumentation of *conceptual spaces* in popular culture and language, i.e. the metaphorical, symbolical, or figurative use of space and spatial relations as a means of rhetoric and intellectual deliberation.[10] Apart from the early examples already introduced in the context of poetic spaces (like the concept of "private" and "political" spaces that promotes the idea of democracy in Ancient Greece, or Plato's allegory of the cave), Augustine delivers a simple but particularly charming example in his musings about memory. He recounts that his ability to memorise things has con-

10 It may be worth noting that the German word for "conceptual space" is "*Denkraum*" ("space of thought"). Cf. also *Drawing for Real – A Quest into the Space of Imagination*, p. 274.

siderably improved after he has begun to imagine his memory as an attic lumber-room. Every time he wants to keep himself from forgetting something, he figuratively imagines himself carrying it up the stairs to the lumber-room in his brain where he files it at a particular place representing a particular context, analogous to a library system. This sort of metaphorical and figurative spatial abstraction or imagination has become a self-evident practice of modern discourses, both in speech and in notional or conceptual thinking, producing countless spatial metaphors and "as-ifs" that are used and understood implicitly in everyday language. Since these conceptual spaces refer to a human condition and thus can be imaginatively shared among communicating subjects, they significantly increase the efficiency of communication in general and eventually become a substantial means of rapprochement and mutual understanding in a globalised world. Today, the word "space" is probably more often used in reference to conceptual and metaphorical spaces than in reference to actual dimensional spaces, maybe even in contexts and disciplines that are explicitly concerned with "space" and "spaces".[11] However, the more commonly these metaphors are used, the more often they are mistaken for realities. Given that the underlying idea of space already implicates considerable metaphorical premises, it is hardly surprising that some of these mistakes occasionally entail irrationalities and absurdities of *real* consequences.

A State of Mind

Space is turned into a metaphor as soon and whenever its conception is attributed to an objectified natural or environmental reality. The attribution implies, among many other things, that the notion of space is derived or abstracted from objective experiences of natural environments and that therefore space is an objectifiable phenomenon in or of nature.[12] In retrospect, such metaphorical premises of the rational idea of space may be regarded as one of the core problems of

11 Whether or how far the overexploitation of conceptual spaces in modern arts and sciences has affected their communicative potential may be left to the respective experts to assess. Most certainly, the potential of *shared* conceptual spaces is compromised by the progressive dispersion of common philosophical concepts and scientific terminologies into so-called "specialised" fields of expertise in the continuing reformation of scientific systems since the late 19th century (cf. also *The Age of Spacisms*, p. 156 et seqq.).

12 Though we will never really know whether such an abstraction of space occurred *before* the intellectual and cultural "dawn of mankind" (and if so, whether "derivation" or "abstraction" are appropriate terms to describe it), it seems very unlikely considering our most primordial spatial experiences. Which is, for instance, the crucial point in the famous mythical "Moonwatcher"-scene of Arthur C. Clarke's and Stanley Kubrick's *2001 – A Space Odyssey* (cf. *All About Space* Volume 1, chapter I.5 *Moonwatcher*).

"empiricist" and "rationalist" epistemology in the 16th, 17th, and 18th century. As we have put it above, the problem boils down to bringing the mathematical theories, the poetic practices, and the common experience of space into accord, including their many diverging implications, which turns out to be a logical and physical impossibility precisely because of the metaphorical premises.

On the one hand, space is *not* an experiential phenomenon based on the sensory perception of natural realities, not under the conditions of rational differentiation anyway: What we see or hear or feel or measure are distances, densities, volumes, interstices, resonances, slight differences in the visual, acoustic, topographic, or physical manifestation of objects situated in different locations of a given environment. On the other hand, space is not a purely rational conception or construction either: Unlike numbers, geometrical shapes, or formal logical principles, it cannot possibly be derived or represented by the means of abstract thought only in any deductive or inductive way because, like time, it is *always* there, from the very beginning, and it always immediately relates to a perceptual or experiential world. However, though we cannot perceive it in a sensory way, we *sense* it at *any given conscious moment* in time *at once*. When we close our eyes and ears, when we empty our minds of all thoughts and emotions and sensory perceptions (by means of methodical meditation, for instance), space is still there. It may seem "empty" (i.e. empty of objects), but we are still *in it*. Moreover, this basic intuitive spatial experience is evidently there all along for *all of us* as the basis of our common sense of reality.

Apparently, space *is* an experiential phenomenon but, like the experience of time, it is neither abstracted from perceptions of natural phenomena nor from any logical principles. In fact, it is the other way round: We project the principles of space and time onto the perceptions of the natural world. That is why there is neither a specific word nor a specific notion of space in the rational sense before the totality of the abovementioned sensations (the spatial "world as a whole") is translated into the mathematical metaphor of a three-dimensional reality. In other words, space cannot possibly be objectified in any way. There is no Archimedean point. It remains a mysterious or exceptional experience because we simply cannot imagine or think of anything "real" that is *not* in space (unless we give up on the difference between realities and abstractions, of course, which is definitely neither a rational nor a reasonable option). Space is not only *beyond the objects*, it is the *ultimate precondition of any objectifiable reality* human beings can relate to. It is, as Immanuel Kant finally puts it, a transcendental "aesthetical intuition a priori". It is a principal and primordial human state of mind: an anthropic principle that determines how humans intuitively comprehend the world they live in (cf. *The Age of Spacisms*, p. 161 et seqq.).

Kant's strikingly simple deconstruction of the rational metaphor in favour of a strictly experiential (or *phenomenological*) notion of space and time, including the string of logical, aesthetical, political, ethical, and scientific consequences he elaborated as from the publication of the *Critique of Pure Reason* in 1781, largely affects the worldviews at the turn of the 19th century (and is occasionally paraphrased as "the Copernican revolution of philosophy"). But, like many other intellectual achievements of the Enlightenment period, it is also broadly and deliberately ignored in *practical* terms and thus, though cited and referred to extensively ever after, decontextualised in order to justify all sorts of modernist ideas and ideologies. Hence, in common practice and understanding, the rational metaphor of space basically outlasts all modernities and modernisms as a widely uncontested implicit conception. And soon enough, it is also commonly mistaken for a natural fact.

Empty spaces

Initially, and from a purely pragmatic or utilitarian point of view, neither the rational metaphor itself nor its confusion with reality presents an obvious problem. After all, the rational conception of space comes significantly closer to an accurate and calculable analytical description of the spatial features and relations of objects and thus delivers a perfect theoretical basis for the modernisation of the natural and technical sciences. As one of the foundational ideas of the modern era altogether, it accelerates the accumulation of information about the natural world, the organisation and transformation of this information into knowledge, and, based on that knowledge, both the development of new and the enhancement of existing technologies. Moreover, it opens up all new possibilities of economic exploitation of natural and human resources. And at the turn of the 20th century, the natural sciences arrive at conceptions of space (and time) that cannot possibly be described or formulated beyond metaphors and mathematical formulas anyway. Apart from that, it might be argued that all of the precedent conceptions of space we have encountered so far have also been based on metaphorical premises.

However, what appears to be inacceptable about the rational metaphor of space is its qualitative emptiness and conceptual definiteness, *especially* if it is mistaken for a reality. To implement this mathematical emptiness in the conception of our environments or the real world does not only mean to empty it from "mystic forces", from spirits and gods, superstitions and illusionary "misbeliefs" – assuming that were possible. It also means to empty this real world from a great many reasons for assuming moral, political, and existential responsibilities, accountabilities, and obligations that come along with acting in and upon space and spaces; common values und responsibilities that we would probably subsume as "ecological" or "sustainable" today and that are based on the common awareness that each of these spaces once was and sometime will be a *future space* experienced by future human beings. Furthermore, it tends to exclude (and eventually stigmatise) all sensations and experiences of space that do not fit into this empty dimensional conception of reality as "false", "unreal", "artificial" or "illusionary", as errors, irrational misperceptions, or pathological delusions. In other words: On the assumption that it is essentially empty, space (as an *experiential* phenomenon) becomes essentially meaningless and insignificant, a mere technical formality so to speak – *unless* it is filled with meaningful objects, of course. Thus, the universal metaphor purporting an abstract and metaphorical reality of space as a "three-dimensional void" diverges significantly from the spatial human condition as we have come to know it.

As set out above, spatial experiences are based on the *instantaneous* comprehension of the spatial reality as a whole (or: as an environmental "totality") at any given conscious moment in time. *This* reality – the reality of our spatial consciousness – is *never* empty for the simple reason alone that we are always in it. It is never a *perfect* deep black silent void, not even in the deepest or most withdrawn meditative states of the mind. It always and immediately involves sentiments, sensations, notions, desires, imaginations, conjectures, memories, projections, possibilities, ideas, fantasies, or illusions of some kind. These sensations and sentiments are undoubtedly real, even under rationalist assumptions. And they bring us back to one of the essential contents of the cosmogonies we have started out from: the assertion of a sharp and absolute boundary between nothing and something, implying that, on *this* side of the boundary, there never was and never will be any essential emptiness, and, therefore, no essential meaninglessness either. This principal and ultimate line of defence against the all too human (and all too existentially justified) "*horror vacui*" has always been the most primordial and existential basis of the spatial human condition. Quite probably, it is also the very origin of intelligent cognition and behaviour. And, of course, it defines the very original, primordial, and ineluctable idea of space.

Obviously, "empty spaces" suggest to human beings that they need (or are supposed) to be filled. Accordingly, trying to fill all kinds of empty spaces with all kinds of objects and conceptions and space-consuming behaviours keeps us busy all through the "age of rational space" and up to the present day; an occupation that is perfectly corresponding with a modernity that becomes increasingly obsessed with the notions of creativity, originality, technical innovation, and economic growth – and their confusion with one another. With this in mind, some of the recurring cultural countermovements against rationalist worldviews in the 19th and the 20th century (such as "early" and "high romanticism", some of the classic avantgardisms in the fine arts, or certain upmarket subdomains of the "fantasy" and "science fiction" genre) might be considered from a slightly different perspective. According to the terminology we have introduced, one common objective of these heterogeneous and mostly transdisciplinary objections against increasingly rationalised realities might be outlined as a continuing "search for the lost magic of space": as a continuing attempt to recover the experiential wholeness and integrity of space, and to refill the empty spaces with equivalents of the forces and energies that have been ubiquitously present in their pre-rational conception: with myths and mysteries, dreams and nightmares, stories and sensations, with memories, projections, imaginations, desires, and with all kinds of transcendental and transrational *experiences*. Evidently, such a modernised magic approach to space cannot be conceived of by means of purely intuitive symbolisms and narratives anymore now that the rational idea of it has become a prevalent and commonly accepted conception. It has to be sublimated and explicated in mental, psychological, or supernatural experiences of space, in aestheticisms, surrealisms, pararealisms, paranaturalisms, and, eventually, in straightforward irrationalisms.

However, as from the exemplary "early romanticist" movement at the turn of the 19th century, these characteristics of a modernist recovery of "magic spaces" are not only a remaining and rather explicit topic of western art and literature, they also cover an ever-increasing popular demand. And before such counterrational movements and strategies are converted into distinct poetologies and "genres" – before they, as such, lose their ability to seriously shake the general confidence in simple rationalist and materialist conceptions of the world (or before they become part of a commercialised escapist entertainment culture) – the recovery of an experiential magic of space, if we may stick to the expression for a moment, proves to be a very serious political and intellectual endeavour that is essentially grounded in the Enlightenment idea and its vigorous stand against rationalist worldviews.

A both famous and representative example is Voltaire's (i.e. François-Marie Arouet's, 1694–1778) philosophical novel „*Candide ou l'Optimisme*", published in 1759 as a satirical reply to Gottfried Wilhelm Leibniz' rationalist thesis that we live in "the best possible of all worlds" (or: "the best of all possible worlds"). In its vehement accusation of rationalist sophisms, the novel implies that the intrinsic irrationality of rationalism can be easily disconfirmed by simply employing rationalist thinking on experiential realities. Seeking for "reasonable" rather than "rational" conceptions, the Enlightenment philosophers are thoroughly aware that the rationalist separation of conceptual and experiential realities is well on the way to become the ideological basis of a cynical utilitarian individualism (and, eventually, a delusional solipsism) that is going to impose many of the abovementioned collective responsibilities and accountabilities on the individual human being. They are aware that the rational idea of spatial realities also provides the ideational background of many modernist reconceptions that inevitably are going to be derived from it and, consequently, are going to be corrupted by the underlying idea of "empty spaces": concepts like "architecture", "art", "body", "boundary", "community", "economy", "freedom" (including all kinds of "unfreedom"), "home", "intelligence", "liberty", "matter", "mind", "movement", "nature", "perception", "privacy" and "publicity", "science", "society", "the world" and, of course, "reality" itself (eventually including all kinds of "artificial realities"). Moreover, they are aware that the momentous discrepancy between experiential realities and rational conceptions of space must be considered as an infinite source of modernist irrationalities. In particular, even though restricted by the lack of a respective terminology, many of them anticipate the collective psychotic potential of this discrepancy or inconsistency in the sense of a "derealisation" and "alienation" that definitely fits in with the forthcoming psychological conceptions, diagnostics, and formal stigmatisations. Drawing on Kant's work and extensive studies in Brahmanic and Buddhist philosophy, Arthur Schopenhauer's (1788–1860) main work *The World as Will and Representation* (published in two volumes in 1819 and 1859) frames this fundamental criticism against rationalist dogmata in a very articulate way by introducing, among many other basics of modernist thinking, the conceptual matrix of modern psychology. Needless to say, the conceptual matrix of modern psychology is based upon the experience of space and time.

These philosophical concerns are explicitly received and reflected by the so-called "early romanticists". In marked contrast to most of their successors in the High Romantic era who have little to offer in reply to rationalist claims but reactionary escapism, they feel obliged to live up to the intellectual and political inheritance of the Enlightenment idea, not least in opposition to the restorative developments following the disgraceful failure of the French Revolution. For instance, Ludwig von Beethoven's (1770–1827) groundbreaking and often desperate attempts to turn music from a mere aesthetic experience of systematised harmonics into an experience of collective spatial and temporal imagination, are also a pointedly humanist attempt to reclaim the primacy of experiential comprehensions of reality against the impositions of rationalist ideologies, as well as William Blake's (1757–1827), George Gordon Byron's (1788–1824), and Percy Shelley's (1792–1822) early romanticist poetry, or Francisco de

Goya's (1746–1828) late pictorial and graphical oeuvre.[13] The prototypical gothic novels of the time, from Matthew Gregory Lewis's *The Monk* (1796) to Mary Shelley's *Frankenstein or: The Modern Prometheus* (1816/18) and E. T. A. Hoffmann's (1776–1822) style-forming "ghost stories", are definitely beyond need of further explanation in this context. And Georg Büchner's (1813–1837) unfinished fragment *Lenz*, based on the true case history of the 27-year-old German poet Jakob Michael Reinhold Lenz recorded by the Alsatian pastor Johann Friedrich Oberlin in 1778, may be considered as an exemplary, both concussive and stunningly exact description of the psychotic dimension attached to the discrepancy of experiential realities and rational conceptions of space, anticipating derealisation "disorders" that are going to be diagnosed in millions of cases in the centuries to come. Referring to verbalisations in the original text, Büchner's decidedly empathic "diagnosis" (he works as a doctor in Zurich and dies there at the age of 24) might be paraphrased as the *unbearable silence of essentially empty spaces* or the *horror vacui* itself in its most existential form.

In spite of their disparate approaches to the topic, there is an implicit understanding among the exponents of the early romanticist movement that the intellectual, artistic, poetic, and occasionally magic "monstrosities" they invoke against the spirit of their times are far more acceptable and humane than those that eventually are going to creep out of the disenchanted emptiness of rationalised realities. Most certainly, that is one of the many issues Francisco de Goya addresses by the ingenious ambiguousness of his "Capricho" No. 43: "*The dream* (or: *the sleep*) *of reason produces monsters*".

13 Goya's late paintings and graphics represent an unprecedented outburst of artistic accusations against the contemporary political and ideological conditions, in terms of allegoric content as well as in terms of his proto-surrealistic style. The fact that both Goya and Beethoven, the painter and graphic artist as well as the musician and composer, were confronted with progressive deafness might be taken into account with regard to their innovative "translations" of spatial imagination in their respective artistic fields. Cf. *Confessions of an Exile*, p. 142.

Francisco de Goya; *The sleep* (or: *the dream*) *of reason produces monsters* (No. 43), from *Los Caprichos*, 1799

In summary, we acknowledge that the discovery – or rather: the *disclosure* – of the idea of space as a three-dimensional void is a tremendously productive core idea of modernity, both in tangible and in intellectual terms. However, in the course of the 20th century, it has not only resulted in most diverse forms of physical space consumption of increasingly irrational proportions but also in a plurality of conceptual spaces that, at some time, may have crossed the boundaries of common sense, including the progressive convergence of what we have referred to as "magic", "poetic", and "rational" theories and practices, which appear to be less and less differentiable in recent times. In the wake of this rampant poetry of delirious productivity, the self-conception of architecture has gradually been expanded by an explicative approach to space, which may be evident at an early stage in the context of the arising landscape architecture and the resurrecting urban planning in the 17th century. Along with the development from a craftsmanship to a modern discipline of spatial design, the former poetry of spatial objects begins to shift towards a poetry of creative "spacing": towards a visual and topographical practice of making spaces explicit and objective in their aesthetic and/or purposive "functionality" (and maybe, now and again, of camouflaging their essential emptiness). In hindsight, this explicative aspect is not only a definitional criterion of "modern architecture" but also one of its most essential contributions to the ongoing rationalisation of space (up to the occasional and rather presumptuous poetic conception of spatial explication as "creation" and "production of space").

With regard to the "age of rational space" in general, and in view of its historical consequences (including the global ecological challenges of the 21st century), we cannot fail to note that, at a certain point, the implementation of the rational idea of space as a common understanding of reality has also opened a bottomless pit of inhumane inspirations. As has been discussed above, ideas do not vanish or disappear just like that. They cannot be "erased" from our collective memory. They can only be repressed by alternative ideas: alternative ideas that make common sense.

Blackmail

St. Paul's Churchyard, London, 18th Mai 1692, just before dawn[14]

"I'm glad you could come, Sir."

"Good morning to you, Madam. Do we know each other?"

"No, we don't. Not in person, that is. We have been in correspondence. You have received my confirmation of this meeting in writing yesterday, just before noon."

"I did? – Well, to be honest, Madam, if that were so, I would be expecting to meet a certain *Mister* Keller here."

"Mr Keller from Zurich, I assume? – Given the *cause* of our acquaintance, Sir, would you have agreed to meet a *lady* in a matter as delicate as this?"

"Now, I'm ... no, most probably not."

"All the more, I feel deeply honoured by your confidence, Mr Wren, and I assure you that I am perfectly aware of your personal interests to keep this a secret. Are you carrying the item with you?"

"What kind of item would that be?"

"Look, Mr Wren, as matters stand, you are not in a position to play games with me. You have brought this upon yourself when you decided to withhold Mr Hawksmoor's discovery from the Brotherhood and the Fellows of the Royal Society. You are susceptible to my threats, and I am absolutely willing to act on them."

"I'm sure you will understand that I need to demand an explanation as to *how exactly* you have come to know about all this. No one has ever seen or heard of the Map except for Mr Hawksmoor and myself, Miss ... –"

"Keller."

"... Miss Keller. Was it Nicholas himself who blabbed it?"

"No, not at all. To my knowledge, Mr Hawksmoor has not betrayed your trust. To be quite candid with you, I am the very person who has actually *drawn* the *Orbis Intelligentiae*."

"With respect, that is a most impertinent and transparent *lie*. If you really do want to blackmail me, Miss, you should not take me for a fool."

"Believe me, Mr Wren, I don't. You had no idea about the significance of the Map until you learned of the legend of the Seven Architects less than a year ago, in a starry night in June. It was just a few

14 After the Great Fire of London in August 1666, leaving around 100'000 inhabitants homeless, the self-taught English architect and rather eccentric experimental scientist Christopher Wren (1632–1722) was commissioned to conduct the rebuilding of the vastly destroyed city. He was a founding member of the *Royal Society of London for Improving Natural Knowledge*. His most famous work is the design and construction of the new St. Paul's Cathedral on Ludgate Hill, replacing the original church that was founded on the site of a Roman Diana temple in 604 and rebuilt in 675 and 1314 when it became one of the highest buildings in Europe (149 m).

In 1679, Christopher Wren employed the 18-year-old Nicholas Hawksmoor (1661–1736), later to become one of the leading architects of London's rebuilding himself, as his personal assistant. Wren was knighted in 1673 and joined the Freemasons on the 18th of May 1691 in a ceremony at the partly finished new St. Paul's Cathedral. On the 24th of June 1717, the three already existing London Freemason lodges conjoined with a Westminster lodge at the *Goose and Gridiron Ale House* in St. Paul's Churchyard. Anthony Sayer was elected to the chair as Grand Master of the first Grand Lodge in Freemason history, succeeded by George Payne a year later. By the late 19th century, in the Victorian era, the Grand Lodge of London had become the most influential unofficial political power in the capital of the United Kingdom.

The date 1498 refers to the sanctioning of a common legislation of the German and Swiss Freemason brotherhoods by Roman-German emperor Maximilian I. The rise of Freemasonry in Europe, originating from the stonemason guilds in the Alsace and Breisgau region, dates back to the 11th century.

steps from where we stand now, wasn't it, at the *Goose and Gridiron* ale house, when you learned about the legend from your Brothers in spirit for the first time: how it was passed down among the Fellows from generation to generation for centuries, from the Dionysiacs to the Templars and on to the Freemasons. Under normal circumstances, a man like you would take a tale like that for a cock-and-bull story. But you didn't. It dawned on you quite instantly that night: The legendary Map of the Human Mind actually *existed*, and *you* were in possession of it. Now, what would we expect an honest member of the Brotherhood to do in a situation like that? – With regard to its great value to all Freemason guilds, we would expect him to confide the secret to his fellow Brothers, wouldn't we? – But, for whatever the reason, you didn't. Maybe you thought that you might use the Map in favour of your personal power and influence one day. Maybe you did not want to share knowledge as precious and *useful* to an architect on His Majesties service like yourself. Or maybe you were just frightened of the powers of a possibly magic object that has fallen into your hands so unexpectedly."

"There are no magic objects in this world. Not anymore. Magic is superstitious nonsense and make-believe concocted by those who do not know better. In *this* world, there is only matter and power. That is all there is to it. Anyway, you are not entitled to know any of ... all this. You are ... –"

"... a *woman*. Yes I am. I bring the furious spirit of Diana upon you, preserved in the remains of the old temple beneath St. Paul's amongst which Mr Hawksmoor has discovered the Map of the Human Mind. Nonetheless, I am very much familiar with the mysteries and mysticisms of the Brotherhood. I was there when the holy rules were sanctioned in 1498. And, incidentally, I am thinking about founding a lodge myself in Zurich some time soon."

"By Jahbulon, you cannot do that! It would be an unforgiveable sacrilege!"

"Calm yourself down, Mr Wren, people might take notice of us. – Now tell me, do you believe in the legend and in what it *represents*?"

"Of course I do, but you can't ... –"

"If your belief is so imperturbable as it should be, then why would you dishonour yourself by doubting the obvious? – I was also there when the Seven Architects set sail in the harbour of Cnossos three thousand years ago, Mr Wren. I was one of them. I was, as you should have guessed by now, *Leto of Cnossos* herself."

"No. No. This is ... –"

"Do yourself a favour, Mr Wren. Just give me the Map. It is beyond your comprehension anyway."

"Oh ... no, please, I ... I can't breathe, I ... aawoo-ooh!" – – –

"Accept my deepest thanks, Mr Wren. I give you my word that you shall never hear from me again. – Oh, and by the way, I really admire your plans for the new cathedral. I can assure you that your St. Paul's will be a pinnacle of contemporary architecture and that it will outlast centuries. Not even the Blitz will damage it. Your work – and Mr Hawksmoore's of course – most certainly will go down in history. Goodbye to you, Sir." –

Unauthorised drawing of the Goose and Gridiron Ale House, St Paul's Churchyard, London, around 1700

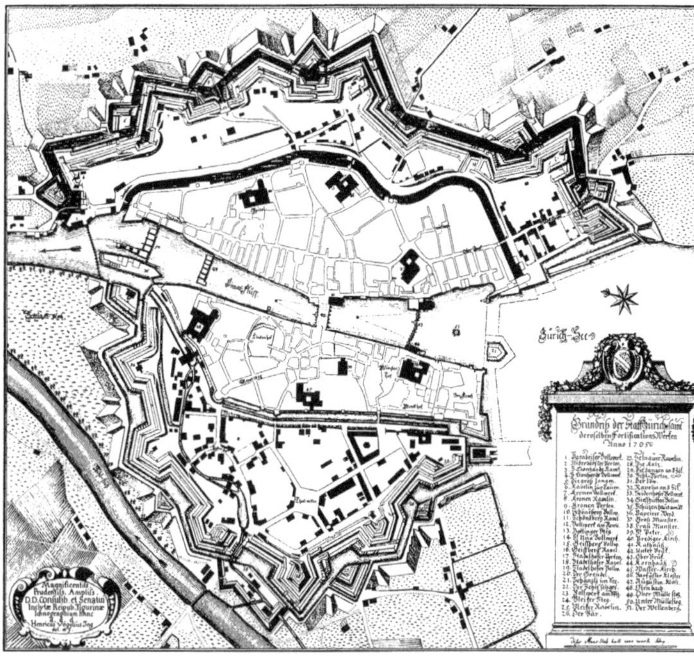

• The City of Zurich with fortifications, Henricus Vogelius, 1705

1712

The English ironmonger Thomas Newcomen (1663–1729) applies the first *steam engine* for mine drainage in a coalmine in Staffordshire. In 1769, James Watt (1736–1819) is granted a patent for an improved application of the technology, which subsequently becomes a key factor of early industrialisation, mass production, automation and rationalisation of work processes. As from the 19th century, the respective changes of labour and social situations in developed countries rapidly and substantially reshape the living, habitation, and environmental conditions of a large majority of citizens referred to as the "working class".

1722

Based on the mathematisation of acoustics, Johann Sebastian Bach (1685–1750) develops the first part of his programmatic collection of preludes and fugues under the title *The Well-Tempered Clavier*, thus introducing the symphonious principles of modern western music.

1751 – 1772

The "*Encyclopédie*" (*Encyclopedia, or a Systematic Dictionary of the Sciences, Arts, and Crafts*), edited by Denis Diderot and Jean le Rond d'Alambert, is published in France. Arguably, it is the central project of the sociopolitical Age of Enlightenment in the 18th century and the ideational model of all subsequent encyclopaedic projects.

1759

The Scottish moral philosopher Adam Smith (1723–1790) publishes his *Inquiry into the Nature and Causes of the Wealth of Nations* after returning to his hometown Kirkcaldy from an educational journey. Though (or because of) being completely out of touch with the economic realities (and "natural laws") it is concerned with, it becomes an instant international bestseller and shapes the initial axioms and premises of capitalist economics as well as the largely poor level of its criticism to the present day. However, if considered with philosophical thoroughness, it clearly outlines the basic capitalist theorems as the ideological counter-principles of morals, which most probably was not Smith's original intent but the obvious and inevitable consequence of his theoretical construct.

1762

In *Du contrat sociale (The Social Contract)*, the Genevan philosopher, writer, education theorist and composer Jean-Jacques Rousseau (1712–1778) takes up Thomas Hobbes' and John Locke's early liberal considerations, though starting out from a quite contrary, generally degenerative anthropological view, and defines both the political order and the conditions of modern democratic-republican systems. As is often the case, the "political order" is received much more meticulously than the "conditions". However, the book is broadly referred to as a key work paving the way for liberalist ideas and the French Revolution in 1789.

1776

After a year of open revolutionary war against the British colonial power, the American "Continental Congress" votes for the *Unanimous Declaration of The Thirteen United States of America*, mostly formulated by Thomas Jefferson, on the 4th of July. The war continues until the British defeat in the Battle of Yorktown in 1781 and is officially ended on 3rd September 1783 when the Treaty of Paris is signed. Around 135 years later, in the wake of the First World War, the systematic genocide of the indigenous cultures of the Americas, started by the Spanish colonial forces in the 16th century, is almost complete, and the United States of America have risen to become the leading world power in almost every respect except for cultural and political self-awareness.[15]

1781

The German philosopher Immanuel Kant (1724–1804) reformulates the basic problems of philosophy under the modern cognitional conditions of the Enlightenment, i.e. in terms of "reason". *In Critique of Pure Reason* (1781), he defines the conditions of epistemology and the understanding of the external world. Among other things, he defines space and time as primary intuitional categories of the human mind's conception of reality. In his writing on morals (1785–1797), he develops the "Categorical Imperative": "Act only according to that maxim whereby you can, at the same time, will that it should become a universal law" (in one of several formulations), and in *Critique of Practical Reason* (1788) he analyses the conditions of freedom. The comprehensiveness of his thinking encourages the metaphor of a "Copernican revolution in philosophy".

1782

After centuries of witch-hunt and systematic persecution of people of either sex being accused of practicing magic or associating with the devil, the *last legal execution of a witch* in Europe happens in Glarus, Switzerland: 48-year-old serving maid Anna Göldi(n) is sentenced to death by the sword for sorcery on 13th June 1782 after having confessed under torture.

Most of these executions were judicial murders in connection with political or sexual motives. And most of them were applied to women. The last known illegal execution of a witch is dated to 1793 in Posen, Preussia.

15 Cf. also chapter IV.1 *The Greatest Day for Freedom* in Dieter Dietz / Matthias Michel/ Daniel Zamarbide (ed.): *All About Space*, Volume 1: *The Invention of Space*, Zurich 2016.

1789 On the 14th of July, after looting an armoury, citizens of Paris storm the state prison "Bastille". The *civic revolution* opens into years of political chaos and unrest until Napoleon Bonaparte's coup d'état on 9th November 1799.

• Survey map of the city of Zurich ("Müllerplan"), 1793

1799 In spring 1798 Napoleon Bonaparte has unopposedly invaded Switzerland and modernised its political structure into the "Helvetic Republic". Because of its central strategic position, the other major European powers ally to expel the French army from the Swiss territory. After a series of combats in north-east Switzerland, the allied imperial army of Austria, Russia, Great Britain, Portugal, Naples, and the Ottoman Empire under Archduke Charles of Austria attack Napoleon Bonaparte's imperial occupation troops under general André Masséna in Zurich from the east on the 4th June 1799, outnumbering it by a factor of three. This "First *Battle of Zurich*" results in a no-win situation after heavy combats in the woods around "Zürichberg" hill causing huge casualties on the French side. At the request of the Zurich authorities, Masséna negotiates a truce and withdraws his troops to the western suburbs on 5th June, thus preventing the city from being destroyed in street battles.

On the 25th of September, the French troops attack all the allied emplacements around Zurich at once, compensating for their numerical inferiority by feints and by concentrating on the weakest Russian sectors of the front along the river "Limmat". In the "Second Battle of Zurich", the imperial army is drubbed, subsequently chased across the central and eastern Alpine passes and finally expelled from the Swiss territory within less than two weeks. Again, the city of Zurich evades a seemingly inevitable destruction.

After Napoleon's ultimate defeat in the Battle of Waterloo, the national borders of Switzerland are internationally accepted on the occasion of the *Congress of Vienna* in 1815. As a modern federal state, Switzerland is founded in 1848 after a minor civil war-like conflict between the conservative catholic and the progressive liberal cantons, which is settled in favour of the latter.

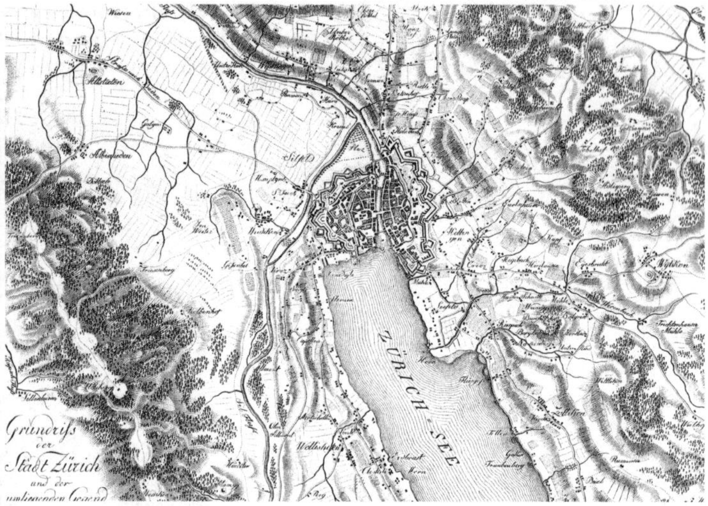

Zurich map 1799 by Heinrich Keller, 1800

Confessions of an Exile

Two letters written by Ludwig von Beethoven in October 1802 and in July 1812[16]

Heiligenstadt, October 6th, 1802.

O you men who think or say that I am malevolent, stubborn or misanthropic, how greatly do you wrong me, you do not know the secret causes of my semblance. From childhood, my heart and mind were disposed to the gentle feelings of good will, I was always eager to accomplish great deeds. But think of it that for six years I have been a hopeless case, aggravated by senseless physicians, cheated year after year in the hope of improvement, finally compelled to face the prospect of a lasting malady (the cure of which may take years or may be even impossible), born with an ardent and lively temperament, even susceptible to the diversions of society, I was compelled early to isolate myself, to live in loneliness. When, at times, I tried to get over all this, o how harshly was I repulsed by the doubly sad experience of my bad hearing, and yet it was impossible for me to ask: Speak louder, shout, for I am deaf. Alas, how could I possibly admit such an infirmity in the one sense which should have been more perfect in me than in others, a sense which I once possessed in highest perfection, a perfection such as few surely in my profession enjoy or have enjoyed. – O I cannot. Therefore forgive me when you see me draw back when I would gladly mingle with you, my misfortune is doubly painful because it must lead to my being misunderstood. For me, there can be no recreation in human society, in refined interlocution, in mutual exchange of ideas, only just as little as the greatest needs command I may participate in society, I must live like an exile. When I approach people, I am seized by hot anxiety, the fear that my condition might be observed.

Thus it has been during the past year, which I have spent in the country, commanded by my reasonable physician to spare my hearing as much as possible, in this almost meeting my natural disposition, although I some-

16 The translation is based on transcripts of the original documents compiled in Dieter Rexroth; *Beethoven. Leben. Werke. Dokumente*, Mainz 1982. The woman addressed as "my immortal beloved" in the second letter has not been identified to the present day.

times gave in to my inclination for society. But what a humiliation when someone stood beside me and heard a flute in the distance and I heard nothing, or someone heard the shepherd singing and, again, I heard nothing. Such incidents brought me to the verge of despair, and I very nearly put an end to my life. – Only art it was that withheld me, it seemed impossible to leave the world until I had produced all that I felt like producing, and so I endured this miserable, truly miserable existence [...] – With joy I hasten towards death; – if it comes before I shall have had an opportunity to show all my artistic capabilities, it will, despite my hard fate, still come too early, and I would probably wish it had come later. – But even then I am content, will it not free me from my state of endless suffering? – Come whenever you will, I shall meet you bravely. – Farewell, and do not forget me completely in my death, I deserve this of you having often thought of you in my life, and how to make you happy; be so. –

Ludwig van Beethoven
[Seal]
For my brothers Carl and – – to be read and executed after my death.

In the evening, Monday, July 6th –

[...] What a life!!! So!!! Without you – Pursued by the goodness of the people here and there, which I think — to want to earn just as little as to earn them – Humbleness of man towards men – it hurts me – and when I consider myself in the overall context of the universe, what am I, and what is He – whom one calls the greatest – and yet – again, herein lies the divine of man. [...]

Good morning on July 7th –

In bed already, my ideas yearn towards you, my immortal beloved, here and there joyfully, then again sadly, awaiting whether fate will answer us. I can only live either all together with you or not at all. [...] Be calm – love me – today – yesterday – What a longing in tears for you – you – you – my life – my all – farewell – oh, go on loving me – never misjudge the most faithful of hearts

Of your beloved
L.
Ever yours
Ever mine
Ever ours

1804	The British engineer and inventor Richard Trevithick (1771–1833) puts the first *steam locomotive* into operation.
1815	The Congress of Vienna puts an end to the Napoleonic Wars and to the republican visions of a denationalised Europe. The feudal monarchies are reinstated and a new era of European nationalism begins. As a consequence of the "Restoration", many universities, especially in the German-speaking world, are submitted to strict political control. Political activities of professors and students are broadly prohibited. Thus, Europe becomes subject to transboundary political conditions that enable a rapid and extensive implementation of industrialist power structures and *modern national economies*, which are, following the English example and the general outline of Smith's approach to the "wealth of nations", based on entrepreneurship and exploitative wage labour, on continuous growth of technology and population. By the second half of the 19th century, the respective capitalist

differentiation of modern societies, including its cultural and demographic consequences, is fully fledged in central and western Europe. Industrialists ascend to join the financial aristocracies and, organised as "liberals" and so-called "radicals", begin to gain considerable influence on local and, subsequently, national policies.

1826 The French inventor Joseph "Nicéphore" Niépce (1765–1833) produces the earliest surviving photograph (*View from the Window at Le Gras*), applying a heliographic procedure. Subsequently, his partner Louis Daguerre develops the technique towards the light-sensitive silver halides of the "daguerreotype" process until 1837.

1856 The most powerful Swiss politician and economic leader of the 19th century, *Johann Heinrich Alfred Escher* (1819–1882), descendent of an old and notorious family of Zurich's financial aristocracy, founds the first international bank in Zurich, the "Swiss Credit Institute" ("Schweizerische Kreditanstalt"), to finance and realise his railroad projects independently from foreign creditors. In 1873, the bank's headquarters, designed by architect Jakob Friedrich Wanner,[17] are built at the "Paradeplatz", a former pig and livestock market place, which has been gradually upgraded since the beginning of the slighting of the city's fortifications in 1833. Due to mistaken speculations that it would become the site of the Zurich main rail station (opened in 1871), the "Paradeplatz" has turned into the most prestigious and valuable real estate site in Switzerland and, subsequently, the centre of Switzerland's financial industry.

Following his radical-liberal convictions and using his financial and political powers, Alfred Escher shapes Zurich into a modern city and a transport hub, initiating, among other things, the foundation of the Swiss Federal Institute of Technology (ETH) in 1854, built by the German architect Gottfried Semper. However, despite Zurich's rise to become one of the wealthiest cities in the world, the Swiss Federation ranks among the poorest countries in Europe until the end of the World Wars.

1859 The British naturalist and biologist Charles Darwin (1809–1882) publishes *On the Origin of Species by Means of Natural Selection, or The Preservation of Favoured Races in the Struggle for Life* and thus puts forward the theory of evolution.

1867 Karl Marx (1818–1883), a central agitator in the revolutionary activities of 1848, publishes the first volume of his monumental work *Capital* in cooperation with Friedrich Engels. The other two volumes are published posthumously in 1885 and 1894. "*Das Kapital*" remains the only comprehensive theory of capitalist economy to date, being discussed controversially but hardly ever received or understood in its entirety. However, its publication also represents the sustainable triumph of materialistic worldviews.

17 Cf. photograph on p. 14

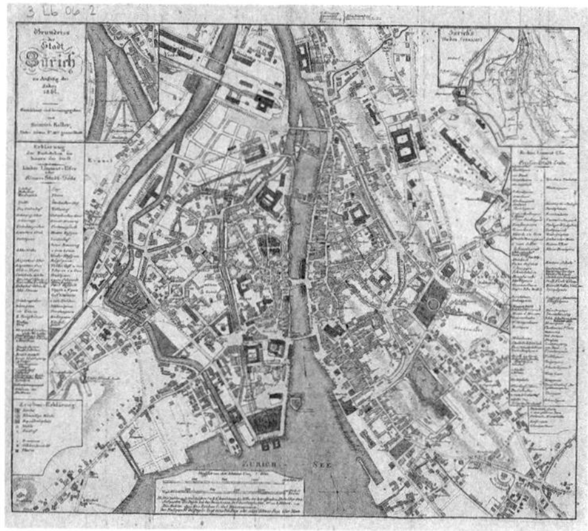

- Survey map of the city of Zurich (1 : 2’500), 1860
- Layout plan of the city of Zurich (1 : 6’600) by Heinrich Keller, 1864

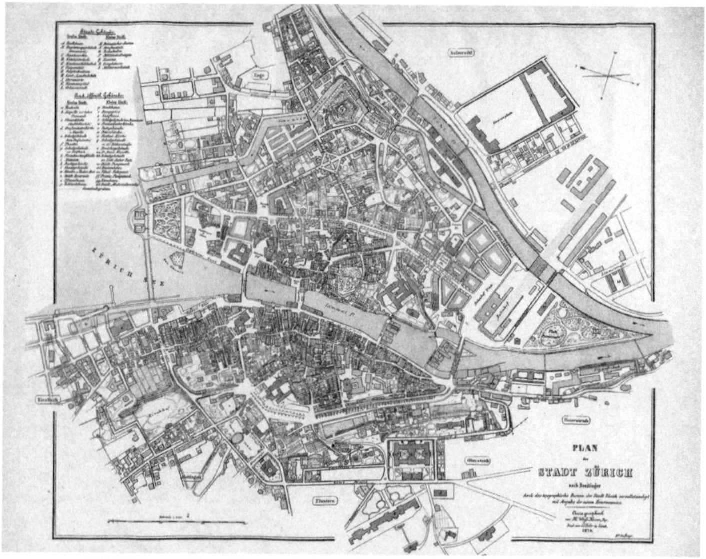

- Zürich in 1874, based on Josef Breitinger, completed by Heinrich Weiss-Keiser on behalf of the typographical bureau of the city of Zurich, 1874

1888

At least once in July or early August, one Alois Hitler, customs officer in Braunau (Upper Austria), illegitimate son of Anna Maria Schicklgruber and Johann Nepomuk Hiedler or his brother, has sexual intercourse with his niece and third wife Klara Hitler-Pölzl. On this occasion, Klara conceives a son who is born on the 20th April of the following year and is given the name Adolf. The child grows up to be a would-be artist and architect, a convinced occultist, a private in the First World War, a sociopath, and eventually the most famous and infamous dictator in history. As from 1923, when his political career picks up pace, Adolf Hitler smothers up his descent and forces his family members to deny the kinship with him.

With regard to science and technology, the two decades between the late 1870s and the late 1890s in Europe and the United States arguably represent the technologically most innovative decade in human history. In fact, most of the scientific and technical discoveries, inventions, and applications that would later define the cultural and technological realities of the 20th century (telecommunication, electrification, motorised vehicles, electromagnetic radiation and early particle physics, various audio-visual and consumer technologies etc.) occur in a period of just a few years peaking around 1888. Until 1910, Thomas Alva Edison (1847–1931) alone has applied for 1093 patents in the United States and for 1239 patents in other countries around the globe, not including those he is forced to assign to other inventors and companies.

Simultaneously with the heyday of industrialisation, a similar innovation period occurs in the visual arts (impressionism, early expressionism, graphic arts, and other avant-garde movements) and in scientific education (early implementations of the social, anthropological, and psychological sciences). To what extent exactly these developments and their contemporary cultural reflection in literature, philosophy, and politics have to be considered as intertwined in an overall context is hard to determine. However, in retrospect, they convey the impression of a feverish and frenetic collective heading for an inevitable climax.

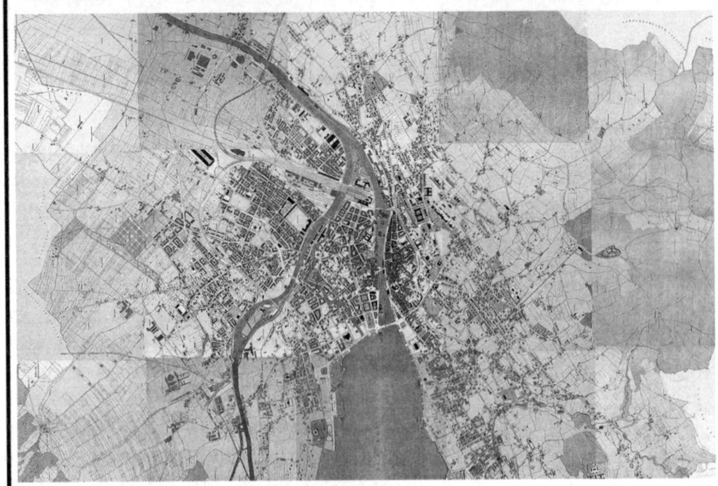

- Heinrich Siegfried; *Vue générale de Zurich prise de la Waid*, 1884. / Zurich, 1900.
- Official survey map of the Zurich area, 1900

THE AGE OF SPACISMS OR: THE BLACK SQUARE AND THE BLUE MARBLE

MULTIPLE EXPLICATIONS

2018

What kind of reality is this that imitates a metaphor? – "It's completely impossible," he said aloud. [...] He was fiction. He belonged to a world that was not real.

(Haruki Murakami; *1Q84*, Volume 1, 2009)

The history of ideas of space, as far as we have tried to understand it so far, appears to be structured in ideational strata of intertwining "ages" rather than in consecutive "times", meaning that these ages do not actually succeed one another but rather are layered one upon the other. Thus, this history of ideas may be chronicled along a historical timeline for reasons of representation, but in a comprehensive view, it is not a "horizontal" but rather a "vertical" history in which ideas are continuously overlaid and interwoven. Correspondingly, reconstructing it in terms of a "brief history of space" is, structurally speaking, an archaeological rather than a historical endeavour suggesting, among other things, that in the wake of major historical upheavals older and lower ideational sediments may partially cover the surface of newer und upper ones.

Against this background, we have not chosen the "most important" historical events to set up this chronicle but rather some that seem to be representative for specific developments in the general conception of space. And it worked pretty well up to the last entry. We have dug up a history of ideas of space that leads from a quite self-evident intuitional conception of the spatial environment as a whole up to the poetic conception of a virtually indefinite natural resource of shapeable and explorable interstices, and, finally, up to a universal metaphor based on the mathematical abstraction of a three-dimensional void, which allows rational, transcultural, and transideological discourses on spatial conditions. Although a multiplicity of spaces can only be conceived of in terms of this conceptual and rational abstraction, we have alternately used the word "space" in the singular and the plural from the very beginning because, apart from the principal aspects of the "magic", the "poetic", and the "rational" idea of space, we have deemed it reasonable to acknowledge the diversity of spatial conceptions within these ideational layers on a global scale. Moreover, since we look at these ideas of space from a 21st century perspective, we have to take into account that, as from the dawn of modernity, the notion of a multiplicity of spaces has been adopted in everyday speech and the general notion of space itself.

As has been discussed before, this modernist notion of multiplicities of abstracted, diversely conceptualised and designable spaces sets the stage for many irrational implications that are based upon one simple categorical mistake: the conceptual objectification of space by employing the theoretical assumption of an Archimedean point used in mathematical computations and constructions of three-dimensional objects on the cognitional (and anything but theoretical) *experience* of space. Or: the long-known confusion of interstices with "spaces" and vice versa, which is already inherent to the etymology of the word itself (to the roots of both the Latin word *spatium* and the Old High German word *rūm*, cf. p. 58). As soon as this categorical mistake is commonly adapted to the experience and to the common notion of realities, the idea of space quite literally disintegrates into an ever-increasing pluralism of spatial conceptions, metaphors, and analogies that soon enough cease to be reasonably referable to a consistent idea (or a common sense) of space beyond the mathematical metaphor. The trivial fact alone that these so-called "spaces" can be perceived and experienced differently according to different perspectives, viewpoints, imaginations, ideologies, or living conditions of individual – or rather: individualised – human beings at the same time, gives rise to essentially pointless debates and discourses. In these discourses on "spaces", multitudes of particular spatial situations and relations have to be explicated – or rather: made explicit – in reference to their particular "contexts", which provides us, on the one hand, with seemingly unlimited possibilities of spatial poetry, speculation, and experimentation. On the other hand, precisely as multiple explications, these contextually bounded and multiply poetised spaces are inevitably turned into cognitional *objects* and thus, at some point, into essentially artificial (i.e. mostly "technical") *simulations* of space. At this point, the rational idea of space begins to relapse into a mere cognitional implication of the "poetic" idea of interstices in between objects: a poetic idea in the disguise of rational discourses.

And at this point precisely, when, on the one hand, the scattered discourses on "space", "spaces", and "spatialities" get into full flow and, on the other hand, the idea of space can no longer be based on a common comprehension that what we refer to as space is *nothing but* the human experience of given environments at given moments in time, we hesitate to continue the chronicle in terms of a history of "ideas of space" for obvious reasons. – What are we supposed to do? – Should we open a new chapter under the title "The Age of Irrational Spaces"? – Or should we simply declare that the history of ideas of space has come to a provisional end (and find solace in the fact that, eventually, the *dissolution* of the conventional idea of space has not even spared the natural sciences in general and the universal theories of physics in particular)? – Then again, both conclusions would be too simple and rather disappointing, wouldn't they? –

What if we would try to take the coexistence and convergence of multiple situational, contextual, and eventually incommensurable ideas and simulations of "rational", "poetic", and "magic" spaces seriously and declare that, at this point precisely, we enter into the "age of *spacisms*"? –

What we would refer to by the term of "spacism" would be a multitude of simulated spaces and spatial simulations. We would do that from a 21st century perspective; a perspective that involves many-faceted everyday experiences with various simulations of spaces, discourses, communications, and values, including the many simulated everyday problems caused by the many mistakes of metaphors and simulations for realities. For instance, we would have witnessed the pointless debates about metaphors like "virtual spaces" or "artificial intelligence" for decades now. We would *know* that most of these debates are essentially pointless because they are based on the essential confusion of the terminological metaphor with the real thing (or the mistake of its *explication* for *comprehension*): For the time being, we would still *know* that there are no "spaces" involved in technical data capacities, and that there is no such thing as "intelligent" processing of knowledge and experience involved in the advanced technical computing of information, wouldn't we? –

In other words, we would know better than ever before that it is not only possible but also strikingly easy for human beings to live in metaphorical realities for an indeterminate period of time, as long as the explications of the metaphors or simulations involved remain commonly accepted and unquestioned. We would have long since got used to realities in which these simulations are perfectly explicit and broadly uncomprehended at the same time.

Evidently, this capability to live under the conditions of metaphorical and simulated realities is based on the capability of volitional or *intentional ignorance*. Like any other natural predisposition, intentional ignorance is not a good or bad faculty in itself. Its effect depends on the intent and the extent to which it is exercised in particular contexts or situations. However, intentional ignorance quite obviously turns into a malign state of mind at the very moment when the metaphors that justify it are explicitly mistaken for natural facts. At that very moment, the occasionally charming humbleness of ignorance turns into mere stupidity: into the arrogate denial of reality we usually refer to as hypocrisy. Simple notions turn into presumptuous "ideas", the ideas turn into ideologies, and the ideologies turn into "truths". The explications of these truths turn into empty formulas and slogans that have no further use or purpose than the denial of their implications. In consequence, new metaphors and simulations are produced, seemingly confirming the validity of the metaphorical realities they are based on in a vicious circle of self-fulfilling prophecy: questions are raised to produce the answers that are already given in advance. At some point, two people can look at the same natural fact and cannot make the slightest common sense of it. Reality turns into an infinite loop of uncomprehended present that cannot be referred back to its past or causation anymore. And even less, it can be referred forward to any reasonable perspective on possible futures or future possibilities.[1]

1 As has been suggested in the closing chapter VII. *The Dissolution of Space* of *All About Space* Volume 1, the simulation of spaces (or: the progressing production of "simulacrums" of space) implies, at some point sooner or later, a phenomenology of "nothingness" as against the void of an "empty space": a nothingness that is *anything but* absence or inexistence or emptiness. On the contrary, it is a phenomenological state of complete fullness: a world full of nothing.

Remarkably enough, the problem of nothingness in its modern philosophical formulation, mostly associated with existential philosophy as from the turn of the 20th century, emerges more or less simultaneously with the irrationalisation of spatial representations in the classic avant-garde movements. In a very pointed manner of speaking, these experimentations in art and literature gradually converge to the oft-quoted formula that "nothing is true" and "everything is permitted". Purportedly, these were the last words of Hassan as-Sabbāh, spiritual leader of the Nizārī Ismailites and founder of the legendary "Fedayeen order of the Hashshashin". The myth of the "Hashshashin" as a sworn elite community of trained contract killers, their association with the drug hashish, and the etymology of the modern word "assassin" are mainly based on one of the accounts in Marco Polo's travelogues (cf. p. 107).

Hassan as-Sabbāh died in the mountains of northern Persia in 1124, and up to the present day, "*Nothing is true, everything is permitted*" has been interpreted in many contexts and variations. Most probably, it was originally associated with the mental ability to temporarily concentrate on a certain task or idea in a way that allows to blind out usual restrictions of reality and thus accomplish things that are beyond ordinary

In broad outline, that is what we would have to expect if we would actually enter into the "age of spacisms". And since we have already become familiar with the primary spacist principle in the context of rational spaces, we might as well put it down in writing to begin with:

The 1st principle of Spacism:
The simulation of experiential realities in metaphorical spaces.

Nevertheless, against the background of all we have come to understand about the idea of space so far, we would try our best not to be fooled into confusing simulated with real spatial experiences, wouldn't we? –

1888

However, what forces us to abandon the form of a chronicle with regard to the 20th century is *not* the exponentially increasing amount of available information, the unleashing of uncomprehended technological complexities, or the falling apart of a long since globalised world into social, scientific, intellectual, and political fragments of all kinds of ideas of natural, artificial, and conceptual spaces that characterise the "age of spacisms". It is the simple fact that the listed entries of the chronicle would appear to be representative of a global continuity of progressive events and ideas. It would suggest reasonable strategies or sensible and logical decisions based on the solid ground of a common sense and understanding of space, resulting in rational and consecutive global developments. In other words, with respect to the 20th century, it would be a fake. Evidently, there *have* been strategies and decisions. And most of them certainly were rational to the limits of cynicism and beyond. But, as we know by now, they have led us way beyond reasonability. They only seem reasonable because we have become so incredibly good at justifying the irrational consequences of our thoughts and

mental or physical possibilities. However, in most cases, the sentence is interpreted as a statement about the perception of reality or even about reality itself (in the approximate sense of: "Nothing is real, *therefore* everything is possible"). Conceived of in this epistemological sense, the formula evidently involves many intriguing and inspiring implications with regard to postmodern cultural conceptions and conditions.

The American "beat generation" writer William S. Burroughs (1914–1997) initiated a sustainable revival of both the formula and its legendary historical origins by repeatedly referring to them in his works. Subsequently, "*Nothing is true, everything is permitted*" became a very popular idiom in the countercultures of the 1960s, not least because its undetermined meaning seemed to be so perfectly applicable to the spirit and the cultural conditions of postmodernist times. In 2007, it was readopted in the popular video game series *Assassin's Creed*, a typical contemporary mix-up of trivialised secret society mysticisms and historical factoids.

actions and behaviours in rational terms. Nevertheless, we demand reasonable explanations, don't we? –

With regard to the last entry in the chronicle, the best we can do is to refer to a few conspicuous events that may be thought of as representative for the beginning of the "age of spacisms", defining the three decades before the outbreak of the First World War as sort of a prologue or foreplay. After all, we have pinpointed the beginning of this "prelude" around the year 1888. It is, for instance, the year when Heinrich Hertz objectifies electromagnetic waves, when John Boyd Dunlop invents the tubed tyre, George Eastman popularises the roll film, which leads directly to the invention of motion pictures and the film camera associated with names like Eadweard Muybridge, Thomas Edison, the Lumière brothers, or Georges Méliès. It is the year of the so-called "Jack the Ripper" murders in London's Whitechapel district, the investigations being seriously hampered by representatives of the Victorian government (involving cover-ups, suppression of evidence, and false convictions) for reasons that are still discussed in terms of conspiracy theories today. And it is the year when Friedrich Nietzsche's (1844–1900) "anti-Apollonian" polemic *On the Genealogy of Morality*, published in November 1887, starts to be received in the context of his previous aphoristic works *Thus Spoke Zarathustra* (1883–1885) and *Beyond Good and Evil: Prelude of a Philosophy of the Future* (1886), which radically denounce the idea of progress in cultural history and, along with it, the deceitfulness of (deductive) reason. Nietzsche's writings eventually provoke rather daring responses among the intellectuals of the time.

> *EVE: Nietzsche said that God is dead, didn't he? – Damn right he was. ADAM: What he actually said is that* we have killed *Him. That's something else entirely, now isn't it?*
>
> (Aaron Zucker; *The Fabulous Adventures of Adam and Eve – A strictly intellectual stage play*, 1899)
>
> *The principal reason for the contradictions and disingenuousness of the common conception of god is the maleness of his anthropomorphic features. [...] The centre of gravity of pessimism lies in the conception of man. The only true and righteous illumination of the world lies in his critical humiliation.*
>
> (Helene von Druskowitz; *Pessimistische Kardinalsätze: ein Vademekum für die freiesten Geister*, "Pessimistic Key Sentences: A vade mecum for the most libertine spirits", 1905. Re-issued in 1988 as *Der Mann als logische und sittliche Unmöglichkeit und als Fluch der Welt*, "Man as a logical and moral impracticality and as the curse of the world".)
>
> *War? – Of course! It is our only hope, the legitimation of our existence, and it is our will! ... Yes! War against you who die too slowly, and against all the dead who block our way! ... Indeed, our nerves call for war! ... We prefer a violent death, we glorify it as the only humane way to die: the way of a predator!*
>
> (Filippo Tommaso Marinetti; *Death to the Moonshine!*, 1909)

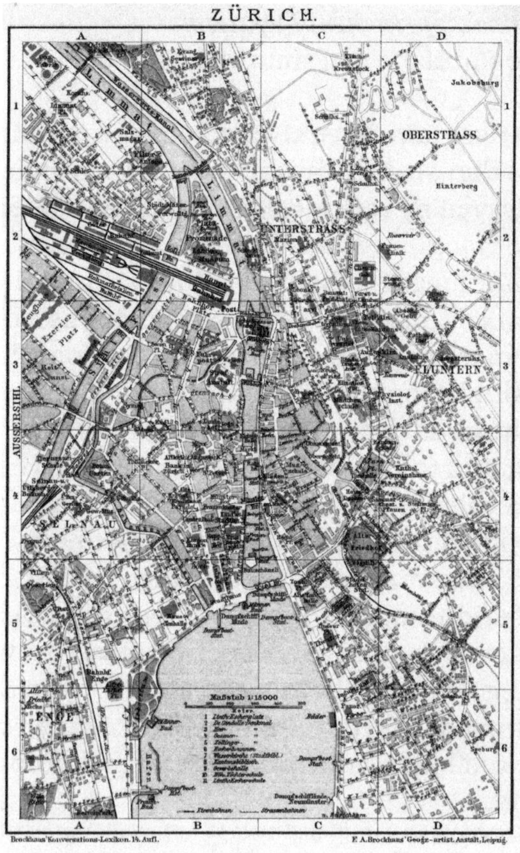

Zurich city map (1 : 15'000) published by "F. A. Brockhaus Geographische Anstalt", Leipzig, 1898

What the abovementioned events have in common, along with many other more important or more trivial ones, is that they introduce technical, communicative, political, and intellectual means of perceiving, designing, reproducing, accelerating, slowing down, manipulating, conditioning, and conceptualising spatial realities in "real time" – or in a way that converges to the experience of *simultaneity*, which certainly represents a major aesthetical change in the common perception of space. The general idea of a categorical consecutiveness of events in space and time and, consequently, the reliability of conclusive reasoning begins to be put in question in many more or less obvious ways. We might even go as far as to formulate

The 2nd principle of Spacism: The simulation of simultaneity.

Experiences of simultaneity are (and have always been) essentially "magic" experiences, precisely because they seem to escape the common logics of cause and effect. Though mostly conveyed by technical applications of electricity at the time, they inevitably evoke "magic" responses. Evidently, the use of the word "magic" in this context is not meant to be metaphorical at all. It refers rather precisely to the experiential conditions that have been discussed earlier in the context of *Magic Spaces*. Remarkably enough, even professional "magic" trickery (which becomes increasingly popular at the turn of the 20th century) is mainly based on techniques of simultaneity.

However, first and foremost we have chosen the year 1888 for the last entry in the chronicle because most of the basic scientific and technical discoveries, inventions, and applications that would later define the spatial realities of the 20th century (like telecommunication, electrification, motorised vehicles, electromagnetic radiation and early particle physics, various audio-visual and consumer technologies etc.) occur in a short period of just a few years around the 1880s and 1890s, implying, among other things, that, as from the end of that particular period, the irrational self-extermination of the human civilisation on planet Earth, based on rational ideas and motives and technologies, is within reach of technical feasibility.

At this very moment, we see a one-armed male torso nailed to a rotten supporting beam of a trench, the entrails gushing out between the torn apart ribs, and we can see that this ghastly work of sculptural poetry is supposed to mean something. In the background, we see muzzle flashes, ceaseless lightning of deafening explosions blowing up clouds of black smoke and grey soil all across the plains. – We see secret circles of occultists gathering in darkened secluded rooms, reviving the magic practices of past ages in all new interpretations, invoking spirits and forces of the hereafters in order to attain wisdom. – Then we see a woman in a saucy evening dress with a cocktail glass in her hand, screaming "Don't you dare to touch me, you bastard!" – For a split second, we see a close-up on Sigmund Freud trying to standardise psychological behaviour by translating mythical, Schopenhauerian, and Nietzschean concepts and metaphors into general models of the human psyche, kept awake by cocaine flashes. – We see the American Airlines Flight 11 plane crashing into the northern façade of the World Trade Center's north tower in New York City. We see United Airlines Flight 175 crashing into the southern façade of the south tower 17 minutes later. – We see a 1967 TV studio full of people dressed up in colourful hippie stuff surrounding the Beatles singing "All you need is love ... love is all you need ..." in the first worldwide satellite TV broadcast in history. – We see another close-up on Ingrid Bergman and Humphrey Bogart kissing passionately in soft-focussed black and white, followed by a glimpse of Kazimir Malevich's *Black Square*. –

What is this? – It feels like everything happens at the same time.

It feels as if the times had begun orbiting in an infinite loop of presence, playback, and re-presentation.

Exactly. What is that supposed to mean?

We don't know yet. But we asked for reasonable explanations, didn't we? –

EVE: And God said: "Let there be light!" – And there it was. Isn't that what God is all about?
ADAM: Well, yes, maybe. – See that red button?
EVE: Yes, of course I see it. What is it for?
ADAM: Now watch it! I press the button, and – at the very same *moment – the light goes on. Now isn't that great? –*
EVE: It sure is. But what is it supposed to mean? Are you implying that ... –
(Aaron Zucker; *The Fabulous Adventures of Adam and Eve – A strictly intellectual stage play*, 1899)

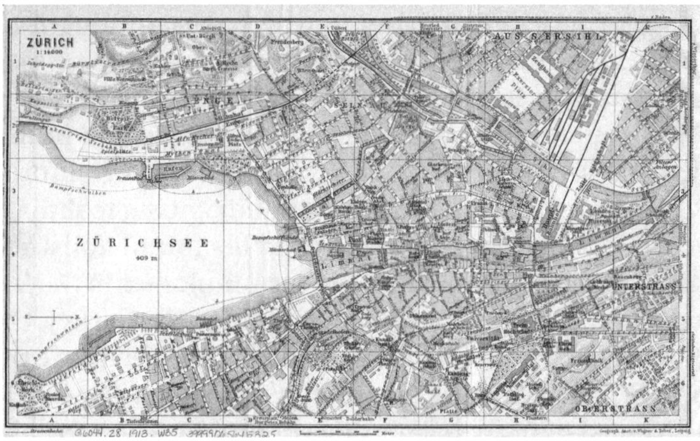

Zurich city map (1 : 14'000) published by "Geographische Anstalt v. Wagner", Leipzig, 1913

1914

Three decades of frenetic inventions, innovations, and technifications, a short period of unprecedented accumulation of capital, of economic and demographic growth have turned the urbanised areas of the developed countries into glistening artificial environments of entertainment, consumption and waste, of hilarious vanguardisms, aestheticisms, and reckless intellectual experimentations, of science fiction, fictional science, and fictitious scientificity. Regarded as spatial environments, the modernist cities in Europe and the US are rather *explicit* places. The buildings are unambiguous spatial explications of the social and political conditions. The transport axes are explications of acceleration and spatial mobility. The lighting, the density, and the linkage of spaces explicate economical efficiency, rationalisation, productivity and profitability. Increasingly detached from the rural surroundings and societies, these urban areas have most explicitly grown into a *multiplexed multitude of conditioned spaces*, into exciting, technically optimised dreamworlds of incessant rush, busyness, and consumption, full of sensual, emotional, and intellectual thrills, vertically and horizontally accelerated, electrified, and trafficable.

However, although (or precisely because) these spaces are as explicit as they can possibly be, although they are extensively reflected in contemporary art and literature and represented on thousands of cinema screens, they remain broadly unrecognised and uncomprehended with regard to what they imply: the radical changes of spatial perceptions, experiences, and behaviours, the foundation of these magnificent constructions on global imperialism, economic exploitation, social depravation, slavery, moral bigotry, and dubious rationales, and, most of all, the momentous redefinition of the human condition as the condition of *mass societies* and *mass cultures*. Among many other things, the condition of mass societies evidently amounts to the devaluation of individual self-experiences and the individual human being as such. And just as evidently, it provokes *compensatory* responses, ideas, and behaviours.

The general unawareness with regard to the immediate consequences of mass cultures is not only due to intentional or unintentional ignorance or the ecstasy caused by the staggeringly advancing technisation of everyday environments. It is also due to a concurrent decline of holistic, systemic, and integrative philosophical conceptions and terminologies in the intellectual and academic discourses of the time. At the turn of the 20th century, these humanistic discourses are broadly split up into new specialised fields of expertise like sociology, anthropology, psychology, and economics that are, for the time being, neither based on consistent theories or methodologies nor on coherent ideas of what they are supposed to find out or comment on exactly, thus becoming a fertile soil for dispersed and competing ideologies.[2] Driven by the avant-garde spirit of the times and by advanced opportunities of public communication, the pri-

2 Friedrich Nietzsche himself may be regarded as a protagonist of this development. After his early attempts in philosophical writing, he adopted a polemic and aphoristic style, which distinguished his chief works of the 1880s and allowed him to express his thinking in incisive assertions beyond reasonable argumentation. Consequently, he did not think of himself as a philosopher anymore but rather as a "psychologist", although, in retrospect, he might just as well be referred to as sort of an aesthetic theologian and cultural critic. However, his writings became one of the most influential sources of inspiration for the delirious avant-garde artists and intellectuals of the early 20th century precisely because he could be received in polemic and ambivalent citations instead of tedious argumentation.

This "evasion of philosophy" was even more explicit in the academic culture of the United States that had no intellectual tradition of its own at the time. Based on Ralph Waldo Emerson's (1803–1882) claims for a spiritual and intellectual emancipation of the United States in the mid-19th century, the founding fathers of modern American academia like William James (1842–1910) or John Dewey (1859–1952) established a philosophical culture of mere cultural criticism that broadly and deliberately ignored the precedent achievements of the humanities and the liberal arts. Revealingly, this specific American kind of unburdened intellectualism was referred to as *pragmatism* (cf., among others, Cornel West; *The American Evasion of Philosophy – A Genealogy of Pragmatism*, Madison/Wisconsin, 1989).

mary merit of these new theoretical approaches and perspectives is to problematise and explicate facts and realities and fields of interest that have been implicitly taken for granted before. However, making things explicit, turning them inside out so to speak, entails the risk of either trivialising them or bringing problems to light that had better been left in the dark as long as there are no concepts of how to *explain* them properly or how to deal with their *implications*. In the wake of the rapid conventionalisation and popularisation of explicative methodologies in the social and anthropological sciences, the cultural, scientific, and technological history of the 20th century may well appear to be a never-ending story of premature explication and explicitness that always remains short on comprehension and explanations.

The 3rd principle of Spacism:
Simulation follows explication. Comprehension follows simulation.

What becomes explicit but remains unexplained, inevitably (and quite literally) explains itself in disclosing and revelatory events: in "apocalypses". All of a sudden, like a thunderbolt out of a clear sky, though not unexpected or unanticipated at all, the irrationalities buried beneath the delirium of rational thought burst open like purulent boils. The supressed and marginalised social energies discharge in an orgy of strange desires, obscene phantasies, long-concealed anger, and furious violence. Additionally, the seed of mindless nationalism, intentionally and carelessly cultivated over a hundred years of European history since the Congress of Vienna back in 1815, bears its bitter fruit. The dreamworlds turn into nightmares.

> We see dusk. We see cold rain. We see dirt and mud smacking beneath thousands of combat boots. We see a one-armed male torso nailed to a rotten supporting beam of a trench, the entrails gushing out between the torn apart ribs, and we can see that this ghastly work of sculptural poetry is supposed to mean something. In the background, we see muzzle flashes, ceaseless lightning of deafening explosions blowing up clouds of black smoke and grey soil all across the plains. We hear the fighter planes rattling across the grey sky, dropping their deadly freight. We see poisonous hazes of gas escaping from detonated grenades. We see myriads of mutilated bodies, some of them dead, some of them alive, screaming in unbearable pain and inconceivable horror, ripped apart and bleeding to death like slashed pigs. We smell the nauseous stench of burnt flesh. We see a seventeen-year old chap stumbling straight into hell along with hundreds of thousands of other nameless young men, sent to their slaughter like sheep by degenerate aristocrats, perverted generals, and immensely rich industrialist sociopaths who sit in their bathtubs or by their chimney fires, counting up their sales or the supplies of their human resources or both. We see pretty girls and ugly old hags chanting nationalist slogans in the streets of their hometowns, getting even more agitated by every new message of another son, another boyfriend, or another husband who has "heroically fallen in battle".

The psychosis of modernity takes its toll in a first episode of deliberate mass destruction and mass extermination. Ten million casualties in four odd years, twenty million grievously wounded and crippled, another twenty-five million fatalities during the 1918 Spanish flu pandemic, an unknown number of incurably traumatised. As is well known, the "Great War" has been sparked for no conclusively substantiated political reason. However, everybody seems to have expected it to happen.

You say that it is the good cause, which sanctifies the war? – I tell you: It is the good war, which sanctifies everything.
(Friedrich Nietzsche; *Thus Spoke Zarathustra*, Part One, 1883–1885)

Kazimir Malevich; *Black Square*, oil on linen canvas, 1915

And then: sudden darkness. Meaningless silence. If we listen closely, we can hear the rollicking rhythms of dance music in the distance of the near future. And we can hear voices, mostly women's voices. We can hear the sobbing and moaning, the "Ahs" and "Oohs" and "Oh my gods" of desperate survivors making love: the background sound of the "Roaring Twenties".

The degenerated aristocrats have been removed from power and forced to discreetly mingle with the immensely rich industrialist sociopaths. The glistening cities are still standing. They still look the same, they still are full of entertainment and busyness and flamboyance, but there is an all-new indefinite sadness about them. Walking through the shady streets feels like straying through labyrinths. The people look distanced, detached, forlorn, trapped in their individual spaces, even in the bars and cabarets and dancing halls where they try to surrender to the immediate lusts and needs of consumers trying to persuade themselves that they are still able to feel happy once in a while. Many of them have been granted the right to vote recently. But for the time being, they don't mind about the future. They are too busy coming to terms with the past. And this is just the beginning.

We see distanced, detached and forlorn people, trapped in their individual spaces, straying through the labyrinths of glistening cities, staring into empty spaces. – We see Malevich's *Black Square* again. – We see Alfred Binet and Théodore Simon developing the first applicable statistical method of "measuring" human intelligence in a standardised test in 1905. – Once more, we see Sigmund Freud trying to standardise psychological behaviour in general models of the human psyche. – We see a medium shot of Friedrich von Hayek reciting passages of his bestseller *The Road to Serfdom* (published in 1944) at the foundation meeting of the Mont-Pèlerin Society in Vevey, Switzerland, in April 1947. The assembled economists, businessmen, and journalists listen to his sermon devotionally. It is about freedom, libertarian market principles, and the tyranny of collectivisms (such as Communism or Nazism and the like), which are, in Mr Hayek's final analysis, nothing but economic misconceptions. We get the indefinite impression that it won't be long until the immensely rich industrialist sociopaths join the party. – Again, we see secret circles of occultists gathering in darkened secluded rooms, reviving the magic practices of past ages in all new interpretations, invoking spirits and forces of the hereafters in order to attain wisdom.

So if you meet me, have some courtesy, have some sympathy and some taste
Use all your well-learned politesse or I'll lay your soul to waste
Pleased to meet you, hope you guess my name
But what's puzzling you, is the nature of my game ...
(Mick Jagger & Keith Richard; *Sympathy for the Devil*, 1968)

The easiest and most explicit way to cope with the challenges of mass phenomena without bothering to thoroughly comprehend them is to mystify them in large numbers. Thus, one of the principal conceptual – or: cognitive – formulas of progressiveness in the 20th century is the description of realities in statistics and other quantitative methods of "measurement". Irrespective of whether they are originally motivated in post-rationalist and post-ideological attempts to recover objectifiable truths (which was most certainly the case in the wake of traumatic collective experiences such as the Thirty Years' and the World Wars) or simply ideologies in their own right mistaking mathematical for natural truths, statistical inquiries and assertions that are expressed in numeric relations (instead of absolute numbers) mostly and systematically produce fake realities – and are misused in that way precisely – because they inevitably (and thus rather predictably) abstract and decontextualise the realities they pretend to describe "objectively".

The 4th principle of Spacism:
The simulation of facticity in statistical quantifications, relations, and standardisations.

The rational decisions and strategies that have defined the spatial realities of the 20th century are essentially based on quantitative thinking and practices. Given the intentional ignorance inherent in the obsession with abstracting realities in increasing and decreasing numbers, small wonder that a hundred years of experiences with globalised mass societies and mass cultures, with aerial warfare, chemical and biological weapons, rational mass destruction and mass extermination are not enough to finally understand the global spatial condition as essentially *spherical*, atmospherical and, consequently, ecological. Small wonder that taking *appropriate* actions with regard to this human condition seem to remain out of reach for so long. And small wonder that these mass societies and cultures cannot seem to find another way to conceive of their condition than either rationalise it in large numbers or simply ignore it in retrograde ideologies and fundamentalisms.

EVE: Are we aware that we're about to associate some of the leading sciences of the 20th century with irrational theories and practices?
ADAM: Yes, for the time being, we are. I mean, when it comes to taste the fruit of the tree of knowledge, we are the experts, aren't we?
EVE: But seriously, my love, who would even want *to see it that way?*
ADAM: That is precisely the point. On the other hand, we are confronted with the consequences of irrational thought and behaviour every day. We are perfectly familiar with the logics of large numbers. We are perfectly aware of the implicit metaphorologies of modern social and political theories. We have read Auguste Comte, haven't we? – We have read Adam Smith, Alexis de Tocqueville, Karl Marx, and all the others, haven't we? – Furthermore, we know perfectly well that each and every fundamental precondition of modern economics is a tendentious mathematical idealisation serving the purpose of subjecting socio-economical realities to rational quantifications. In other words, we know that none of the authoritative economic theories we have ever heard of would survive a serious discussion of whether every economic situation whatsoever is a situation of shortage (which would amount to the irrational compulsion to incessant economic growth); whether human beings are first and foremost driven by selfish motives, urges, and instincts (which would not only contradict all principles of self-responsibility but also all conceptions of human intelligence we have ever known); whether there has ever been a simple competitive market situation of supply and demand that

conforms to the ideal preconditions of economic market theories beyond selling the lowest possible value at the highest possible price (which would mean that we might just as well do without any tutelage of theoretical economics); or, for that matter, whether there has ever been any real or reasonable correlation between monetary and tangible values. Fact is that each of these preconditions can easily be falsified. Which would not even be worth mentioning if we would not accept them as if they were laws of nature. *Taking ideologies for laws of nature, that's what I would call "irrational".*
EVE: I agree. But we were actually discussing the topic of space and time, were we not?
ADAM: Of course we were. And we still are. This is all *about space and time. I mean, we have read* Kant, *haven't we?* –
(Aaron Zucker; *More Fabulous Adventures of Adam and Eve – Another strictly intellectual stage play*, 1929)

1781

When Immanuel Kant described space and time as primary intuitional categories of human cognition in one of his early essays in 1770[3] and then, after ten "silent years", included them as "intuitional aesthetic notions a priori" in the introduction to his *Critique of Pure Reason* in 1781, he probably did not think of it as an original or particularly inventive idea. He rather thought of it as the most *reasonable* way of explaining how the human mind conceives of an external spatial and temporal reality that is more or less consistent with sensory perceptions and logical thinking under rational conditions. However, he evidently was determined to put an end to the metaphorical rationalist conceptions of space. And since his liberal thinking was not only dedicated to the epistemological and political aims of the Enlightenment but also to a perspective of phenomenological common sense (which is why he is so hard to read and so easy to understand), he did not dilute the simple precision of his introductory description by involving its many and most momentous implications.[4] He simply stuck to his motto *Sapere aude*![5] and saved the implications for later.

3 Immanuel Kant; *De mundi sensibilis atque intelligibilis forma et principiis*, 1770.

4 The introduction of "common sense" as a philosophical term is usually ascribed to the English analytic philosopher George Edward Moore (1873–1958). However, the word, the meaning, and the attitude attached to it have been in common use for centuries, especially in the German expression "(gesunder) Menschenverstand". Kant does not explicitly appeal to the term as such, but the attitude of accepting common sense as a principal and decisive criterion of philosophical thought is implied and commented on throughout his work as from the *Critique of Pure Reason*.

5 Three years later, in his essay *Answering the Question: What is Enlightenment?* (1784), Kant adapted this citation of the Roman poet Horace from the 1st century BC to encapsulate the principal idea of the period of Enlightenment: "*Dare to know!*" or "*Dare to use your common sense and think for yourself!*".

1. Space is not a conception abstracted from outer experiences. For, in order that certain sensations may relate to something without me (that is, to something which occupies a different part of space from that in which I am), and, in like manner, in order that I may represent them not merely as without, of, and near to *each other, but also in separate places, the representation of space must already exist as a foundation. Consequently, the representation of space cannot be borrowed from the relations of external phenomena through experience; but, on the contrary, this external experience is itself only possible through the aforesaid antecedent representation.*

2. Space then is a necessary representation a priori, which serves as the foundation of all external intuitions. We never can imagine or make a representation to ourselves of the non-existence of space, though we may easily enough think that no objects are found in it. It must, therefore, be considered as the condition of the possibility of phenomena, and by no means as a determination dependent on them, and is a representation a priori, which necessarily supplies the basis for external phenomena.

3. Space is no discursive, or as we say, general conception of the relations of things, but a pure intuition. For, in the first place, we can only represent to ourselves one space, and, when we talk of multiple spaces, we mean only parts of one and the same space. Moreover, these [multiple] parts cannot antecede this one all-embracing space as the component parts (from which the aggregate can be made up), but can only be thought of as existing in it. *Space is essentially one. The multiplicity in it, and consequently the general notion of spaces, of this or that space, depends solely upon limitations. Hence it follows that an a priori intuition (which is not empirical) lies at the root of all our conceptions of space. Thus, moreover, the principles of geometry (for example, that "in a triangle, two sides together are greater than the third") are never deduced from general conceptions (of line and triangle), but from intuition, and this a priori and with apodictic certainty.*

4. Space is represented as an infinite given *quantity. Now every conception must indeed be considered as a representation contained in an infinite multitude of different possible representations, which, therefore, comprises these representations under itself, based on their common features. But no conception, as such, can be conceived as if it contained* within itself *an infinite multitude of representations. Nevertheless, space is conceived of that way because all parts of space are equally capable of being produced to infinity. Consequently, the original representation of space is an* intuition *a priori, and not a conception.*

(Immanuel Kant; *Kritik der reinen Vernunft – Critique of Pure Reason*, chapter I. *Transcendental Doctrine of Elements*, § 2., 1781)[6]

Beyond doubt, these lines still represent the most comprehensive, unambiguous, and commonly acceptable explanation of space in historical times. Even if we take a pass on the preliminary and conclusive comments, it is obvious that this explanation is neither based on theoretical nor definitional preconditions. It is *strictly experiential*. Moreover, in the light of the previously outlined history of ideas of space, we realise that Kant's description, although he certainly did not think in terms of a history of ideas of space as we do, quite naturally includes all the basic conceptions of space we have encountered so far, particularly also those we have discussed in terms of "magic spaces". The latter are implied as the

6 This translation is based on the terminology of the J. M. D. Meiklejohn translation as published in 2003 and updated in 2018 by the Project Gutenberg (www.gutenberg.org).

intuitive idea of space as the totality of our experiential environments at any given moment in time, containing *all* objects *at once*, irrespective of whether we think of them as "real" objects or projections of imagination. The so-called "poetic spaces" are implied as creative interventions in space that purposely "structure" or "restructure" it by the means of designed objects. The interstices are articulately attributed to the objects: they are not manifestations of space. If they need to be considered as "spatial" interventions for practical reasons, they must necessarily relate or refer back to space in its totality somehow. And finally, the "rational spaces" are implied as the basic idea of space as a cognitional entity that can be measured and comprehended and designed in abstractions of the spatial relations of objects according to the given dimensional preconditions of our intellect and imagination: views, volumes, densities, interstices in between objects. Thus, in the phenomenological comprehension of space and time as anthropic principles, rational theories involving them as objectifiable natural phenomena are discarded and disproved for good.

However, this is just the explicit part of Kant's approach. The implications, discussed in the following parts of the *Critique of Pure Reason* and others of Kant's groundbreaking works, go much further. Referring to the history of conceptions of space from a present day's point of view, some of these implications immediately leap out at us, first of all the simple ones that concern the idea of space itself:

1. Space is beyond the object. However, it cannot be defined as some sort of "absence of objects". On the contrary, objects are structural elements of *or* in *space.*

To perceive these elements, their structures and dispositions, is the way a human central nervous system constructs the exterior world as a whole. The construction of this exterior world as a whole to which we refer to as "reality" takes place at once: at each and every conscious moment, over and over again. Quite arguably, to comprehend these structures and dispositions can be understood as an *act of imagination*. This continuous act of *imaginative comprehension* is what we usually call "human intelligence".

2. There are no amounts or quantities of space. By definition, there can be only one infinite *space.*

Therefore, within the boundaries of human intelligence, the only appropriate way to intellectually represent this cognitional infinity (or boundlessness) in dimensional form is spherical. Spatial thinking is *spherical thinking* (or *hemispherical* thinking, respectively): a way of thinking that broadens in all spatial directions equally and simultaneously, being fully aware that there is no end to it (cf. The Map of the Human Mind, pp. 78, 101, and 178).

3. As a notion, an idea, or a phenomenon, "space" cannot be defined in absolute terms, because there is no conception out of or beyond space, at least not for human beings.

Accordingly, Kant didn't even try to "define" space. Space can only be *described* or *explained* according to respective *common experiences*. Therefore, the only reasonable method to scientifically access or investigate space is a *phenomenological* method.[7] All other methods inevitably lead to inquiries into objects.

These implications restricted to space in a narrower sense evidently involve epistemic consequences:

4. All human cognition of reality is necessarily conveyed, "mediated", and conditioned by spatial representation and imagination. These essentially spatial cognitions are reflected and organised according to a second "intuition a priori", which structures the interior world of the human mind: the sense of time (or the successive order and logic of comprehension). Thus, intellectual conceptions like thoughts or ideas emerge.

In the second chapter of the *Critique of Pure Reason*, Kant explains that time is not an abstraction of experiences of natural realities but rather an arraying projection of the human sense of time onto these experiences; an assertion that has been sustained and corroborated by the cognitional sciences ever since. That is why the human mind usually conceives of the sense of time as phenomenologically "prior" to the sense of space.[8] Remarkably enough, Kant's description of the space-time-relation is more than just slightly reminiscent of the "architectural" intuition of time discussed in the context of "magic spaces" (cf. p. 59).

5. The capability of imagination (or spatial representation following a temporal logic) refers directly to the capability of intelligence and vice versa. Therefore, if there is any reasonable way of qualifying or quantifying (collective or individual) human intelligence, it must be based upon a qualification or quantification of the (collective or individual) faculty of spatial and temporal imagination and mental representation.

This being correspondent to the common and easy-to-verify everyday experience that any decrease or increase of imaginative capability inevitably leads to a correlating decrease or increase of a human being's intelligent and communicative behaviour.

6. In terms of epistemology, it is completely irrelevant whether (or to what extent) the mental representations of space and spatial objects refer to realities that exist independently of these representations or not because, to every human being, these representations are as real as reality can be.

7 We use the indefinite article here to emphasise that we refer to a general concept of phenomenological methodology (such as Kant's description of space and time) and not to the specific methodology of "phenomenological reduction" introduced by Edmund Husserl in his *Logical Investigations* in 1900 and 1901.

8 Cf. chapter I.2. *The Priority of Time: There was rhythm before there was imagination* in: *All About Space*, Volume 1: *The Invention of Space*.

In other words, space as an "intuition a priori" does not raise any specific epistemological questions about the "realness" of realities.

Which inevitably leads us to the moral and political implications:[9]

7. The division of space into multiple spaces is, to a certain degree, a practical and existential necessity in terms of the human condition. In short, it is the only way that enables intelligent human beings to act upon space under the conditions of their existential finiteness and limitation.

However, at the same time, the (poetic or rational) division of space into multiple, enclosed, or separated spaces produces multiple simulations of space: "fake spaces", if you will, or "metaphors". Acting upon space without being aware of that inevitably involves a fundamental denial of reality. And it initiates a vicious circle of intentional ignorance mistaking the simulations and metaphors for realities.

8. The intuition "a priori" of space (and time) is shared *among* all *human beings. To put it in a somewhat declamatory nutshell: There is only* one space *for all of us.*

From a present day perspective, this is the quintessential conclusion of the multiple ideational "globalisation" processes we have gone through during the past millennium. Different places are not different spaces. Ultimately, every act upon space is an act upon our spatial environment as a whole, and the common intuitions of space and time are the primordial basis of any common sense. Hence, imposing individual, specific, or ideationally determined representations of space on other human beings *as given realities* is not only a violation of common sense, it is a fundamentally immoral act. The spatial condition of human beings is, whether we like it or not, also a *moral* and a *political* condition (right up to Kant's famous "categorical imperative").

For this categorical reason, any attempt to systematise or generalise economic affairs in political terms, irrespective of its intents and objectives, is bound to result in a complete failure of morality, both in theory and in practice: By definition, neither space nor the spatial human condition can be subject to economic principles because spatial conditions are neither quantifiable nor divisible beyond mathematical simulations or their fraudulent imposition on spatial realities in which we all *coexist*. For the very same reason, any attempt to systemically individualise ecological affairs in political terms is bound to result in a perversion of moral accountability: Since the spatial condition is not divisible beyond mathematical simulations, it cannot be subject to individual principles or responsibilities (such as the "causative principle") by definition, most certainly not in a globalised world.

9 Considering the postmodern ambiguity of the word, it might be worth noting that we, along with Kant, refer to the primary meaning of "moral" and "morals" in the sense of a principal moral consciousness, which is attributed to every individual human being as against social, political, cultural or ethical theories, standards, imperatives, or conventions.

9. Quite obviously, and as appears to have been evident even to the earliest human societies we can possibly refer to, the ecological principle of balance and equilibrium is the ultimate political implication of the spatial condition.[10]

Two things fill the mind with ever-increasing wonder and awe, the more often and the more intensely the mind of thought is drawn to them: the starry heavens above me and the moral law within me.
(Immanuel Kant; *Kritik der praktischen Vernunft – "Critique of Practical Reason"*, 1788)

1919

And what about the arts? – What do we see? –

We see lots of movies, shot on very fancy film sets. In retrospect, they look exaggeratedly symbolistic, including the actors' performances. – We see Malevich's *Black Square* again, invoking the association of a black screen for a moment. We see Duchamp's *Fountain*. We see all kinds of great works of art associated with forthright explicit and pretentious categories like "cubism", "futurism", "suprematism", "surrealism", "constructivism", "abstract expressionism", and so forth. After having seen them over and over again, we get the impression that, despite their explicitness, they are way beyond our comprehension in their depiction of multiplexed multitudes of fragmented and distorted spaces or realities or whatever, all the way up to what appears to be mere activist sensationalism. – We see innumerable explicitly modernist buildings in all their explicitly functional and explicitly representative designs based on explicitly rational conceptions. We see "Bauhaus", constructivist propaganda and advertising designs, and a few decades later, we see innumerable deconstructivists deconstructing constructivism, over and over again. – We see Lady Gaga wearing a dress made of raw beef at the 2010 MTV Video Music Awards and there is no doubt that it is supposed to *mean* something. However, we cannot think of what it is. – We see the glistening Twin Towers still standing, and they are faintly reminiscent of the Twin Obelisks we have encountered at some point on our way up through the brief history of space.

EVE: It feels like the spaces and times were converging to an infinite loop of presence, playback, and re-presentation in mysterious ways.
ADAM: I think you have a point there.
(Aaron Zucker; *More Fabulous Adventures of Adam and Eve – Another strictly intellectual stage play*, 1929)

10 Chapter IV. *The Politics of Space* in *All About Space* Volume 1 closes with a seemingly pretentious short excursus into the morals of space derived from a confrontation of the terms "freedom" and "liberty" and their respective spatial implications. Against the background of Kant's conception of space, the two contradicting moral conclusions presented there (entitled *Growth* and *Resonance*) may be comprehensible in a less hermetic and more systemic way: as pointed emphases of a principally economic and a principally ecological approach to space.

1934

We see a kid reading a superhero comic in a bedraggled living room in Brooklyn. – We see the Nazi Party Congress at Nuremberg in panoramic view as chronicled in Leni Riefenstahl's film *Triumph of the Will*, showing, among many other repulsive things, hundreds of uniformed and insecure young men in an arena and thousands of almost uniformed and, in an all too conspicuous way, sexually famished women fanatically cheering and rejoicing at them on the spectator's stands. We see their outstretched right arms, and we hear them chanting the magic spell. – Yet again, we see Malevich's *Black Square*. – Then we see survivors of the Second World War, gobbling potato chips and gazing at a flickering TV screen as if they had been braindead for quite some time now. They look distanced, detached, and alienated, trapped in their individual spaces.

After the stock market crash in 1929, following upon the overheated cyclical economic recovery driven by the reconstruction and redevelopment of a broadly collapsed Europe, and after enough female consumers have produced enough male teenagers to make up for the deficiency of army personnel, preparations for a next Great War appear to have become a sufficiently rational option. The applied poetry of rationalised mass destruction and mass extermination enters its second loop.

Again, we see perverted generals and immensely rich industrialist sociopaths sitting by their chimney fires, counting up their sales or the supplies of their human resources or both. – We see St. Paul's Cathedral outlasting, against all odds, the relentless bombings of the city of London. The aircrafts are not rattling anymore. They are roaring now. – We see submarines torpedoing passenger ships in the North Atlantic. – We see German soldiers and officers unbuttoning their trousers to commit racial defilement with spindly Slavic women. – We see Russian soldiers and officers committing mass rapes with freed German women, claiming that this is but revenge for Stalingrad. – We see cattle wagons full of men, women, and children at the forecourt of hell. We can see there is a common understanding that their lives are *worthless* lives. A moment later, we see their dead bodies – or what's left of them after they have been disposed of their profitable parts – piled up in thousands. – The Brooklyn kid has grown up by now. He stands there in his US army uniform, staring at the piles in Dachau, incapable of accepting what he sees.

The 5th principle of Spacism:
The simulation of plurality in mass hypocrisy.

What makes it so plausible to assume that hypocrisy is the vice of vices is that integrity can indeed exist under the cover of all other vices except this one. […] The hypocrite is really rotten to the core.
(Hannah Arendt; *On Revolution*, Chapter 2., 1963)
The longer one listened to him, the more obvious it became that his inability to speak was closely connected with an inability to think, namely to think from the standpoint of somebody else. No communication was possible with him,

not because he lied but because he was surrounded by the most reliable of all safeguards against the words and the presence of others, *and hence against* reality as such.
(Hannah Arendt; *Eichmann in Jerusalem: A report on the banality of evil*, Ch. III., 1963)[11]
The ideal subject of totalitarian rule is not the convinced Nazi or the convinced Communist, but people for whom the distinction between fact and fiction (i.e., the reality of experience*) and the distinction between true and false (i.e. the standards of thought) no longer exist.*
(Hannah Arendt; *The Origins of Totalitarianism*, Part 3, Ch. 13, § 3., 1951.)
We see Neil Armstrong's first steps on the moon in 1969. A fancy cream-coloured spaceship hovers into sight from the left and softly lands beside the Stars and Stripes flag. Only now we realise that it is a vacuum cleaner. (Or is it a hair dryer?) The zoom-out reveals the detached and alienated survivors watching a TV commercial in 1972, still gobbling potato chips. – We see John Williamson, chief economist and vice president of the World Bank, at a speaker's desk, sketching out the concept of the *Washington Consensus* in 1989. In summary, the concept amounts to the conclusion that the step-by-step privatisation of public institutions along with a monetary plutocratic totalitarianism exercised by immensely rich sociopaths on a global scale is the best possible strategy to prevent the world from other totalitarian threats. – We see British Conservative Party leader Margaret Thatcher at one of her regular business lunches at the *Institute of Economic Affairs* (IEA), founded by poultry industrialist Antony Fisher in 1975. She recites a passage from Friedrich von Hayek's *The Road to Serfdom*. It is about freedom, libertarian market principles, and the tyranny of collectivisms. A moment later, we see her at a meeting with Shah Reza Pahlavi in a conference room of the Niavaran Palace in 1978. And then: yet another meeting, but this cosy little chat with General Augusto Pinochet appears to be highly unofficial. – We look into the face of a screaming Vietnamese girl fleeing in terror from a group of US soldiers. A few seconds later, she is shot in the back. – We see distanced, detached and alienated people, trapped in their individual spaces. Some of them are straying through the labyrinths of glistening cities, others through infinite wastelands. We cannot make out exactly what they are gazing at.

11 The notion of the „banality of evil" in the title of Hannah Arendt's journalistic work for *The New Yorker* was received very controversially in 1963. Adolf Eichmann was an important Nazi bureaucrat who was, among other things, charged with the logistics, statistics, and the accounting of transportations to the concentration and extermination camps. In 1961, he was put on trial in Jerusalem and finally sentenced to death. He tenaciously denied his guilt by asseverating that he had only been following orders.

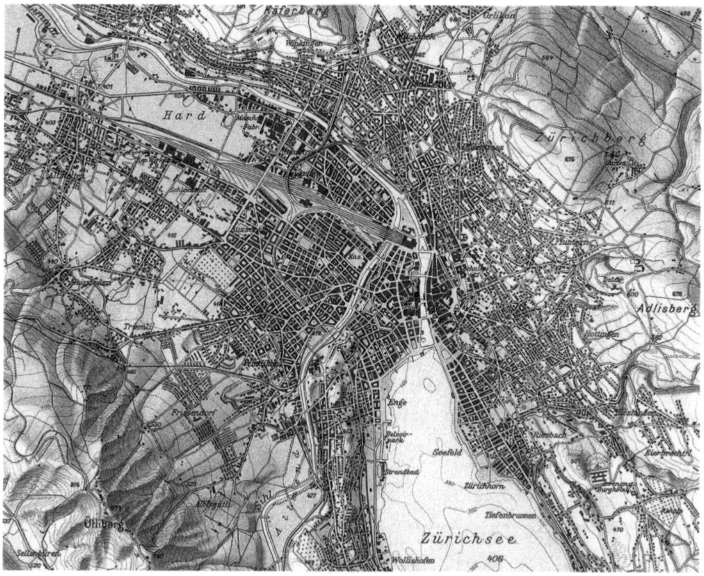

Zürich 1979, Swiss World Atlas edited by the Swiss Conference of Cantonal Ministers of Education, 1979

I saw the best minds of my generation destroyed by madness, starving hysterical naked,
dragging themselves through the negro streets at dawn looking for an angry fix,
angelheaded hipsters burning for the ancient heavenly connection to the starry dynamo in the machinery of night,
who poverty and tatters and hollow-eyed and high sat up smoking in the supernatural darkness of cold-water flats floating across the tops of cities contemplating jazz,
who bared their brains to Heaven under the El and saw Mohammedan angels staggering on tenement roofs illuminated ...
(Allen Ginsberg; *Howl*, 1955/1956)

1945

We see an ocean horizon in Super-Panavision-Metrocolor. We are not sure which ocean it is. A colourful sun is rising. It looks slightly blurred. And as we watch it rising higher and higher, the colours rapidly fade into white. We think we see Ingrid Bergman and Humphrey Bogart kissing passionately one more time in the blazing white light. A sudden thrashing heat. We hear a majestic orchestral C major chord turning into a dramatic c minor. It feels like we have known all along what we are going to see when the trampling beat of the kettledrums sets in ... – We have seen and heard this before, right? – Is it a movie? – Is it a recurring dream, maybe?

All we can say is that it still feels as if the spaces and times were orbiting in an infinite loop of presence, playback, and re-presentation. After having claimed approximately 65 million casualties, most of them civilians, the Second World War ends on August 6th and 9th 1945 when two atomic bombs are dropped over Hiroshima and Nagasaki. The first bomb is called "Little Boy". The second is called "Fat Man". Neither the people killed immediately nor the casualties of the long-term damages can ever be numbered beyond rough estimates in the hundreds of thousands.

The remains of Old Europe have definitely ceased to exist. The leadership of global politics is handed over to an immature but highly motivated and self-assured nation of immigrants armed to the teeth; its greatness is largely built on genocide and slavery, but unburdened with cultural and intellectual heritages of centuries. In the course of the continuing global decolonisation, Planet Earth is divided in a First, a Second, and a Third World. Based on that conception, the applied poetry of rational mass destruction is extraterritorialised to the developing countries and enters its third loop referred to as "the Cold War". After a short-term decrease of war casualties in the 1950s, the average amount of civilian casualties in the wars of the second half of the 20th century continuously rises up to over 90%. The statisticians are still counting. However, since the 1970s, these figures are highly outnumbered by the casualty figures of environmental damage and pollution caused by the global economic disequilibrium, by excessive consumption, and financial speculation in values and commodities of subsistence. At the turn of the 21st century, the approximate annual figures of deaths from starvation can be numbered in fatalities per second. This extends to the figures of fatalities of "destitution" and of so-called "armed conflicts". And this is just the beginning.

The 6th principle of Spacism:
The simulation of progress in the constant positive multiplication of what is already there.

Most obviously, there are natural and logical limits to growth. Nevertheless, we cannot fail to admit that this principle is particularly hard to break once it has been globally implemented. We can actually *sense* how the metaphorical, the purportedly "empty" and "open" spaces are getting filled and stuffed and standardised in every conceivable respect. Moreover, we realise that the principles of spacism follow a relentlessly consecutive logic of stereotyping and massification, up to the insidiously implicit revaluation of the existential precepts of natality and mortality. In its utmost eschatological consequence, the

6th principle implies that the present is not the beginning of the future but rather the end of the past.[12]

> *What matters is that there is no outside anymore. The world is closed up. The situation has become a situation of mankind.*
> (Karl Jaspers; *Vom Ursprung und Ziel der Geschichte*, "*The Origin and Goal of History*", 1947/1949)

What is this "situation of mankind"? – What do we see? –

> We see the "Blue Marble": A colour photograph of planet Earth shot by NASA astronauts during the Apollo 17 mission in 1972. Usually it is presented upside down to conform to the common expectation that the northern hemisphere is at the top. But we see it in its original orientation. – What is it supposed to mean?

We think it means that, although the "space age" has remained but an episode of the Cold War, the perspective from the Archimedean point has finally become a reality, if only for a fleeting moment and within the absolute limits of human existence. What we see is one space containing all spaces: all the magic and poetic and rational and irrational spaces we have ever conceived of simultaneously converging into one. And it only confirms what we have known all along:

In the end, there is only *one space* for *all* of us.

12 This line of reasoning is a keynote rationale of most eschatological concepts, from the doomsday, "salvation" and ultimate "redemption" scenarios up to Nietzsche's suggestive evocation of the "Übermensch" or, to some extent and in a considerably less irrational way, Marx' idea of communism as the inevitable final condition of human societies. With the exception of the latter, these concepts are evidently based on the pretext that human beings and/or societies are either incapable or unworthy *in principle* to create better futures out of a given present. In consequence, the future-oriented human capabilities like the intellect or the power of imagination are deliberately and systematically controverted and devalorised. One of the recurring and most effective suggestions of such concepts is the idea that it is more valuable und honourable to *die for a cause* than to *live* for it.

The ideological revival of this kind of thinking in popular politics and storytelling at the turn of the 21st century is unmistakeably obvious. And, disastrously enough, it leaves its mark on many topics and debates and decision-making processes that seem or purport to be free of such ideological prejudices.

The "Blue Marble" photographed by astronauts aboard Apollo 17 in 1972

2018

We see a zoom-in on the "Blue Marble" in 2018. The view pierces through the sphere of space garbage and enters the atmosphere. Although we don't know for sure whether the zoom-in is a virtual or a photographed one, and although most of the planet's surface is covered by widespread cloud fields, we cannot help getting the cliché impression that the recent growth of human population and the unrestrained exploitation of natural resources has affected the planet like a malignant tumour. The impression is not based on any visual indications. It's just a projection of our intellectual imagination. In the background, we hear Leonard Cohen's haunting voice:
When they said: Repent, repent!
I wonder what they meant
When they said: Repent, repent!
I wonder what they meant...
(Leonard Cohen; *The Future*, 1992)

In fact, the imagination is based upon bits and pieces of recurring news like "Two thirds of the dry land species declared extinct or on the brink of extinction in no more than an average human lifetime" or "The climatic conditions disbalanced beyond reasonable predictability". However, we are not *really* sure whether we *really* know these things. They are just alleged scientific facts we have heard of or read about, aren't they? – According to the pluralist principle of freedom of opinion, we are free to believe that they are true or that they are just the usual inputs of panic-mongering designed by wicked messengers who trade in bad news, right? –

The 7th principle of Spacism:
The simulation of knowledge in the availability of processed information.

The zoom-in continues. We get the impression of diving into the fuzzy blanket of clouds. All we see is amorphous grey-white haze tickling our fancy. For a split second, we think we see Neil Armstrong's first step on the moon. – We think we see the Brooklyn kid in his US army uniform again, incapable of accepting what he sees. – The woman in the saucy evening dress, a cocktail glass in her hand. She screams: "Don't you dare to touch me, you bastard!" – On a computer screen, we see a list of 60 gender identities to choose from for people who bother to let the public know who they are in 2017, followed by an online report about images of the "Willendorf Venus" figurine that have been banned from Facebook sites as "dangerously pornographic" depictions in February 2018.[13] – Then we see a boy desperately gasping for breath in a bombed out street in Saraqib, Syria, dying from nerve gas intoxication. In the background, we still hear Leonard Cohen's haunting voice:
Give me back my broken night
My mirrored room, my secret life
It's lonely here, there's no one left to torture
Give me absolute control
Over every living soul
And lie beside me, baby, that's an order!
Things are going to slide in all directions
Won't be nothing you can measure anymore
The blizzard of the world has crossed the threshold

13 The "Willendorf Venus" is a more than 25'000 years old figurine and ranks among the oldest manmade sculptural artefacts ever found (cf. p. 41).

And it has overturned the order of the soul
When they said: Repent, repent!
I wonder what they meant…
(Leonard Cohen; *The Future*, 1992)

Official tourist map of the City of Zurich (1 : 10'000), 1997

We see distanced, detached, and alienated people, trapped in their individual spaces, straying through the labyrinths of all kinds of glistening and derelict cities, gazing at their smartphone screens as if they had become comfortably numb a long time ago. What they are gazing at is referred to as "virtual space" or "virtual reality" or simply "virtuality". Extensive parts of this virtual reality are referred to as "social media", which, at this very moment, appears to be a rather sarcastic denotation because, the longer we observe them, the more obvious it becomes that their inability to talk sense is closely connected with an inability to think, namely to think from the standpoint of somebody else. No communication seems to be possible with them, not because they lie or refuse to communicate (quite evidently they don't), but because they are surrounded by the most reliable of all safeguards against the words and the presence of others, and hence against *reality as such*. For a moment, we think that we have heard this one before. However, the zoom-in through the blurry blanket of clouds continues.

Give me back the Berlin wall
Give me Stalin and St. Paul
Give me Christ or give me Hiroshima
Destroy another foetus now
We don't like children anyhow
I've seen the future, baby: It is murder!
When they said: Repent, repent!
I wonder what they meant
When they said: Repent, repent!
I wonder what they meant…
(Leonard Cohen; *The Future*, 1992)

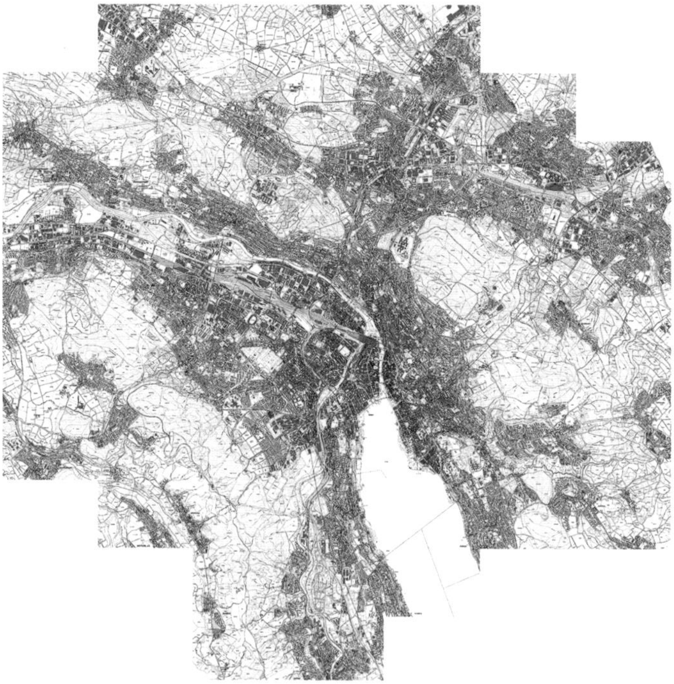

Official plot plan of the City of Zurich, 2017

While we are waiting for the clouds to dissipate, we still ponder on Karl Jaspers' literally conclusive assertion that, at the end of the age of rational space, *there is no outside anymore*. In principle, the assertion makes perfect sense to us: The situation has *definitely* become a "situation of mankind". In fact, it was already a situation of mankind long before we entered into the "age of spacisms". But how does the general awareness of this situation impact on our spatial conceptions and practises? – What about, for instance, the poetic idea of space that proceeds on the assumption that there is always an inside and an outside to spaces (which is, as we have presumed earlier, one of the main reasons why it has never progressed beyond the object, particularly not in architecture and spatial design)? – Does this poetic idea still produce concepts of "cultural" insides and "natural" outsides, or has the "situation of mankind" resulted in alternative practices? – Anyway, and just to be sure, if we accept Karl Jaspers' conclusive assertion, then we should prepare ourselves for the disclosure of a world that is completely filled up with insides. But then again, how are we supposed to imagine or conceive of a world like this: a *totality of insides*, a hermetic system of inside environments and inside perspectives? –

Referring to our experiences with the living conditions in so-called post-war "affluent societies" that are primarily organised according to the basically economic doctrines and compulsions of the 4th, the 5th, and the 6th principle of spacism, we assume that people living in a totality of insides *either* must have abandoned their illusions of individual freedom (which essentially depend on the belief in intact environmental outsides) and developed strategies to renounce the consecutive logic of ever-growing mass cultures: multiple *strategies of relinquishment* and *reduction*, both in physical and in ideational terms, including multiple strategies to *enjoy* it. *Or* they must have submitted themselves to

The 8th principle of Spacism:
The simulation and virtualisation of inside and outside perspectives.

> The zoom-in continues, but the background sound has changed just now.
> *Ah, ooh, I love to love you baby, ooh, love to love you baby, uh-huh uh-huh, love to love you baby, ooh, ah, I love to love you baby ...!*
> (*Love To Love You Baby*, 16:48-minute-long early disco hit performed by Donna Summer, 1975)

Given the known facts and circumstances, we admit that the second assumption is much more plausible than the first one. And proceeding from it, we would have to imagine a world of perfectly conditioned and broadly standardised simulations of spaces, of multiplexed feel-good and feel-bad worlds, composed of various spatial simulations like "phenotopes" (*perceptual spaces*), "ergotopes" (*labouring* and *exercising spaces*), "aggelotopes" (*communication spaces*), "chariotopes" (*entertainment spaces*), "polemotopes" (*conflict spaces*), "erototopes" (*erotic spaces*), "uterotopes" (*breeding spaces*), "nootopes" (*spaces of thought*), "alethotopes" (*spaces of knowledge*), "scandalotopes" (*spaces of excitement*), "technotopes" (*spaces of feasibility*), and "chirotopes" (*spaces of management*).[14] Their virtuality would be perfectly camouflaged in their explicit purposiveness and practicability: the labouring spaces would appear to be perfectly explicit offices or production facilities, the communication spaces would appear to be perfectly explicit conference surroundings or interactive user interfaces, the breeding spaces would appear to be perfectly explicit nurseries, daycare and education centres, the erotic spaces would appear to be perfectly explicit pornographic amusement zones, and the recreation spaces would appear to be perfectly explicit holiday environments. They would be full of fancy spatial magic and poetry, full of resonances confirming their facticity and meaningfulness, and their implementations would appear to be perfectly rational. However, as simulations of spaces, they wouldn't be perfect if they would allow any outside perspective. After all, that is how perfect simulations work, isn't it? – Thus, these simulative spaces, including all the

14 Some of these derivations from Ancient Greek terminologies are used, in a much more elaborated and differentiated context, in the third volume of Peter Sloterdijk's comprehensive discussion of sphericity as the global spatial condition of mankind, published under the collective title *Sphären* ("*Spheres*") as Volume I *Bubbles*, 1998, Volume II *Globes*, 1999, and Volume III *Foams*, 2004.

explicit facts and factoids, realities and virtualities contained in them, would have to be completely and gaplessly intertwined with each other in one global simulation of a "chreiotope": a perfectly explicit consumer space of continuous supply and demand, of unquestioned and endlessly recurring simulated needs and satisfactions: multiplexed multitudes of spaces full of distractive sensual, emotional, and intellectual thrills, highly entertaining, technically accelerated, vertically, horizontally, and transversely trafficable spatial explications of the social and political conditions: a perfectly directed *economy of spaces*.

Then again, we know from *experience* that a system as perfect as this cannot exist. No system is perfect. Therefore, the institutionalisation of hypocrisy and intentional ignorance of past and future spaces[15] according to the 5th, the 7th, and the 8th principle of spacism would have to be developed far enough to rule out any philosophical inquiries into the matter of spacisms. In *this* world, there would be no professionals. There would be only experts.

The 9th principle of Spacism:
And this is just the beginning.

> *"Do you see that spider?" "Yes," said Balaki, "I see the spider moving along its web." "We are like the spider," said the king. "We weave our life, and then move along in it. We are like the dreamer who dreams and then lives inside the dream. This is true for the entire world [we inhabit]. That is why it is said, 'Having created the creation, the Creator entered into it'. And this is true for us. We create our world, and then enter into that world. We live in the world that we have created."*
> (Brihadaranyaka Upanishad, India, around 700 BC)
> As the zoom-in continues, the clouds finally disperse. It feels like we have known all along what we are going to see next.

"Welcome to the real world!"

15 Cf. chapter VII.4. *Future Spaces* in *All About Space*, Volume 1.

(Hemi-)Spherical Thinking

Broadening in all spatial directions equally and simultaneously, being fully aware that there is no end to it

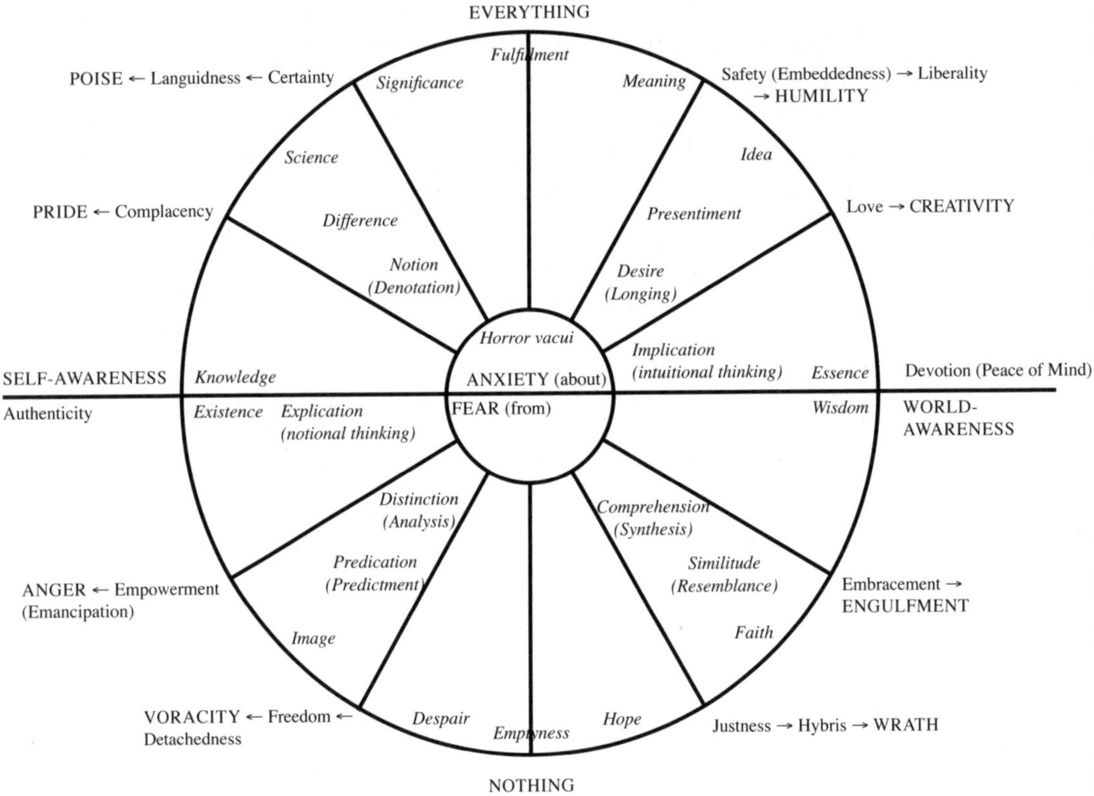

Transcript of an English version of the "Map of the Human Mind" found in the estate of one Captain William Arthur Shelley, a notorious libertarian buccaneer on behalf of the Crown who sailed the Caribbean and the Pacific Sea in the late 18th and early 19th century. He died in fall 1836 at the age of 74 in Plymouth, Devon, and left his legacy to his unmarried daughter Eleanor. This version of *The Map of the Human Mind* has been presented and discussed by Zurich neuropsychiatrist Claus Friedrich Berg in 1994 at the World Congress of Neurosciences in Barcelona chaired by Dr Lucia Penelope Pessoa de Fátima.

And that is all there is to it.
The very idea of space.
The whole story as far as it can be told ...

Unless ...
... the multitudes and multiplicities were nothing but another beginning.
The parts and bits and pieces put together again, reassembled, reconnected, reintegrated into a whole.

If that were so ...
... then, in the end, there would be everything.
Space and Time turned into one, and both lessons learned.
A complete history as far as it can be comprehended.

Cuneiform inscription in two columns on clay tablet, Part 2, 2025 BC. Buried in the ruins of Ur, most probably the very first city human beings ever built, but never found in the course of archaeological excavations on site.

II.
ZURICH MAPS

THE CIRCLE OF SPACE

The Pentagon

5.1 Entrance to the "St. Josef" Hotel, "Hirschengraben" No. 64/68
5.2 Passageway to "Blaufahnenstrasse" No. 14
5.3 Public toilet facility, Tram Stop "Paradeplatz"
5.4 Southwest corner of the Synagogue "Löwenstrasse"
5.5 Alfred-Escher-Memorial, "Bahnhofplatz" (Zurich Main Station)

The Heptagon

7.1 Entrance to the "St. Josef" Hotel, "Hirschengraben" No. 64/68
7.2 "Susanna-Gossweiler-Platz"
7.3 Choir of the "Wasserkirche" ("Water Church")
7.4 Credit Suisse Bank headquarters, southwest corner, "Paradeplatz"
7.5 Entrance to the "Paddy Reilly's" Pub, "Talstrasse"
7.6 West corner of "Löwenplatz"
7.7 Southeast corner of the Zurich Main Station building

THE CIRCLE OF TIME

The Dodecagon

12.1 "Zürichberg" woods, to the north of "Reservoir-Weg"
12.2 "Wolfbachtobelweg", to the west of the "Doldertal" Retirement Home
12.3 Street corner "Minervastrasse"/ "Apollosrasse", west side of "St. Antonius" Church
12.4 Southbound fairway of the official Zurich Lake shipping
12.5 Northeast side of the "Sihlberg" Castle premises
12.6 Passageway at the "Gold-brunnenplatz" Tram Stop
12.7 Street corner "Norastrasse", south side of the municipal "Hardau" high-rise buildings
12.8 Forecourt of the main entrance to the Zurich University of the Arts ("Toni-Areal") under the bifurcation of a railway viaduct
12.9 Southeast corner of the "Waid" Municipal Hospital
12.10 Crossroads "Hofwiesen-" and "Wehntaler-Strasse"
12.11 West driveway of the Animal Hospital "Irchel"
12.12 Footpath to the north of the "Waldhüsli" cottage in the "Zürichberg" woods

INTERSECTION POINTS

Centre points

x.1 Centre point of the Circle of Space on the top of "Lindenhof" hill (430 metres a. s. l.)
x.2 Centre point of the Circle of Time at the "Mattensteg" footbridge, "Platzspitz" Park, confluence of the rivers "Limmat" and "Sihl"

Main Diagonal of the Circle of Space

x.3 Wood glade to the west of the "Zürichberg" broadcasting tower, intersection point of the diagonal and the Circle of Time
x.4 "Escherhöhe", hilltop of the "Zürichberg" (676 metres a. s. l.), intersection point of the diagonal and the Dodecagon
x.5 Small cupola at the entrance to the "Semper" Observatory, Swiss Federal Institute of Technology (ETH)
5.1/7.1 Entrance to the "St. Josef" Hotel, "Hirschengraben" No. 64/68
x.6 Movie screen of the "Filmpodium" Cinema, intersection point of the diagonal and the Heptagon
x.7 Restaurant "La Piazzetta", "Pelikanplatz", intersection point of the diagonal and the Circle of Space
x.8 Uncompleted concrete bridge, motorway access Zurich South, intersection point of the diagonal and the Circle of Time
x.9 Top of the "Uetliberg" mountain (869 metres a. s. l.)

Main Diagonal of the Circle of Time

x.10 Stone pyramid to the east of the "Kanzlei" school building, "Helvetiaplatz"

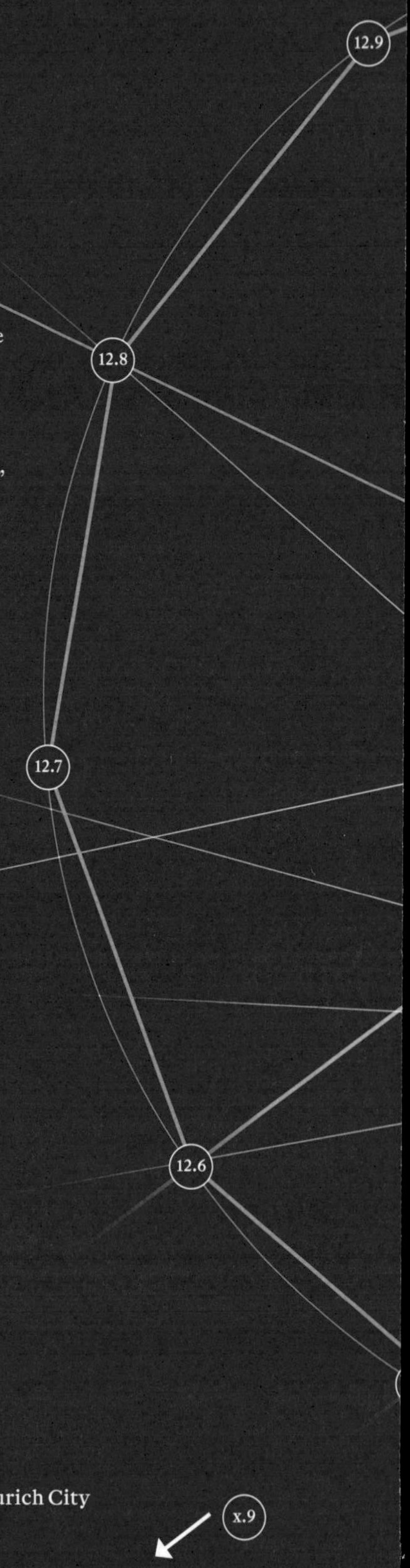

Main System Map of the circles of Space and Time, Zurich City

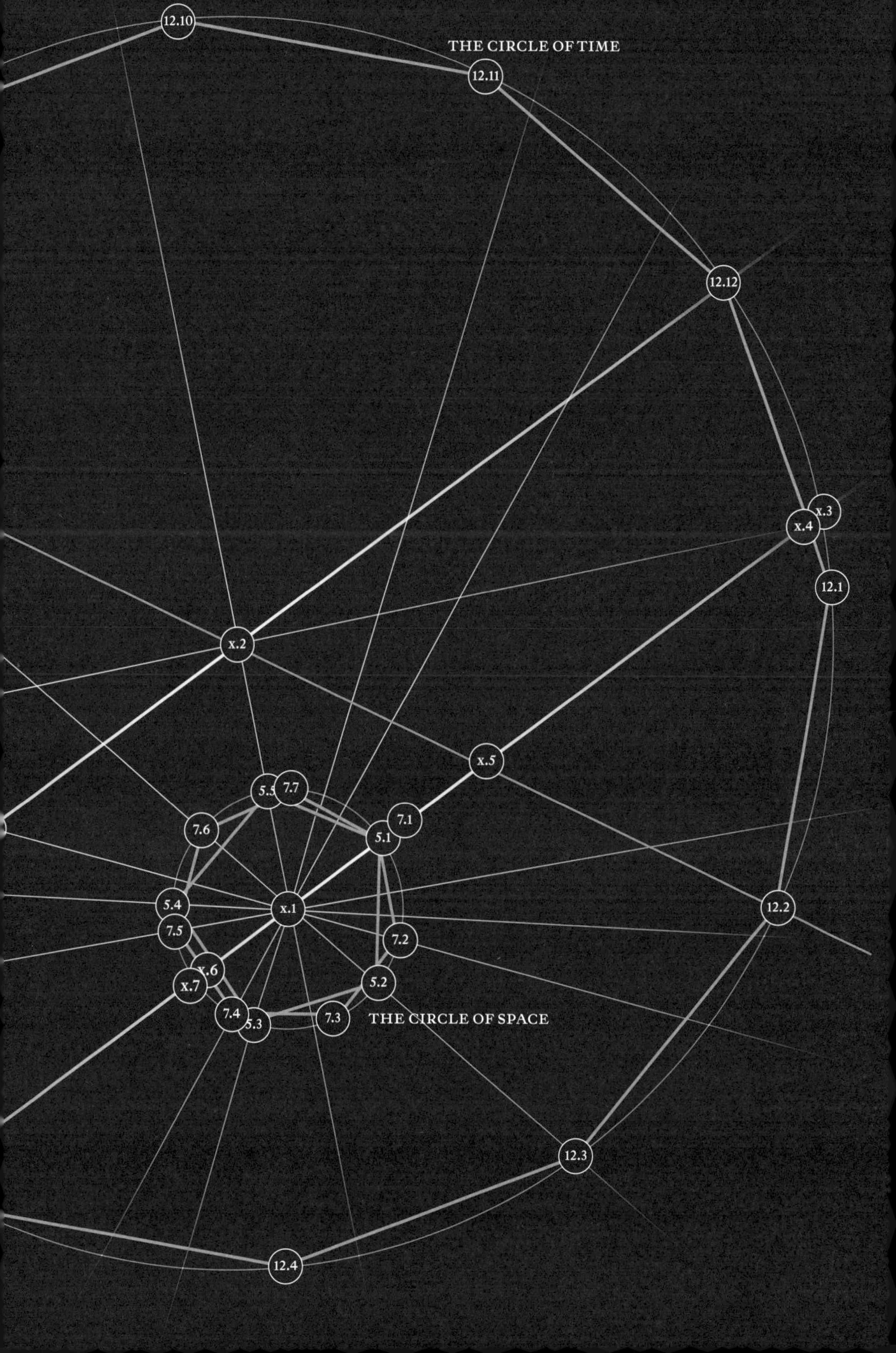
THE CIRCLE OF TIME
12.10
12.11
12.12
x.3
x.4
12.1
x.2
x.5
5.5
7.7
7.1
5.1
7.6
5.4
x.1
12.2
7.5
7.2
x.6
x.7
5.2
7.4
5.3
7.3
THE CIRCLE OF SPACE
12.3
12.4

View of the city of Zurich, xylography by Josua Murer, 1576.

t vnd gelägenheit / wie sy zů diser zyt in wä
Josen Murer / vnd durch Christoffel
getruckt / Im M.D.LXXVI. Jar.
AMPLISS. SENATUI, POPULO, TOTIQUE CIVITATI TIGURINÆ, PATRIÆ DILECTISS. JODOCUS MURER, AMORIS ET GRATITUDINIS ERGO DEDICAVIT.
Rathuß
Wettinger hof
Wasserkilch
Wellenberg

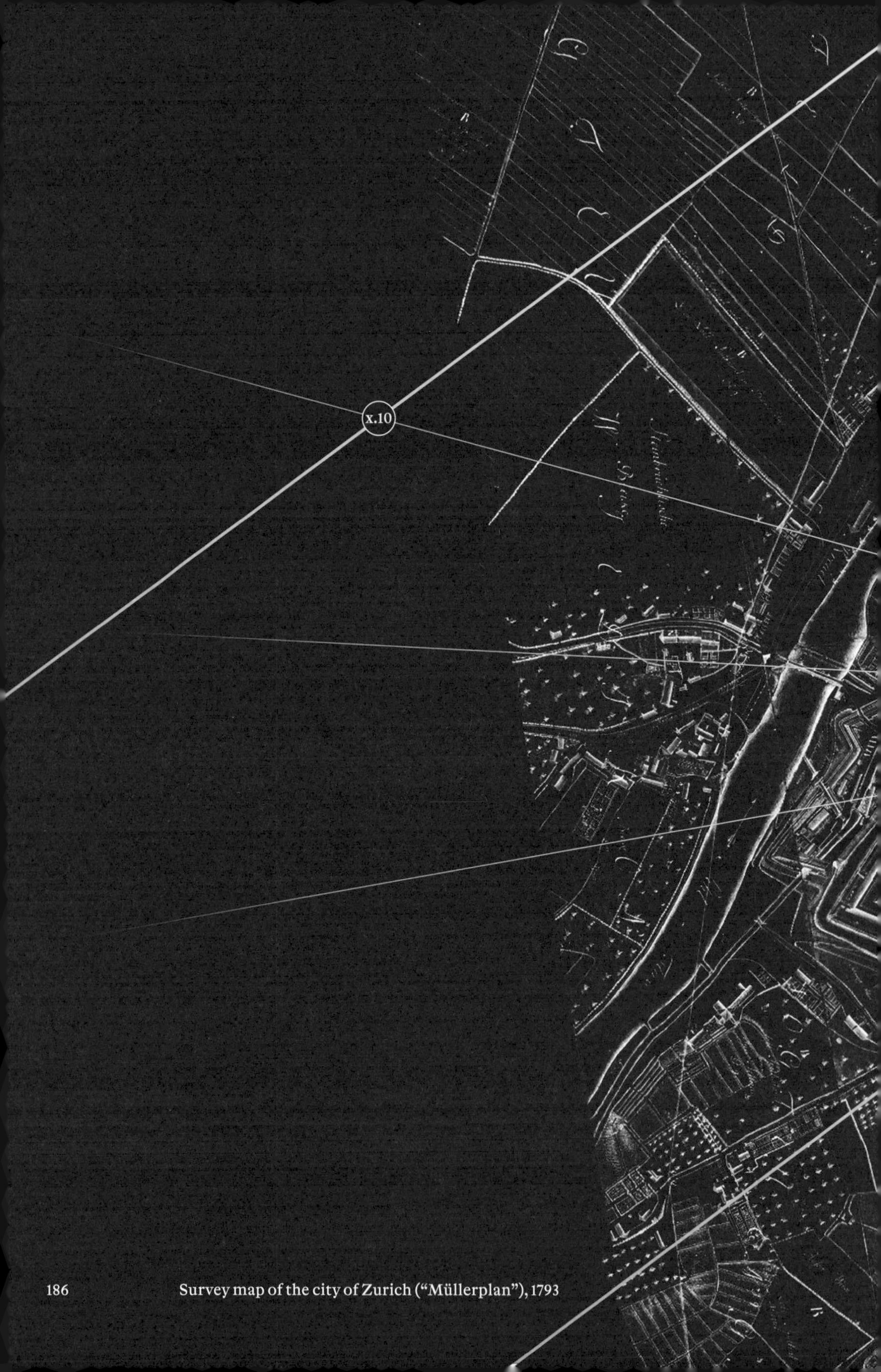

Survey map of the city of Zurich (“Müllerplan”), 1793

5.5
7.6
5.1
5.4
x.1
x.6
5.2
7.4
7.3

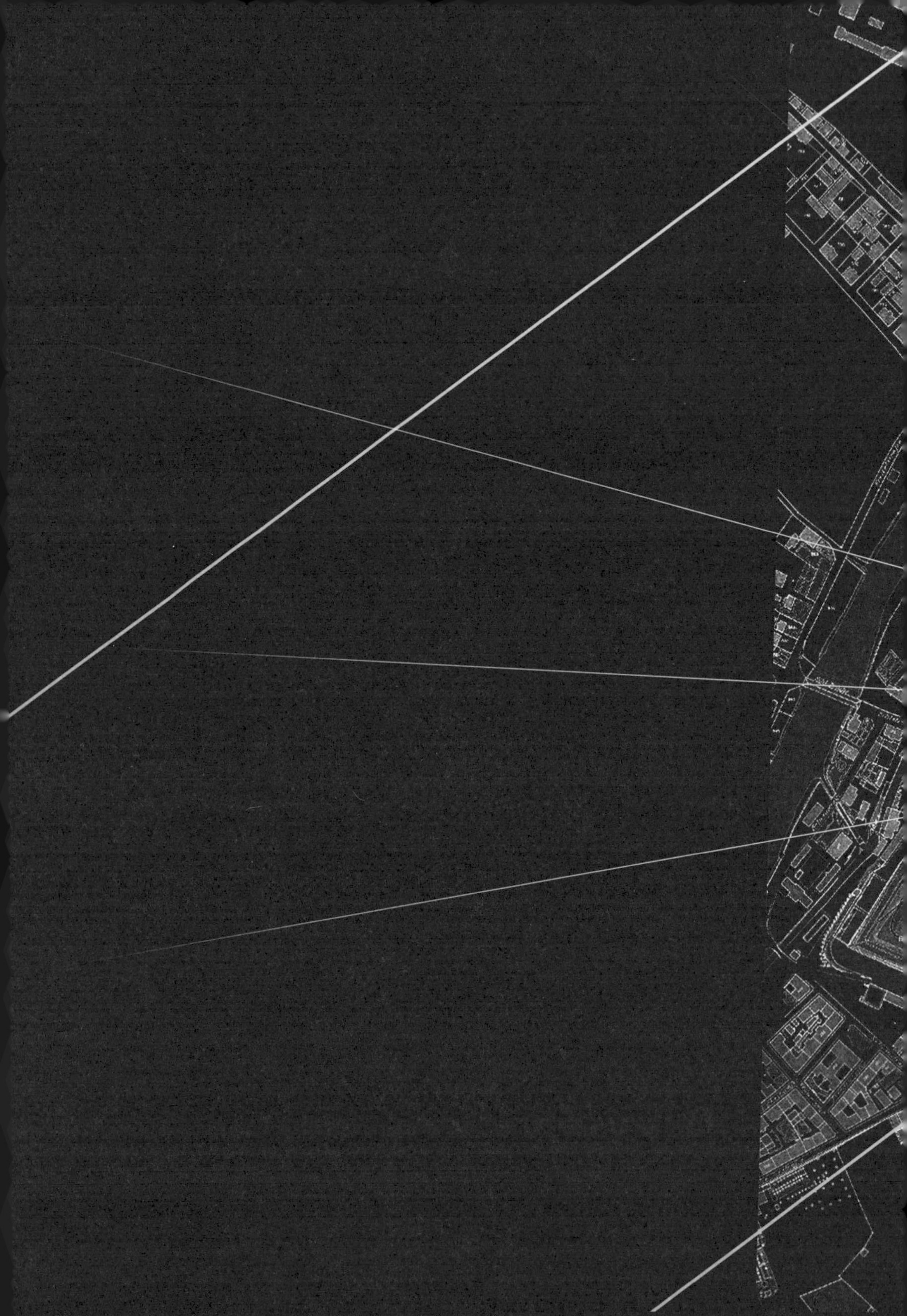

Survey map of the city of Zurich (1 : 2’500), 1860

5.5
7.7
Exercierplatz
Sihl
7.6
Limmat
7.1
5.4
x.1
7.2
x.7
Münsterhof
5.3
7.3
Schanzengraben

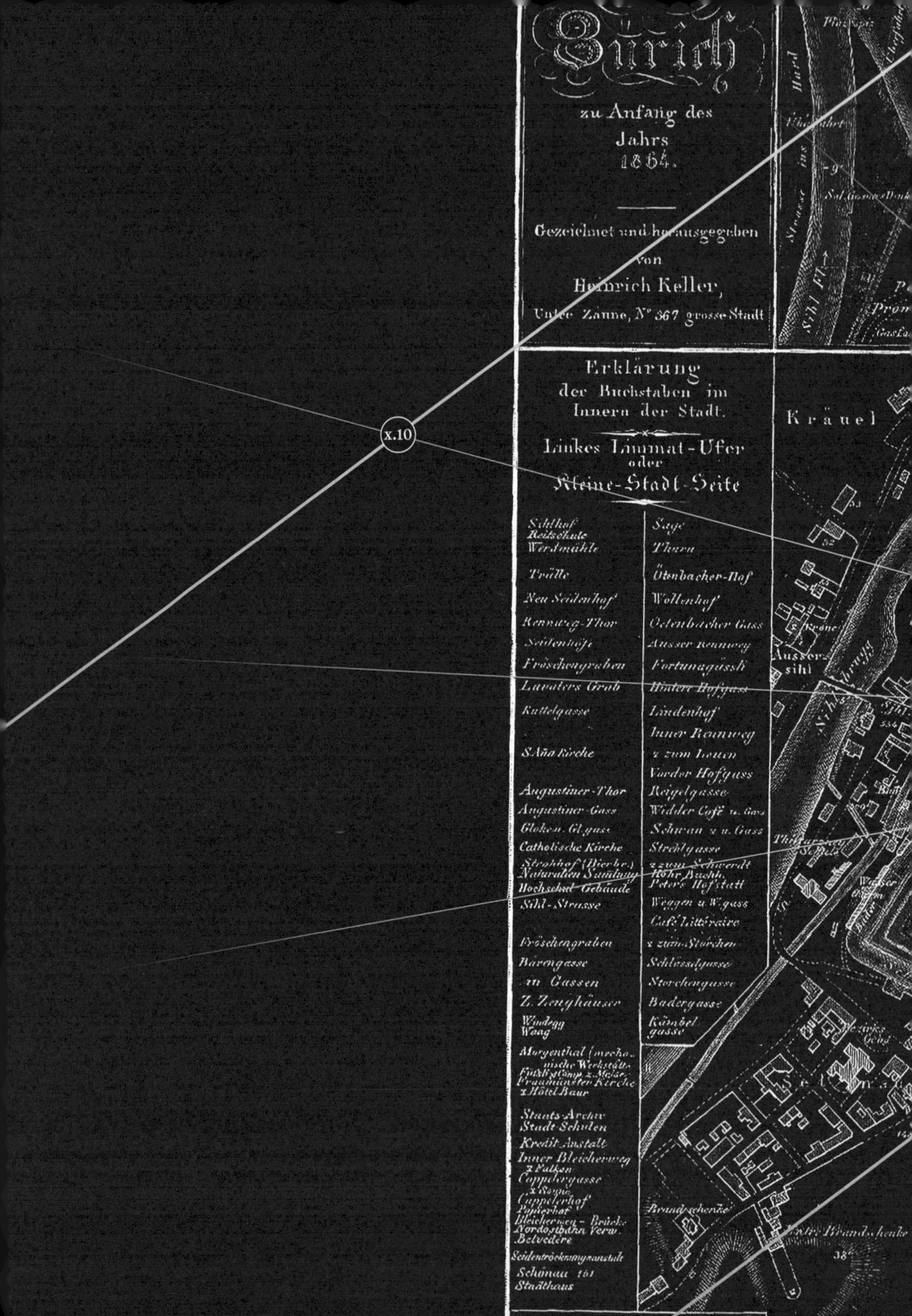

Layout plan of the city of Zurich (1 : 6'600) by Heinrich Keller, 1864

5.5
7.7
7.6
5.1
x.1
7.5
7.2
x.6
5.3
7.3
Kornhalle
Sihl
Limmat
Post
Strasse
Münsterhof

Official survey map of the Zurich area, 1900

x.4
12.1
x.2
x.5
5.5
7.1
5.4
x.1
12.2
5.2
5.3
7.3
12.3
12.4

Official tourist map of the City of Zurich (1 : 10'000), 1997

Unterstrass
Oberstrass
Fluntern
Hottingen
Enge
Dold
ZÜRICHBERG
12.11
x.1
x.2
x.3
12.2
12.3
12.4

12.8
12.6

12.10
12.11
12.12
x.3
x.4
12.1
x.2
x.5
5.5
5.1
5.4
x.1
7.5
7.2
x.6
7.4
7.3
12.3

Official plot plan of the City of Zurich, 2017

12.10
12.11
12.12
x.3
x.4
12.1
x.2
x.5
5.5
7.7
7.1
7.6
5.1
5.4
x.1
12.2
7.5
7.2
x.6
x.7
5.2
7.4
5.3
7.3
12.3
Zürich
12.4

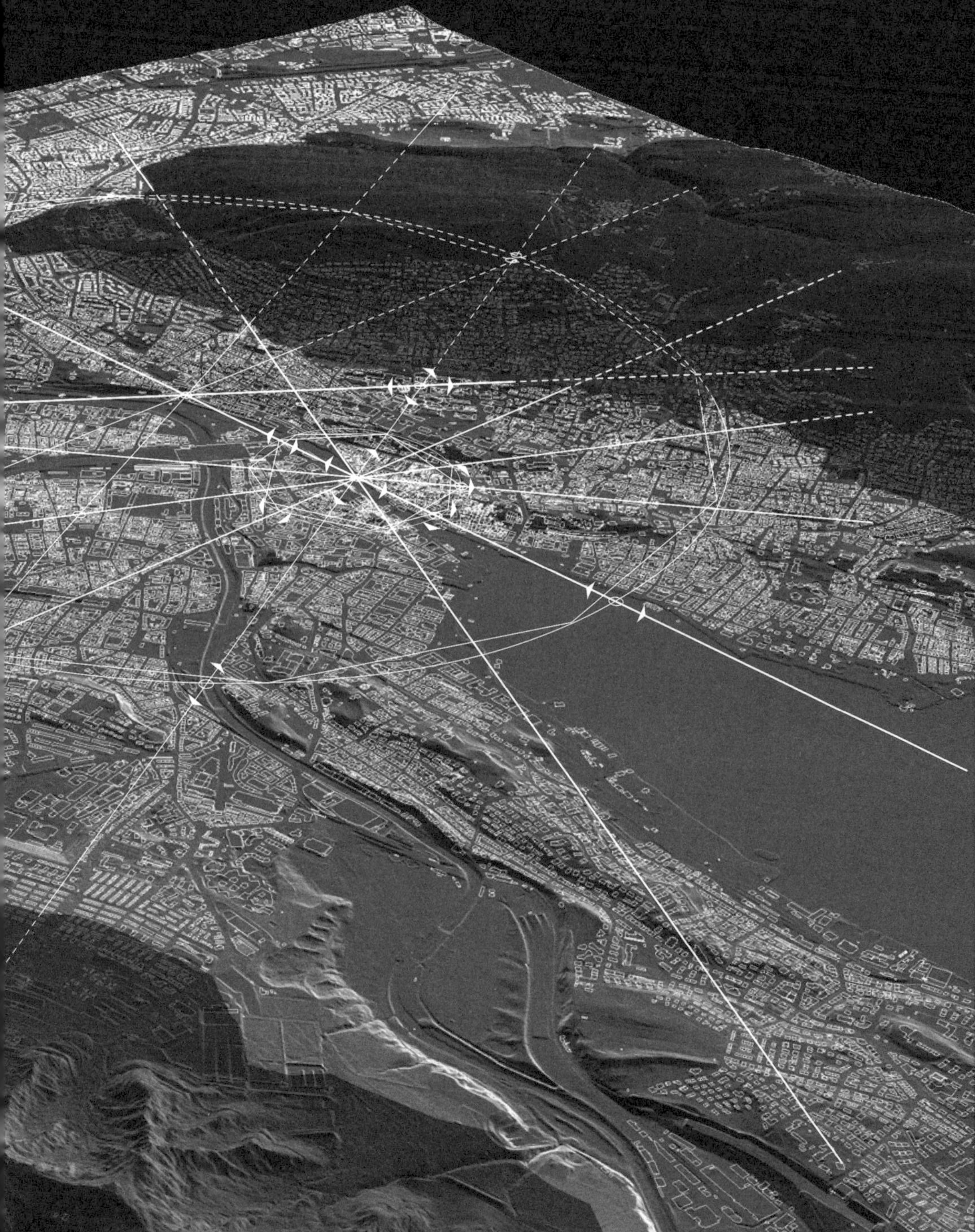

5.5 Alfred-Escher-Memorial, "Bahnhofplatz" (Zurich Main Station)

12.6 Passageway at the "Goldbrunnenplatz" Tram Stop

Coordinates

N 47.3763°, E 8.547°

N 47.37°, E 8.5129°

x.1 Centre point of the Circle of Space on the top of "Lindenhof" hill (430 metres a. s. l.)

x.2 Centre point of the Circle of Time at the "Mattensteg" footbridge, "Platzspitz" Park, confluence of the rivers "Limmat" and "Sihl"

N 47.3736°, E 8.5412°

N 47.3813°, E 8.5388°

5.3 Public toilet facility, Tram Stop “Paradeplatz”

12.5 “Sihlberg” Castle premises

N 47.369°, E 8.5386°

N 47.363°, E 8.5244°

7.2 “Susanna-Gossweiler-Platz”

5.4 Southwest corner of the Synagogue “Löwenstrasse”

N 47.3719°, E 8.547°

N 47.374°, E 8.5345°

7.3 Choir of the "Wasserkirche" ("Water Church")

N 47.3691°, E 8.5424°

III. THE IMAGINATION OF SPACE

Zurich Spaces

Dylan Perrenoud

SWISSCO

ZURICH A DRAWING IN WORDS

Dieter Dietz

As I engage now in writing, in thinking about drawing, noting how I would attempt to draw Zurich, the place of my birth and a part of my life, noting right now at the outset, first attempts that I will soon engage in, not sitting in a train as I am now but having spaces in mind and in front of my inner eye, I am hesitating, whether to work on a framework first, not so much a frame but a structure that will lead me through writing, or to just drop myself into a first, concrete point of departure, imagined as I am not there but here, sitting on a train, writing.

Perspectives are shifting as my gaze travels across a lake, in the mist, fog just lifting, revealing first contours of an island passing by, Saint Peters. Shifting perspective, also faint, a vantage point in time rather than in view, Zurich, my destination.

Light reflects mauve on trees, no leaves. Curtains of willows, in a rapidly passing foreground. Stems all robed in ivy, or the white of birch trees ascending into the sky. Occasional boats passing by, not with fishermen as at dawn when I am travelling in the opposite direction, but anchored and passing as I move on by.

And now, roads, cars. Another station, a voice in the loudspeakers announcing a small city, known for its watch making companies.

I am not drawing, but writing, as I travel.

The concept of drawing deals with time. It denotes moments at a specific space, in specific modes. It includes time, in specific ways.

A line may capture a moment, an essential aspect (revealed to us *en face*, as seen, a-spect) condensed, figured. It will travel for a few seconds over the surface of a paper, an expression of the 'imago' that has been formed in front of my eyes and my inner eye nearly simultaneously. This line will persist, as a moment's trace, an interaction between a person, a conscious being situated in space, in time, in a situation. Drawing / sketching on a page.

LOGBOOK

Zurich, February 8th 2018, 12:46,
Drawing the site of HOUSE 2, 7 months after its disappearance on June 18th, 2017
Grey skies and light snow, temperature 0° Celsius
I am sitting on a stool where Reeds in wooden sections of 2.5 by 5 cm formed a part of the HOUSE 2 programmatic sequence. The place where a short violoncello concert took place on June 1st 2017. I note with my pen: Bach: Cello Suite #1 In G, BWV 1007 - 1. Praeludium,, Bach: Cello Suite #1 In G, BWV 1007 - 2. Allemande, and Bach: Cello Suite #1 In G, BWV 1007 - 3. Courante, hour 11.42. The note placed as a memory on the lower edge of the paper, hardly legible.
Coordinates 47.390476 N, 8.510727 E
Coordinates 47.374819 N, 8.547504 E, grey skies, 2.5 ç Celsius

The tip of my ball-point now just lifted off the paper, a long line getting slower towards the end, the ball rolling, turning…two swirls in the opposite direction…orthogonally?

Again I am pressed against the paper, fingers holding me lightly, a dance of nearly parallel lines now starting, just slightly foreshortened.

Above the bridges, curved lines. And a broad mass, two nearly vertical lines on the paper, the façade of the Toni Areal appearing as a line ending at the mass, several windows indicated, rapidly, the workshops. Closer by: the stairs, lines nearly parallel. Just slightly foreshortened. Vertical lines delineating the volume of the elevator next to the stairs. Now a couple descends the stairs, talking, dressed in a thick jacket, beige, and a longer coat, black. My lines fail to capture the moment.

The sound of trains passing on the bridge. Sissing, shivering frequencies. Eurythmics, 1983: 'You can hear the sound of the underground trains, you know it feels like distant thunder' – Vitruvius' Eurythmia, conceived of 2041 years ago. Crossing the bridge, many lines. The lines on the paper trying to capture sound. Distant voices.

The ballpoint travels on – meshes, crossroads – the surface of the sheet of paper limited, my lines limited, my capacity to draw this space, limited. I am, nonetheless, immersed in the moment. I can feel the void around me, façades, the bridges, the distant field of tracks, the river fairly near. Visual, bodily, mental and mnemonic sensations – skies still grey, only visible as slanted slots.

Ichnographia

A line may also delineate a space that I have carefully measured, meticulously, pacing in space, using measuring tools, threads, tubes, water. Based on my notes, I can commence to plot points, systematically. Draw a plan. The plotted lines, issued from this systematic process, contain time more eternally, the delineations shaping situations, accessibility, exclusions. Space defining elements facilitate movements, gravitationally, on surfaces, or pose barriers – traced lines on a sheet of paper – to access, to view, to warmth, to cold, to odors, to a smiling face. The plan offers an endless field of potential situations. It holds them as a simultaneous plateau of past, present and future moments, traced and contracted into a two-dimensional surface. Contractions take time and care, they can be convulsive, too, mentally. Equally in their construction as traces on paper. We are confronted with a plan that projects a contract of delineations of open and closed potentialities into space, into the city, into the land.

Ichnographia

LOGBOOK

Zurich, February 21st 2018
First attempt to engage in an ichnographic procedure in words.
6 months and 6 days after a walk with Matthias Michel from Lindenhof to battle memorial, memories of unseen places, the Semper Observatory
Coordinates 47.374819 N, 8.547504 E,
Grey skies, 2.5° Celsius
16h 16' 39"

Plotting a first point, mentally. At the bifurcation of the small road leading along the South façade of the ETH building by Gottfried Semper and a short bypass road, leading to the stairs, just below the sharp left turn along the Karl Moser University. Now walk west. The point is situated at the apex of the inner radius defining the boundary between asphalt and some remnants of earth and plants around a tree. Cobble stones. I haven't been looking up. Just surface beneath me. A first point, simple, I place it on my mental page of fluctuating size, still remaining a limited rectangular surface, latently a potential of frame. Figures will appear later.

Immediately the point on my mental page is contrasted by what I physically sense around me. Topography sloping down to the left, the gravitational mass of the Moser building intellectually and physically present. It is sensually there. My peripheral vision barely grasps its contour against the skies, slightly veiled probably by the canopy of the tree, bare of leaves in this season.

16h 16' 55'

An intermediary trajectory from the HOUSE 2 site, in a tram, very cold outside, fragments of English sentences. A trajectory along a line. Shifting perspectives again. Towers, parking lots, a bridge, skies obscured. Heading for the Polybahn Cable Car. Shifting thoughts as well. Typing into the keyboard at an unsteady rhythm. Plotting a further point in that mental drawing will be challenging. I have plotted one point so far.

Plotting a further point 6 days, 20 hours and 37 minutes later. Yet again grey skies, a bit brighter though. Distance 21.354 m. A first line implied. I have now decided on an orientation of the mental page. North aligned with the side of the pages, top facing the pole – most classical format for maps, but how can I define that directionality, where do I plot that second point? Even with a compass my drawing will not be precise, a full survey and a sextant would be necessary. I decide to give it an orientation that resembles north, from my memories. The drawing that will emanate from my first measurements will be turned in time. The point at 21.354 m is, in fact, a slight elevation on the paving, only 'gravel' standing out just 2 cm at the curb-side, on the well maintained bypass between the Polyterrasse Bar and Mensa and Künstlergasse. Then up a stair, 13 lines of risers, I will approximate them. Angle, measured as precisely as possible. Width, 4.35 m. 13 steps up, sharp turn left, 16 steps, slight turn right, 10 steps. Now back at Künstlergasse. To my left the ramp to the Polyterrasse. I have moved up along a semi-octagon, with rounded edges, built in limestone. I have plotted a series of points on the right side of the stair, assuming the geometrically straight line, the angle of which I just measured. The continuous line that has been drawn along the trajectory of my movement on the right side of my body, the hillside, appears now as a sagged, seemingly erratic trace on my mental page – an arrow, a flash of lightning, hard to contextualize without knowing the history of it.

At this point I decide to mix tools. The traced line, in words, mentally referring to what could be the process of delineating measurements that have been plotted onto a horizontal projection plane, has taken time in words, perhaps more than in drawing. I will superimpose this first line with the figure in plan of the octagonal stair that sits at the Künstlergasse, as a bastion harnessing a view across the city – a late 19th century architectural landscape element, not in defense of anything except its own geometry. I will use our third eye, the one that scans over the earth and has so for several decades, a viewpoint calculated of millions of pixels, themselves compiled of millions of satellite photographs. My third eye restlessly pans to and fro according to the clicks and movements of my fingers on the trackpad. Gravitationally dysfunctional - a virtual abyss. Traces of weather conditions and time cycles have been erased, partially, not completely. I extract the figure in redrawing it, as a diagram, black lines on white.

Next I trace the rectangle that is so active spatially, situated in front of the Semper ETH building, above the medieval part of the city, just hovering above the roofs, those roofs that still felt like waves to be immersed into just minutes ago and a few meters further down. What seems to me relevant now, what this drawing should bring forward, is a sequence. I will draw a space defining lines, that, complimented with knowledge and memories will show a spatial continuity, structured through topography, views perceived by a person, and architectures. The horizontal projection plane will hold this transgressional information as a figure, black lines on white, continuities of surface, thresholds of climates, interior and exterior. For the plan drawing of the Semper building, I decide to use a superimposition of an original plan (before Gustav Guhl's intervention at the turn of the century) with today's plan that includes the concrete structures in the Nordhof and the Südhof. The first plan dates from 1858, labelled REZ-DE-CHAUSSEE. The second one is from ironclub2018.ethz.ch. I will not draw the exterior limestone façade, only carve the interior spaces into the white of the mental page. Westvestibül, Antikensaal, and the East Entrance, added by Guhl in 1905, form a beautiful enfilade, a threshold in the fabric of the city.

On my mental page I have now a line, a small figure, the semi-octagon, the rectangle of the Polyterrasse and a more complex organism: the Semper ETH building. The sequence casts potentialities through space and several centuries. It is now time to introduce one of the axes of the Zurich Polygon Map, the axes that Matthias Michel and I have been following on September 19th 2017. The axis dissects Gottfrieds Semper's building nearly exactly in the middle, it slices my view towards Uetliberg and Lindenhof. The hill slopes towards Zurichberg in my back. Angle from true North 60°
12h 11' 35"

This spatial axis guides me through the Semper building, in a slightly oblique angle. It will exit through the door, second left, at Guhl's rotunda. Beyond Rämistrasse it continues between auxiliary infrastructural buildings of the Univeritätsspital along Schmelzberggasse – left over spaces everywhere, a kind of a police station. For the plan drawing I will not trace the boundary lines of this sequence that resembles rather a suburban conglomerate, a consequence of mono-functional considerations. All of a sudden, a small building shows up, accentuated vertically in its proportions, standing awkwardly on a plot, its geometrical orientation not obvious at first sight. In plan the building shows an L-shaped disposition, sitting on a terrace in the terrain. The main wing is topped by a roof-terrace, sitting next to a circular tower with a cupola. If you look closely, a double line reveals its purpose. Today the Collegium Helveticum resides here. The orientation of the building now lets me readjust my drawing on the mental white: The Semper Observatory's façades align with North.
13h 19' 55"

LOGBOOK

Zurich, February 27th 2018
A short sketch to test the idea of an orthographic drawing in words.
Around Schmelzbergstrasse, views from aligning streets and hospital
Coordinates 47.377825 N, 8.551025 E,
Grey skies, 2.0 ç Celsius,
15h 55' 15"

I will draw in profile, on a vertical projection plane. The double line, now in elevation, proves to be the opening through which, from the 1860s onwards, sunspots were observed and catalogued in the Zurich Sunspot Number publications. Today, the series of terraces and garden walls have been aggressively separated from the lanes of the adjacent streets, and the few left over trees and bushes tell of an episode in the city fabric, disintegrated as a nonconnected piece of time. Oddly a little observatory has been added in 1911, and the Sun Tower in the 1950s. They appear in my drawing as lines, partly dotted, as obscured by the terrace and the Semper building itself. The terrace is surmounted by an indication of a plinth and the meticulously proportioned Rez-de-Chaussée built in limestone. Above, yellow render between pilasters. Orthographically I will now note: edges of the plot of land, horizontal lines defining the respective datum of each étage, and the façade covering this structural disposition in section. The balustrade of the roof-terrace forms a dominant horizontal next to the observatory tower. My projection plane, oriented perfectly north-south, will let the buildings scattered around appear as bits and pieces, yet it will stop short in depicting their mutual relationships as space defining relics.

I look at my plan drawing that shows the spatial figure of transitions from Künstlergasse to the Semper Observatory. Mentally I will now allow facades and sections to appear in front of my inner eye. I will unfold them and stretch the lines and lay parallel projection planes along them to project orthogonally, in scale and proportion. The ETH building by Semper, with its façades dissected by the section through the Antikensaal and the Westvestibül, along the axis. The terrain activates slight changes in level, and a large sycamore at the semi-octagon marks a strong drop in Zurich's topography towards the medieval town below. I reference the drop with a datum line indicating 406 m above sea level, the average height of Lake of Zurich, since it has been further regulated in 1949/51. And I draw the second datum, at the vertex of the Semper Observatory Cupola, at 486 m above sea level. It is the datum that will guide our drone flights in early April.
18h 19' 55"

Orthographia.

'Ichnographic drawing contracts elements into hyper-real, yet highly abstract notations of lines. The orthographic drawing shows natural and artificial elements in relative height and in reference to their gravitational location, often anchored into topography. They appear in profile, enunciating their relative proportions in themselves, and towards the world.

Ultimately they reference our body, exclude or include human activity and behavior, stand with or beyond us. In movement, their relative height will constantly be revealed, concealed, or diverted. Shifting foregrounds and panning positions will continuously engage spatial experience in respect to movement and sensorial perception of space, less visual than engaged by our proprioception – visceral. Relations between artificial and natural elements emanate as potential spatial experience and existence. The laughing eyes that were hidden behind the wall just a moment ago, I see them now, as I have moved sidewards, as has she, our gazes crossing diagonally.'

Orthographia.

The observatory stopped its activities on April 1st, 1980. The instruments set 'flat on ground' became dysfunctional by the interferences of new infrastructure and hospital buildings. The Semper Sternwarte projected from the Zurich topography, as a moment, projected its gaze into the universe, trying to make sense of the skies above. Its Cupola is elevated from the terrace by a further band of ornamented panels wrapping the tower, ornate *enclosure* between the implied tectonics holding up a *roof*, here gazing at the *hearth* of our sun system. A small building suspended between the earth, and the skies, literally, crafted on *earthwork*, held by gazes towards the sun.

The constant rhythm of fingers treating my keyboard. Occasional sways of finger tips across the trackpad. Never tactile transmissions otherwise. I emanate light through the screen. The face, vis-à-vis, blue-pale, concentrated. My calculations inanimate.

If we now expand the roof-terrace horizontally, as if water had risen to its tiled pavement, nearly the whole city can be seen as being immersed in the Linth valley. The Semper Observatory's cupola is floating, as does Superstudio's dome of the Santa Maria del Fiore in the waters above Florence. A bit further South, the larger cupola of Guhl's extension, half immersed, half visible on the axis towards Uetliberg

LOGBOOK

Zurich, February 21st 2021
Scenographic drawing in words.
From HOUSE 2 site to Zurich main station
Coordinates: from 47.390476 N, 8.510727 E to 47.378635 N, 8.539786 E ,
Bright skies, 8.3 °Celsius,
10h 35' 35''
Swaying lines across the pages, vanishing point ahead. First initiated moment, motion ahead.

The outset: a scenographic drawing: SCAENOGRAPHIA. To avoid a standstill, this drawing shall consist of a moving viewpoint, in constant transition. First distinction, lateral planes perspectival, orthogonal planes frontal. Lines tracing contours, proportions lost in flight.

Point of departure: Zurich Toni Areal looking east towards ZURICH 1, the building on the left, planar. I draw a rectangle. Curved lines above as if in the sky, bridges crossing. Distant building approaching the vantage point. On the right side, infrastructures, the broad street and beyond, leftover spaces between y-shaped roads and bridges, several rolls of steel cables, 2.3 m in diameter, and behind, a kind of parking lot. The sky is opening up above the vast field with the train tracks. A few lines on the page. In fact, what I describe in words is off-frame. Moving on. A next viewpoint. Lines trace now rectangles to the right and left, Façades along the street in perspective. On my bike I see more ground than sky, moving on, the vantage point shifts upwards towards the upper edge of the mental page that is to hold the scene, superimposed onto the first. Lines mingle, and the lines that are flying towards the vantage point double, triple, multiply. First darker areas start to appear. (As the frozen edges on the lake's coast as I am travelling by in the train.) Moving on: Crossing train lines beneath a viaduct, a bit more than a hundred years old. And now an open lawn, framed by trees. On the skateboard, more skies. The body in transient balance, ensured through speed. Clearly a different sense of gravity and the vantage point shifts towards the lower edge of the page. Further dark areas appear, and expand. Slowly, a latent vertical figure casts itself against the disappearing white near the center of the page.

As I now continue along a street in Kreis 5, along shops and restaurants, more and more lines superimpose the nearly black surfaces in perspectival obliqueness, and I add more and more vantage points to the left, and to the right, never stopping from moving – the act of drawing is an act of contracting time and de-contracting space at the same time. The black on black becoming textures, rhythm, and around the center of the page a lighter area. A loophole into time?

Scaenographia.

In drawing from a particular point in space, physically or mentally, we freeze elements in time. Many modes of collage (collage), of multiplying viewpoints in the same painting or drawing (de Chirico), in disassembling and deconstructing the object (Cubism), in accelerating or decelerating perspective (Teatro Olimpico, Scala Reggia), show ways to overcome the potential death of a spatio-temporal moment if depicted in a frozen state. Photographers imply their vision non-mechanistically and poetically. They engage their artistic eye.

In shifting foregrounds, middle grounds, backgrounds, strange profiles and obscure plans can be imagined. On the other hand a deadlock between coordinates in space and a produced perspectival image by simple and deterministic operation may prove to be a pitfall for the imagination. In drawing however, in creating a vivid imago in front of our inner eye, our imagination will let us conceive millions of diverse possible situations and spatial figurations, again and again. Superimposed imaginations create an open space, to be shared, to be communicated. Places appear as textures: As the white in Sugimoto's theatre photos. The line as the light, of one hour of film, banned on the screen, now luminous and endless in time.

Scaenographia.

Open the page.
As in a drawing consider the available surface.
Let your gaze travel.
Scan for key features, conceive a spatial structure.
Travel mentally between the surface and the space you inhabit, constantly reconsidering your bodily existence in the spatial situation...
Note a point
Let gaze travel
Verify
Repeat

DRAWING FOR REAL A QUEST INTO THE SPACE OF IMAGINATION

Dieter Dietz & Daniel Zamarbide

Introduction: Implications in regard to architectural practice and education
To confront the most vital challenges of our existence today – climate change, human rights, ethical justice and the survival of democracy – are we making the best use of the tools at hand? Have they already been invented? Are they in our hands and minds, or do we need to invent new ones? Of course this essay will not give answers to all those questions. Yet we will try to emphasize one crucial dimension. We, as human beings, must not lose our capacity to imagine. As it is, this capacity may be at peril. We must therefore protect and foster this incredible facility: The power of imagination.

We are convinced that this must come along with a shift in perspective. In western society we have been focusing more and more on objects and quantities that can be defined according to a limited and clear range of criteria. It is now time to immerse ourselves in the in-between.

We see education in architecture as being concerned with these questions. The architectural and educational explorations that we have been carrying out for the past three years now, reflected in the volumes of ALL ABOUT SPACE, do not seem at first to lead us to definite conclusions. But this first impression is in line with one of our aims: We see the quest of the venture as that of constructing open questions rather than closed answers. We do not believe in conclusive truths. Maybe our work raises fair questions as to what architecture is – and particularly important for our endeavor – how space-making and architecture can be taught and learned without preconceptions.

The one thing that we have concentrated our energy on is the exploration of tools as an essential quest of space-making. We commenced our editorial project with the idea that fiction was a great tool for producing space-related stories and that through them, we may approach many of the aspects that need to be understood in the learning of architecture. With a fictional approach the somewhat daring tittle ALL ABOUT SPACE appeared, allowing us to travel all around space matters whilst traversing a broad cultural range. The first volume was literally an explosion of curiosity. Curiosity confronts us with our utmost inner being. As such it looks as much in as it looks out. We have tried to make the book a tangible experience – to be read as a journey, or a novel. In the second volume, the whole Earth Catalogue and Richard Sennett's writings were our companion. These two rather monumental models of thinking oriented our research to tools and their relation to work, logically leading to how society is fabricated and perceived. The built form that supports a given society is our main concern, and as this built form depends on the tools that are used to make it, we have consecrated a very particular focus and interest on how the tools are used collectively. We set up an experiment called HOUSE 1 to put these thoughts into practice. The result is ALL ABOUT SPACE 2. The enquiry into the nature of Tools has by now settled solidly into our educational agenda. In this essay in ALL ABOUT SPACE 3, we will focus on one of these tools, the one we believe to be quintessential in the context of imagination and its translations: Drawing.

We will elaborate on drawing as an important tool that serves two purposes: apprehending our environment and projecting our imagination. The title, Drawing for Real, A Quest into the Space of Imagination, includes in itself the complexity of the subject and presents the main axes on which we want to build our thoughts. Drawing situates itself in a dual and perpetual movement between the material and the virtual, between the immediate and the controlled, between the projected and the observed. Reality is a processed construction. What we see is not an immediate or direct perception. It is a recorded perception that is analyzed or processed, and reconstructed by our brain, to inform us about what we have seen. The eye works as a sensitive support or mediator that captures filtered information (the filters can be multiple depending on cultural, physical and psychic conditions and capabilities) and sends it to the brain, which ultimately will filter and make sense of this process. Realities are thus multiple and complex, and for the purpose of this essay, we place the real in the movement between physical perception and the activities of the brain. Is physical reality more real than our dreams?

1.a Interior and Exterior

As much as drawing evolves in between the virtual and the physical, it evolves equally between interior and exterior. We will start with a few straightforward observations.

The exterior is brought to the drawing and through the act of drawing it can be interiorized, digested. If we are about to draw something that we are perceiving, the process would be roughly the following:

1. To perceive. We look at what we want to draw. A tree.
2. Synthesize. We have to analyze what we are seeing so that it becomes transformable into a drawing form. This operation demands a constant back and forth between abstraction and figuration. How to translate what we see into "drawable" features? Our drawing skills will allow us to synthesize, depending on our capacity to transfigure what we perceive. Many of the details of the tree, such as the leaves may not be figuratively drawn, they will be transformed, simplified, abstracted. What we have seen in the first place will be converted/translated into something other than that which "echoes" the original.
3. The action of drawing which will take place, will produce a drawing, somewhat distant from the original. The tree that we see will be transformed into a drawn shape that we recognize (depending on our cultural background) as a tree represented as a drawing.
4. The bi-dimensional figure that we now perceive – the drawing of the tree – is now a vehicle between the original (the exterior) and the represented – issued from an inner image or a interiorized version.

Through this process the exterior original tree has started a path towards a kind of interiority, one that grasps the source or meaning or content of the tree but does not reflect in pure fidelity its formal features. The inner image of the tree has thus attained a space of intimacy, retained in an interior condition but with the possibility to dialogue with the original model through the drawing,

The opposite movement works in a similar manner, from the inside to the outside. It would happen roughly as follows:

1. The thought of something appears in our mind and we want to stabilize this thought by materializing it formally onto a piece of paper. The image of a tree appears in front of our inner eye.

2. We need to understand the form of this inner image, but it is much less graspable in terms of volume and form than the physical reality. From a hypothetical and blurry comprehension of the images of our thoughts we need to project a "drawable" form. In order to do this, our cultural background usually helps us to categorize a catalogue of "drawable" forms. At this stage, our skills and culture play an important role.
3. The action of drawing takes place and produces a drawing – a figuration of an imagined tree, one that does not need to exist in physical reality. The tree that we have been able to 'project' has been transformed into a drawn shape that we may or may not recognize as the projection of a tree.
4. We are now in front of a drawing of the projection of a tree that moves towards the echo of a physical reality but holds back from it. In order to be assimilated as a tree, it will have to have a tendency towards its physical existence.

These two movements, from the external to the internal and vice versa are the essential traits of drawing. On the one hand, the perceived environment is digested through the act of drawing and assimilated as part of a known context. On the other hand, whatever our imagination is capable to produce and project is measured by a projected figuration of it, opening up a dialogue with the perceived.

1.b A taste of drawing for real

Ink pen. There is something extremely bodily about drawing. Considering the pen as an immediate extension of one's fingers, it is easy to imagine that the ink coming out of the pen as an extension of our own fluids. In a very dynamic manner they travel from our brain to our arm and to our hand to land on a sheet of celluloid. The brain begins the process after having transformed what is perceived into a vision and then sends the necessary messages to move electrons, impulses, liquids towards the body members that will execute the task. The fluid ink thus becomes a recording material as much as an expulsion of some inner movement where the imagined (brain activity) confronts the projected in a graphic form registered on paper.

Pencil. There is something very primitive about drawing. Considering the pencil as a part of our hand, it is easy to imagine that the scraping action between two solid elements (graphite and a material support) is close to our ancestors' means to make fire or shape tools. Through the friction of the two materials it acquires the capability of leaving graphic traces. In the action of scraping one can see a form of violence or material aggression: One material is applied against the other and forces a trace onto the latter. In fact, the pencil is a sophisticated form of trace-making, leaving symbols or marks that usually demand recognition in a non-conclusive form.

Parametrically scripted 3d-modelling/Grasshopper-Plug-in. There is something magical about drawing. Considering the computer as a processor that transforms data into comprehensive information, we can imagine similarities between magic and parametric drawing. A number of actions are presented to the computer. Almost like magic formulas, these actions are processed in calculative ways that we cannot perceive with our senses, making graphic forms appear. The flat computer screen is seen here as a material, bi-dimensional support. As much as the parameters are controlled through the input entered into the computer, the output form is not a direct result of our bodily actions. It "appears" as a calculated and perhaps surprising product, not visually related to the operations that generated it. The layers of data mediation are, in this case multiplied in such a way that the process conceals direct visual relation between the realities at stake (the observed and the imagined).

A radical approach to drawing is proposed by Mathew Barney. In his on-going series entitled *Drawing Restraint* that he began in 1987, drawing performances are developed following the concept of the PATH, consisting of three categories: Situation, Condition and Production:

"Situation is the drive. It is a sexual energy without discipline and direction. It is described by a diagram of the male and female reproductive systems of a six-week-old developing foetus. The sex of the foetus remains undefined for the first seven weeks. 'Situation' is undifferentiated sexual energy, and is characterized by hunger and indiscriminate consumption.

Condition is the visceral funnel. 'Condition' disciplines the oral intake of Situation. In 'Condition' the undifferentiated field of sexual energy begins to take form. 'Condition' functions like the stomach, systematically breaking down the bolus ingested by 'Situation', nourishing and encouraging growth.

Production is the anal output of the path. 'Production' is described by the form of the two-headed dumbbell called the unit BOLUS. The unit BOLUS has the potential to close the three phase PATH, joining the mouth of 'Situation' with the anus of 'Production', enabling a meditation on an endless loop between desire and discipline."[1]

Source!

1 Mathew Barney, in ‚Schaulager-Hefte' series, Laurenz Foundation, Schaulager Basel, 2010

1.c Processing the real. Translations.

Drawing one. Imitation and imagination

The act of imitating is one that characterizes human beings. Many things that we learn as humans and as a species grow from mimetic force. In child development, mechanisms of imitation play an important role. We imitate and at the same time we develop our imagination as an emancipation of this same mechanism. In our daily life (as opposed to our dream life), we stretch the possibilities of imitation in order to find distance between ourselves and the imitating gesture. This distance can only be reached with time and culture, it is not a given and yet, one can only measure freedom when compared to a reference frame that finds itself within the imitation game.

The exercise of imitation does not necessarily call for fidelity to the model and can find its more performative form in what Walter Benjamin has described as *license* or *freedom from the original.* Imitation actually needs imagination. What imagination opens up is a route of translation between the imitated and the imitation. Confronted with the impossibility of copying with literal fidelity what we want to reproduce, we need to abstract and imagine slightly differently what we see. We are thus using our translational power, which is, again, our imagination: To express in another media what we see. The mechanism is complex since it goes through a diversity of perceptual tools and has to travel from vision, complex in itself, through the mind's own, to the recording moment when the pencil touches the paper. Mimetics build up as a long personal history of perception. We build our own culture of perception, and our perception on reproduction of what we have perceived. Memory can be considered as a mimetic tool, one that puts a constant effort in creating a catalogue of what we have seen, heard, touched, tasted, read, etc., as if curating a museum from continuous recordings. Drawing works within this mimetic mechanism, as a tool to record.

Drawing two. Text

Drawing is one of the oldest forms of human expression. Not only human, though: First ochre semi-figurative lines show the capacities of the Neanderthal species to transform their environmental impressions into a graphic and symbolic form: Mainly geometrical shapes and drawing-like figurations of animals. Drawing has proved to be at the origins of writing or a proto-writing form. In fact, this impulse towards symbolic transfiguration precedes by far the existence of architecture or any will for shelter construction by the Neanderthals or the Homo sapiens.

These first line drawings (commonly regarded as paintings or parietal art) are of great interest for our purpose. It is hardly possible to investigate the imaginative abilities of the Neanderthal and Homo sapiens to project unknown phenomena. We do not know how these drawings could reflect prospective thinking. We have therefore to look at these drawings concerning their everyday lives. They were thus made and used in order to comprehend and record what was around them, or even for a third purpose, to share collectively their experiences of hunting and confronting themselves with nature. The drawings may also have had another function, to help create a collective realm and to initiate fiction, or stories to be shared through the establishment of common graphic standards within a group. As if compared to writing, this speaks of the very communicative essence of drawing. Pictograms may have allowed the Neanderthals to embrace their environment and to cope with it collectively through the sharing of drawn symbols. The need for common signs was essential to the development of humans since their strength and distinction from other species was precisely the grouping of knowledge and know-how in large collective projects. This development could not be attained by individual exploits but rather through the *mise en commun* of their efforts – drawing may have, quite importantly, helped in the establishment of collective standards upon which communities developed.

Despite a common cradle found in pictograms, text and drawing divert quite importantly from each other. Drawing, as seen in the previous paragraphs, appears in the movement between figuration of perceptive moments and projective or prospective impulsion. Drawing maintains this essential power in all of the variety of forms it might appear, from diagrams and charts to observation drawings. It always needs an original to which to refer to – in imagination or physical reality. Drawing thus can never be an autonomous figure of representation. It sends us back and forth to other realities than the one presented in the drawing. In fact, cave paintings were clearly done in a mode, distant from the subjects that were drawn or painted and through a process of transposition. These first drawings were not direct imitations of nature. It was an art on its own, a form of art per se. '*Yet,* drawing *is a form. To comprehend it as a form, one must go back the original, for the laws governing the* drawing *lie within the original, contained in the issue of its translatability.*'

Drawing three. Translation

Walter Benjamin's *The task of the Translator* is a very significant essay related to creative thinking and making.[2] The complexity and accuracy of this short text develops a number of ideas that we think are crucial in order to embrace our subject.

2 Walter Benjamin. "Selectied Writings", Vol. 1 1913-1926
Edited by Marcus Bullock and Michael W. Jennings / THE BELKNAP PRESS OF HARVARD UNIVERSITY PRESS, 1996, Cambridge, Massachusetts, London, England
Original Text: Walter Benjamin: "Die Aufgabe des Übersetzers." In: ders. Gesammelte Schriften Bd. IV/1, S. 9-21. Frankfurt/Main 1972.

Translation as a form in itself questions the very core of art making and addresses the very question of how content is addressed to a given reader. It interrogates the transmission of content or meaning of a work of art and outlines how the different layers of conduction of content to a receiver are diverse and complex.

These layers evolve during the life (and 'afterlife' as Benjamin puts it, using several terms: Leben, Fortleben, Nachleben) and development of a work of art and can transform the transmission of meaning into mere communication when the evolution of a work of art limits itself to inform about the original content rather than to provide what Benjamin defines as a 'good translation'. Although Walter Benjamin refers specifically to writing and literature as an art form, we believe that the assumptions and conclusions of the essay are applicable to other forms.

In the last two sentences of the previous chapter we have taken the liberty to quote a passage from Walter Benjamin's text while replacing the word *translation* with *drawing* in order to present a hypothesis where drawing is regarded as a movement of translation. We will continue using quotes from this same text, punctually replacing the word *translation* with *drawing*. The idea is to test our main argument emphasizing the translational character of drawing.

Looking at drawing in this way, we focus with attention on the "translational" aspect of drawing. The prospective one appears more complex to analyze. Although the perceptive and the prospective are two sides of a single coin, when it comes to creative endeavors, we prefer to concentrate on drawing as a tool of translation between realities. First comes the relation to the original subject: In drawing something that we perceive, an existing subject exists before us and we want to capture it to some level, or at least to record its essence or a part of it. We want to be able, through the mediation of the drawing, to convey this captured essence to others, and so, to share our perception and experience. This relation is tense and acquires a complementary status in regard to the original. Furthermore, Benjamin states that it is only through this relation that a larger realm of the real can be attained. The true essence of the content or meaning lies in the complementary nature that exists between the original and its translation. The real would be the sum of the original added to all of the translations of it. This could not be more valid in the case of drawing. The complete reality of a particular subject lies between its physical existence and its recorded perception. All of the drawings of a singular tree plus the tree itself present the very essence of what that particular tree is, since what it is cannot be dissociated from how it is perceived.

The drawing travels, as we have shortly seen in the introduction, through the mechanisms of the perception of reality to translate a certain fact or original state into a perceived one. The notion of translatability is crucial here. The drawing owes as much to the skills of the artists as to the capacity of the subject to be translated (in our case, drawn). Our hypothesis is that some subjects possess more qualities than others in their translatability into drawing form. Here it might be useful to introduce the notions of "fidelity" and "license", as well as "imitation" and "freedom" of and from a subject.

"Translatability is an essential quality of certain works, which is not to say that it is essential for the works themselves that they be translated, it means, rather, that a specific significance inherent to the original manifests itself in its translatability".[3] The capacity of a subject to be translated into drawing form parallels the ability of the artist to actually draw the subject. This ability does not reside in his or her skills to produce resemblances. According to Benjamin, simulation is an inadequate vehicle to attain the core of the original subject, to echo or vibrate with the original in order to complement it and to reach its global meaning and essence. Again we take the liberty to replace 'translation' by 'drawing': *"Drawings do not so much serve the works as owe their existence to it. In them the life of the original attains its latest, continually renewed, and most complete unfolding." "One can demonstrate that no drawing would be possible if in its ultimate essence it strove for likeness of the original."*[4]

Pure figuration is explicitly not at stake in this process. A good drawing is not reliant solely on its imitative qualities. On the contrary, it can take away its capacity to inherently bear the meaning of the translated "original" as the content should be able to be extracted from the drawn form. A drawing does not need to be faithful to its original in its formal representation. By mere fidelity it will not necessarily pass through the meaningfulness of it. This is a crucial point in the comprehension of any art form since it raises the intense and historical debate of figuration in art. What Benjamin proposes, without explicitly referring to abstraction, is that imitation of the real is not essential to the transmission of meaning in a work of art. This assumption opens immediately to non-figurative forms of figuration. The very physical gesture of drawing is thus not constrained to resemblance. It will find its essence in the "echoing" or 'resonance' of the original rather and how this echo is constituted. Thus, it is an open question which touches issues of technicality, culture, practice and perception. Kokoschka's color pencil drawings never imitate the colors and shadows of the physical world or even the forms but provide a perception of them: his own. In this marriage of the physical world and the perception of it by an artist, a more profound meaning of the perceived world and its relation to art can be encountered.

Mathew Barney's *Drawing Restraint* has developed around the idea of drawing as a result of a pure experience. The artist puts himself in conditions

3 ibid
4 ibid

restraining his physical possibilities to actually draw, putting himself in what could be considered athletic situations to actually perform the art. The result is purely Benjaminian in the sense that it uniquely reproduces uniquely the lived moment as a pure result of a number of actions determined by the conditioned environment. The gesture is the drawing as much as it is the situation.

Drawing pursues the life of perceived objects, environments or situations and moves them into other spheres. It provokes a passageway and transports realities into other realities, yet always maintaining a certain kinship to the initial subject. The latter is thus stretched in its form and content and depending on historical and cultural contexts its comprehension evolves, making drawing a constitutive fragment of cognitive evolution.

In the profession, as in education, these processes are imbedded in coded social forms of production. The aim of this essay is not to reconstruct the entire array of tools and processes as they are taught and practiced today. What we will try to pinpoint is a crucial momentum that sits in practices of planning, modeling and projecting: The very moment that ideas are translated from one medium into another, and in particular from the realm of the mind into physical output.

2.a Drawing and Time

In her short essay *Architectonic disposition: ichnography, scenography, orthography*, posted on her blog *monas oikos nomos* on February 20th in 2016, Vera Bühlmann suggests an entirely new reading of key concepts of architectural drawing. She states that "[Vitruvius'] dedicated aim of gathering all the distributed knowledge in architecture has been to generalize from local customs and the ethical/religious meanings attributed to the built works, and to propose rules and conceptual distinctions for addressing and critically evaluating „the establishment of public order" in a manner that can preserve the built environment's „worth".[5]

It can be argued that today the 'worth' of the built environment is still an expression of a ‚public', or at least of a common order. The environment that is the expression of this order is a palimpsest [André Corboz, 1983]. In the European context this palimpsest has incorporated history over centuries, whether continuous history, in a few places with hardly any ruptures such as Zurich, or with major scissions, brought on by wars, earthquakes, conflagrations, or epidemics. This continuous development has seen moments of explosion in the second half of the 20th century. If it is a myth that the living human population has reached a greater size than those who have ever lived since the dawn of

5 Vera Bühlmann. "Architectonic disposition: ichnography, scenography, orthography"
Blog post on monasandnomos.org, posted on February 20 by VERABUEH, 2016 accessed on October 10th, 2017

humanity, this is true for our building stock. In Switzerland, buildings and infrastructure built since 1950 far outnumber all construction from times before. Based on the above statement it can be said that, if the distributed knowledge embodied in the built stock is an expression of our order, we can evaluate it by how well it suits our environment and ourselves as humans. There is today a common consensus, if contested by a few, that our environment has been suffering as result of techno-centric paradigms based on quantitative criteria, aiming first and foremost at short term gain. In terms of space we experience ever-increasing infrastructures of flows, hermetic surfaces, segregated neighborhoods and often less and less porosity between diverting forms of activities or life.

With the quantifiable and the accessibility to data at all times and in any place we have also seen a change in our behavior in respect to knowledge, and even more importantly concerning our capacities to imagine. Policies today seem to imply that messages have to be crafted so as to make the world easier to understand, with no gaps for questions or interpretations, separating the good from the bad, the known from the other, and the us from the them. Simple messages pretend to objectify and break down complex situations to simple 'facts'. There is a broad consensus that, as situations are complex and difficult to comprehend, it suits us well to break them down into objects, separated from one another, focusing on their specific purpose. This is easy to sell and communicate. In the built realm, an architecture of objects is soothing for simple aspirations. However, if our environment asks us to review our paradigms and the way we have chosen to construct our societies and our world, we have to admit that we must review the procedures and the tools that we employ in our ventures for any future transformations and constructions.

In the early 1920s Man Ray discovered a new technique. By accident he turned on the light in the darkroom, forgetting he had a photo-paper lying on the counter. Not wanting to waste the paper, he developed it. Thus he came across the photogram technique, already used in 1839 by William Henry Fox Talbot, who had actually made some of the first photographic images. Man Ray called it the Rayograph. With fascination he observed how an everyday object and light itself started to reveal unseen figurations, emanating from light and enigmatic spatiality, hovering somewhere between 3-dimensional space and the 2-dimensional surface of the photo-paper, a space of mysterious depth and evocative as a dream. Man Ray was delighted: This allowed him to further the techniques with which he approached his investigations into the worlds of the unconscious and of imagination. In particular because the non-perspectival space that appears to literally flow from the Rayographs seemed to offer new ways to articulate his ideas. A non-perspectival space beyond a fixed moment in time.

Man Ray named his first Rayographs '*Champs Délicieux*,' in French, a language hardly known to him at the time. It was 1922.

The problem at stake is a question of translation, both in observing and projecting. In architecture and spatial planning, the realization of a work is not that immediate. Long technological and societal processes are necessary for constructing even a small space or building. If a painter articulates a figure through a gesture of applying a paintbrush onto a canvas, her act produces an immediate reality. The trace on the canvas is the direct result of a physical action in space. And the gesture as a trace, together with the material employed, i.e. the paint and the canvas, become the work. If Jasper Johns decides to relate his gestures to gravity, in turning the canvas into the horizontal, he employs dripping and gravitational forces to accentuate gesture and trace. The work again will embody this situation as an immediate reality. However, if the architect is drawing a line, a sketch, a plan, builds a model, or describes her idea in words, in a film or in a poem, these elements or results of her production are situated in-between – between the realities of her ideas, and those of a conceivable future space or architecture. Temporalities are different, the tools are different and the conceptual consequences are necessarily different. This implies a series of consequences that are fundamental in respect to how we are able to imagine space and act on it.

The account here will be highly generalized. Philosophers, theoreticians, art historians and others have elaborated on the question of cultural meaning and the existential implications at stake in the context of architectural representation and tools. For the purpose of this essay we highlight here four terms, not with the intention of situating them epistemologically in history and cultures, but rather to evaluate their capacity in respect to the production of space and that of architecture. The four terms can be grouped in two pairs or be treated individually. They are the Conceptual and the Physical, and the Virtual and the Immediate.

To begin we will take a look at a first term, the Virtual. Gilles Deleuze, referring to Marcel Proust, uses the term of 'virtual' to hint at aspects of reality that are ideal, yet nonetheless real. As such, the Virtual becomes a concept that is able to travel between realities and therefore will have impact on our cognitive capacities. As to one of its definitions, the aspect of the 'as if' or of simulation is able to create sensations that ask us to evaluate the aspects of some of the properties of an imagined condition, not yet there, yet virtually present. We are here by no means only referring to the virtual, as in 'virtual reality', but to any situation where aspects of the real appear as anything other than immediate physical form. Any simulation, including models can as such become a mode of creating virtual experiences. Accordingly, Deleuze opposes the Virtual not to the real but to the Actual. However, the Virtual is an effect that can be produced by actual causal interactions on the material level. As such the computer screen produces a window that is based on technological processes on a material level, yet as a window it is not actually there. The Virtual is also a potentiality; it can become fulfilled in the Actual. For our context, what is important is exactly that the *staging of potentialities* is fundamental in the processes engaged in the imagination of space. If we refer to the example of the Rayographs, the images they produce of the object as reversed shadows, they keep the virtual image of the object as a memory, yet also open up the possibility of seeing this object in 'another way' or even as another object entirely. Importantly the space that is activated by the object itself, the kind of aura of light, keeps the spatial configuration in suspense, full of potentialities of spaces to be imagined therein.

If we now look at the Immediate, I will choose to consider the Immediate first is by its negation. In German the term *unmittelbar* means that something is actuated without any further means, 'mittelbar' itself (without the 'un') stands for 'mediated through other means than itself'. ('Mittel' remains much more general than the English term, meaning basically 'means'.) The negation of 'immediate' is also in English affirmative. However, it may not be a coincidence that we may often use the phrasing 'not immediate' rather than 'mediate'. Simply because many seem today inclined to think that things and messages are direct and clear, rather than mediated and to be translated and interpreted – that immediacy is a factual condition of all realities. Language tells us otherwise.

In temporal terms immediacy excludes longer periods of time or lapses in reaction. The *immediacy of the gestures* mentioned above in the case of Jackson Pollock creates a nearly perfect temporal union of intention, act, and trace. The result is a work of immanence of correlated meaning and physical presence. Even though recent research in cognitive sciences tells us that there is a slight delay that can be measured between the will to do something and the gesture of it actually happening, we could say that intention, the gesture performing it, and the resulting physical output coincide in Jackson Pollock's work to the utmost degree, both in time and in meaning. Daniel Zamarbide argues in his text, '*Great Apes never built Houses*' that humans may have in fact started to articulate space through gestures in painting, rather than by actually building houses (see All About Space II). In Man Ray's Rayographs the analogy is there, too. At the moment that the light hits the object, and then split-nanoseconds thereafter the photo paper, the immediacy is in the situation of the set up. No intermediary technology, no optics or physics other than the light itself interacts with space and object. One could argue that in a certain sense the photogram portrays the real much more imminently and precisely. The material world is exposed directly, literally: It is only chemicals at work. Time is there, in the length of the exposure and in the distances it has traveled between object and paper, bouncing back and forth. If the visual content is not immediacy as such, the Rayograph still embodies light and the absence of the objects involved in its paper in form of the traces recorded by the chemicals.

Through the Immediate we approach the Physical, or the material world. The compressed moments that we spoke about before engage in the physical world and depend on means of the mind and of time. Crucial in our context is the close relationship that our two examples from the art world maintain between immediacy and the bodily and chemical processes they engage in the physical world. Yet both cases open up a space in the mind that is not fixed and remains open. We could argue that what makes them partially more abstract, makes them also more concrete. In their acts they interact more directly with a physical world rather than with that of simulation or representation.

We suggest to use the term 'Physical' here in its sense of not being of the mind, of having material properties that can be accounted for. In consequence, the Physical refers *also* to that other part of what we define as real: It can be measured. It can be referred to in quantities or absence thereof. In a Rayograph, the Physical can relate both to the material properties of all elements involved, including the chemical reactions and the light causing effects, as well as the overall operational processes that are implied in the production of a Rayograph. The technical aspects form a set of rules that demand action according to material properties. Material and gravitational properties condition in the same manner Pollock's drip paintings. Their physicality literally embodies the material and processual properties that are at play in the action of painting and of being painted.

The Physical, the Virtual, the Immediate; all these terms are concepts. If, in their action or properties, they belong to a more or a less physical state of the real, one of their fundamental properties is that they are figures of the mind, elements with which we construct our thoughts and beliefs. A conception is a specific way to understand a given set of circumstances. The concept is the diagram that we make from it. According to the Oxford dictionary definition, a concept is "An idea or mental image which corresponds to some distinct entity or class of entities, or to its essential features, or determines the application of a term (especially a predicate), and thus plays a part in the use of reason or language." Etymologically, "concept" refers back to the Latin *conceptum*, "something conceived".

Concepts play a key role in cognitive sciences. To reiterate: Concepts are the elements of the construction of our understanding of the world.

Conceptions are readings, and therefore always interpretations of situations in the world. Did Pollock first craft the concept of drip painting, thinking time and again how to go about it, how to make the action happen? Or did he discover it in making, similar to Man Ray, who would only conceptualize the Rayograph once he had discovered it? We don't know. What is important for our purposes is the aspect of transformation: the idea that concepts are translations from one reality into another. As such, they are "reflective", mentally and metaphorically, mediate and not immediate. They imply a delay in time, creating interstices in cognition. They build conceived and perceived realities. In gaps and intervals they open up to potentialities to be activated by our *Vorstellungskraft* (the capacity to make vivid, in front of our inner eyes, the power of imagination) to form for ourselves an *imago*. We believe that in these gaps, in the small and longer delays that are at play in the four concepts of the Virtual, the Immediate, the Physical and the Conceptual (sometimes in varying double pairs), a spatial dimension opens up, a "*Denkraum*", where we will be able to conceive of *space beyond the object*.

The concepts of architectural drawing that Vera Bühlmann refers to in the initial quote are *Ichnographia*, *Orthographia* and *Scaenographia*, Importantly she cites them not as representational tools. She emphasizes: "Vitruv foresees *three dimensions of conception* [author's emphasis], which we know today as ground plan, elevation and perspective. He [Vitruvius] calls these three dimensions of conception *Orthographia* (the natural, potential elements, in renaissance: elevation), *Ichnographia* (the contraction of the potentiabilities of these elements, in renaissance: floorplan) and *Scaenographia* (the operation of contracting, in renaissance: perspective or 3 dimensional plan)."[6] We will come back to these concepts further down. For the time being, let's just add one further quote. In a similar manner to what has been said above about the seemingly simple nature of the object as a graspable and self-sufficient (or even autarkic) entity of reality, in particular when compared to the complex nature of space itself, Vera Bühlmann states: "If Vitruv's triad of architectonic disposition could be demonstrated in a generalized form, then [...] it might provide orientation in how to generalize again from the numerous spreading out of disciplines that fall victim to increasing local seclusion, hermeticism, and what could be called a certain banality of highly technical specialization without systemic overview. Might the conceptual apparatus that constitutes architecture as a *profession* (rather than as an art or as a science) provide a model of how to preserve the "worth" of the public order that is embodied in knowledge?."[7]

6 ibid
7 ibid

2.b *Denkraum*

In his seminal text *The Agency of Mapping*, James Corner quotes Gilles Deleuze and Félix Guattari: "What distinguishes the map from the tracing is that it is entirely oriented toward an experimentation in contact with the real. The map does not reproduce an unconscious closed in upon itself; it constructs the unconscious. It fosters connections between fields, the removal of blockages on bodies without organs, the maximum opening of bodies without organs onto a plane of consistency ... The map has to do with performance, whereas the tracing always involves an 'alleged competence.'"[8] Corner continues: "The distinction here is between mapping as equal to what is ('tracing') and mapping as equal to what is *and* to what is not yet. In other words, the unfolding agency of mapping is most effective when its capacity for description also sets the conditions for new eidetic and physical worlds to emerge. Unlike tracings, which propagate redundancies, mappings discover new worlds within past and present ones; they inaugurate new grounds upon the hidden traces of a living context."[9]

Drawing has seen a continuous decline in the professions that are responsible for planning our environments. In the belief that 3D and BIM-modeling will provide all the necessary information, the classical set of correlated elements of information such as plan, section and elevation have become more and more disregarded. In this process, a lot of the fundamental potentials that reside in drawing as a technique and as tool to stage imagination have been sacrificed. This is true for mapping as much as for architectural practice. J. B. Harley argues: "One effect of accelerated technological change — as manifest in digital cartography and geographical information systems — has been to strengthen its positivist assumptions and [to breed] a new arrogance in geography about its supposed value as a mode of access to reality. If it is true that new fictions of factual representation are daily being foisted upon us, then the case for introducing a social dimension into modern cartography is especially strong. Maps are too important to be left to cartographers alone."[10]

In this part of the text we will focus on the ways that drawing and modes of drawing operate on our thinking and on our imagination. And we will refer back to how a set of correlating systematic and structured codes, can serve as an exploratory field.

If we look at how we can conceive of *Ichnographia*, we see parallels in what Deleuze and Guattari refer to as mapping. As opposed to a simple plan of an object, the ichnographic drawing is concerned with space, with disposition and distribution. In his dictionary of Antiquities of the late 19th century,

8 James Corner, "The Agency of Mapping: Speculation, Critique and Invention." In *Mappings*, edited by Denis Cosgrove. 213-52. London: Reaktion, 1999.

9 ibid

10 J. B. Harley, 'Deconstructing the Map', Carthographica, Volume 26 Issue 2, 1989

Anthony Rich defines *Ichnographia* as follows: "A *chart*, *map* or *ground plan*, made in outline by architects and surveyors for the workmen to build by, or as a map of reference, (Vitruv, 1.2.2).The annexed engraving affords a specimen of Roman mapping from a plan of the city engaged upon slabs of marble, originally forming the pavement of the temple of Romulus and Remus; many fragments of which are preserved in the Capitol. It is supposed to have been executed in the age of Septimus Severus, and when entire, afforded a complete guide to the city, in which every street, house and public edifice was laid down in its proper place, and in sufficient detail to show its gound-plot and architectural design, together with the name of each inscribed upon it."

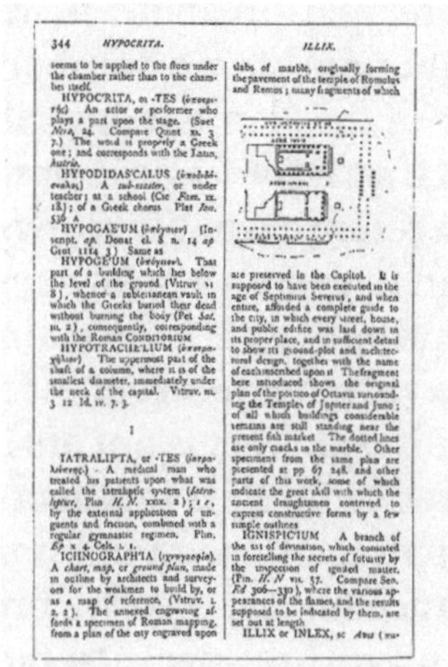

344 *HYPOCRITA.* *ILLIX.*

seems to be applied to the floes under the chamber rather than to the chamber itself.

HYPOCRITA, or -TES. An actor or performer who plays a part upon the stage. (Suet *Nero*, 24. Compare Quint. xi. 3. 7.) The word is properly a Greek one; and corresponds with the Latin *histrio*.

HYPODIDASCALUS. A *sub-master*, or under teacher; at a school (Cic *Fam.* ix. 18); of a Greek chorus. Plat *Ion.* 536 A.

HYPOGAEUM. (Inscript. *ap.* Donat. cl. 8 n. 14 *ap.* Grut. 1114 3.) Same as

HYPOGEUM. That part of a building which lies below the level of the ground (Vitruv. vi. 8), whence a subterranean vault in which the Greeks buried their dead without burning the body (Pet. *Sat.* iii. 2), consequently, corresponding with the Roman CONDITORIUM.

HYPOTRACHELIUM. The uppermost part of the shaft of a column, where it is of the smallest diameter, immediately under the neck of the capital. Vitruv. iii. 3. 12. Id. iv. 7. 3.

I

IATRALIPTA, or -TES. A medical man who treated his patients upon what was called the iatraliptic system (*Iatraliptice*, Plin. *H. N.* xxix. 2); i.e., by the external application of unguents and friction, combined with a regular gymnastic regimen. Plin. *Ep.* x. 4. Cels. i. 1.

ICHNOGRAPHIA. A *chart*, *map*, or *ground plan*, made in outline by architects and surveyors for the workmen to build by, or as a map of reference, (Vitruv. i. 2. 2). The annexed engraving affords a specimen of Roman mapping from a plan of the city engraved upon slabs of marble, originally forming the pavement of the temple of Romulus and Remus; many fragments of which are preserved in the Capitol. It is supposed to have been executed in the age of Septimius Severus, and when entire, afforded a complete guide to the city, in which every street, house, and public edifice was laid down in its proper place, and in sufficient detail to show its ground-plot and architectural design, together with the name of each inscribed upon it. The fragment here introduced shows the original plan of the portico of Octavia surrounding the Temples of Jupiter and Juno; of all which buildings considerable remains are still standing near the present fish market. The dotted lines are only cracks in the marble. Other specimens from the same plan are presented at pp. 67, 248, and other parts of this work, some of which indicate the great skill with which the ancient draughtsmen contrived to express constructive forms by a few simple outlines.

IGNISPICIUM. A branch of the art of divination, which consisted in foretelling the secrets of futurity by the inspection of ignited matter. (Plin. *H. N.* vii. 57. Compare Sen. *Ed.* 306–330), where the various appearances of the flames, and the results supposed to be indicated by them, are set out at length.

ILLIX or INLEX, sc. *Avis* (ru-

Anthony Rich, B.A., "A Dictionary of Roman and Greek Antiquities, London Longmans, Green & Co., 1874

This definition makes clear that we are considering the "situatedness" of the elements of built space, considering of "each element, its form and its placement".

For the time being, following Vera Bühlmann's suggestion, we take the drawing for granted as a "conception" rather than a "representation". Now consider the operation that we are engaging in when we read a map or a plan. We are looking at lines, at figures, projected onto a two-dimensional surface, either virtually in digital space on a screen, or on a sheet of paper. We decipher figures and lines as matter and non-matter, as outlines of space defining walls, demarcations of streets, details in view from above, material qualities. According to time and culture the drawing may be more or less coded. Colors, hatches, line thicknesses, inserts, names, legends, transparencies etc. may refer to other realities than only what can be depicted in projection: To events, conditions, movements, fluctuating quantities etc. The deciphering of codes is one part of the operation. At the same time there is a foundational set of information that we can read without prior knowledge of a code. In our culture we have learned from a certain age onwards to picture the world from above, and we can decipher rivers, streets, or buildings.

It is however of a particular mental capacity, and requires an intellectual labor, to project ourselves as being immersed into such information. The transition to what this two-dimensional information might mean for actual experience requires an effort of transcribing the figure seen flat into an englobing situation. We have to *immerse ourselves mentally into the experienced in space*, to "picture" ourselves in there. However, the line that we see on the two-dimensional surface does not necessarily hold information about its vertical extension. In fact, codes, such as contour lines, or quantitative numbers can provide a systematic account, yet the actual 'height' of the element described is not visible. It is hidden in the third dimension, and if strictly vertical, not able to be depicted in projection. Our mind will have to refer to what it knows or to what it imagines. Accordingly, the reading of a plan or map is also always an act of interpretation. The meaning of what a map contains as information in space is at the same time an act of conception: I will have to reconstruct in front of my inner eye what the drawing is showing me. And, as this act is not entirely determinable, it is necessarily also an act of interpretation. This intellectual operation of reading, interpreting and imagining a spatial situation upon the reading of an ichnographic drawing is of utter importance for any creative process that engages with the imagination of any given and future space. In fact, the ichnographic drawing opens here a gap here, between what is and what a situation could become: A space of and for imagination. Conception in retrospect can here be simultaneous with conception in prospect. This is how I read Bühlmann's "contracted" description of what she reads as Vitruvius' concept of *Ichnographia*: "the contraction of the potentiabilities of these [natural, potential] elements"

"The plotted lines, issued from this systematic process, contain time more eternally – delineations shaping situations, accessibility, exclusions. Space defining elements facilitate movements, gravitationally, on surfaces. Or pose barriers – here traced lines on a paper – to access, to view, to warmth, to cold, to odors, to a smiling face. The plan offers an endless field of potential situations. It holds them as a simultaneous plateau of past, present and futures moments, traced and contracted into a 2-dimensional surface. Contractions take time and care, they can be convulsive, too, mentally. Equally in their construction as traces on paper. We are confronted with a plan that projects a contract of delineations of open and closed potentialities into space, into the city, into the land."[11] In architecture, to conceive of spatial dimensions, we engage in an iterative process, where we employ operations just as described again and again.

11 confer to page …. Dieter Dietz, Zurich, A Drawing in Words

We will read lines on a page or on a screen, and read them with their potentials of what they are and what they might become. The plan evades the deadlock of what orbiting around objects in 3D models may do to our imagination.

While keeping in mind the space of imagination that has just emanated from the ichnographic two-dimensional surface of the plan, let us continue our observations: *Ichnographia* is not a standalone concept. It is complimented by *Orthographia* and *Scaenographia*. Classically, we understand *Orthographia* as elevations and sections that compliment the plan. Looking at a section or an elevation we understand proportions, and we recognize elements more directly than in plan. We are for instance used to looking at a human face in its vertical position. A person in plan, unless lying down, is not easily recognizable. Likewise for a tree or a building. Orthographic projections somehow seem to relate more immediately to our perception of the world. And yet, as there is no foreshortening, it lets us comprehend proportion and relations precisely. In orthographic projection we are able to understand the human dimension. It allows us to conceive of interrelated bodily existence and environment:

"Ichnographic drawing contracts elements into hyper-real, yet highly abstract notations of lines. The orthographic drawing shows natural and artificial elements in relative height and in reference to their gravitational location, often anchored into topography. They appear in profile, enunciating their relative proportions, in themselves and towards the world. Ultimately they reference our body, exclude or include human activity and behavior, stand with or beyond us. In movement their relative height will constantly be revealed, concealed, or diverted. Shifting foregrounds and panning positions will continuously engage spatial experience in respect to movement and sensorial perception of space, less visual than engaged by our proprioception – visceral. Relations between artificial and natural elements emanate as potential spatial experience and existence. The laughing eyes that were hidden behind the wall just a moment ago, I see them now, as I have moved side-wards, as has she, our gazes crossing diagonally."[12]

For our purpose, what counts most is the selective aspect of orthographic projection. As opposed to *Ichnographia*, which could potentially encompass everything, as in Borges' tale of the map of the territory, orthographic projection will always create layerings where foreground may hinder the visibility of what is behind. Furthermore, its relationship to the ichnographic drawing is not entirely fixed. If descriptive geometry since Monge implies an entirely systematic referencing system in order to have full control over coordinates in space at all times, the concepts of *Ichnographia* and *Orthographia* remain more openly related. In fact, that gap that opens up from the plan drawing as an interval of interpretation and imagination, is not closed here. Unlike a 3D-syn-

12 ibid

thesizer that will never allow for ambiguities of where a specific element is located in the virtual 3D-space, *Ichnographia* and *Orthographia*, even if correlated, will still leave that space open. We can interpret further spatial configurations, already more articulated as our first imagination in plan may have suggested, but still open for countless iterations and interpretations. Actively we can work on them, as we draw possible sections from a given plan. *The elements of* Ichnographia *and* Orthographia *are rendered in profile to one another, rather than to a fixed frame of reference.* In *Orthographia* we engage profiles in mutual interrelation to their situation in space and amongst one another. The orthographic drawing portrays possible characters of spatial environments.

The *Scaenographia* can now be interpreted both as an output of the "before" operations of contracting and positioning, or as an origin. It animates the operations of contracting and de-contracting, of delineating and articulating, of erasing and opening up in an iterative and on-going process.

Here, the quality of the drawing as a material practice that relates activities of the mind with those of the hand becomes manifest. As not-yet-contracted elements, space-defining architecture can be experimented with consequential and imaginative lines on paper. It puts into perspective perceived and conceived space to become part of a first actuation that is visual.

Man Ray's Rayographs allow for a further analogy. The objects that have deviated and animated the light on its way to the paper are in fact objects of full actuality, yet have disappeared completely from perspectival space in the photogram. In the surprise that hovers between recognition and wonder when guessing the actual situation that led to the photogram, we connect what we see to the two-dimensional horizontal surface that was the state of the photo paper during the making of the Rayograph, The objects standing on that surface activate the space between. Where they have been standing, only indistinguishable white appears. The rays of light that sculpted space on paper leaves us guessing at the profiles that belong to the now absent objects. We would have to complete in our imagination the emerging possible configuration by the objects that were there, if we chose to do so.

We have been considering the architectonic disposition of a correlated set of drawing concepts for some length now, carefully making sure not to use too often the ubiquitous term 'representation'. Direct translations often fall short in grasping the concepts and notions that reside in one single term in another language. I will give here a personal reading: The Kantian notions of *Anschauung* and *Vorstellung* for instance, are very sensitive to translate. *Anschauung* is often translated in English and French as "intuition", which holds in the original German an aspect which intuition does not necessarily reflect: *Anschauen* as a verb also means "looking at", but not in terms of watching, but in a condition of being vis-à-vis, *en face*, implying that my position in the act is relevant. In *Anschauung* there is therefore always an active act, which engages not simply a sensorial apparatus, but that situates that apparatus in my body consciously, in myself as a person.

In drawing *we do actively take a position vis-à-vis* the drawing. It will speak to us, *en face*. As we are engaging with it, it will become an active partner in the process of conceiving and perceiving. The drawing is able to provide scaffolding for our imagination. As a set of concepts it will open up a space for active imagination.

It is equally difficult to translate a further Kantian term: *Vorstellung*. French and English will often propose "representation". If we would go about it literally, *sich vorstellen* could be translated as "to set up something in front of us", "to stage" perhaps. Taking it slightly further we could also say "to make vivid in front of your inner eye". Another term that translates the German *Vorstellung* is "imagination", going back to the Latin word *imago*, which holds the idea of an image that we make ourselves. In reverse, one possible German translation for "imagination" is *Vorstellungskraft*, the "power to make vivid in front of your inner eye". This power of imagination is to be employed rigorously in acts of perceiving and conceiving the world. It does not come from the outside, as the term "representation" may imply.

It is therefore of utter importance that we do not fall into the trap of creating deadlocks for imagination. Drawings on a two-dimensional surface, allowing us to measure and to explore measure, are powerful auxiliaries to our main and absolutely fundamental tool: Imagination itself. We have to do everything to allow it to breathe, to host it, to welcome it, to give it space, to feed it and to let it speak to us. And to learn to listen to it. Bühlmann interprets Michel Serres' reflections on the concepts of *Ichnographia*, *Orthographia* and *Scaenographia* in *Le Système de Leibniz et ses Modèles Mathématiques* with the conclusion that to Serres it is not mathematics that governs all these aspects of reality (perception, liberty, consciousness, creation, remembering etc.). Instead, he assumes that "there is no relation of cause and effect here, there is a parallelism of structure."[13]

Surprisingly, the power of the concepts of drawing architectonics have been disregarded ever more in the advancements of quantitative approaches to space and the world. Today they seem consumed almost entirely in technophile fascination for computer 3D or BIM-modeling. We could hypothesize whether the output of ever-more hermetic buildings and environments is not related to this same tendency: To a reduction to simplistic frames of reference and to a more and more exclusive reign of mono-functional quantitative models.

13 Vera Bühlmann.
Blog post on monasandnomos.org, posted on February 20 by VERABUEH, 2016 accessed on October 10th, 2017

If we argue that the spaces that open up for imagination between interpretations, between correlated sets of information, of models, of sets of drawings, of poems, (and yes, also of spreadsheets of data), in intervals of time and space, and in particular in gaps of not knowing and ambiguity, that these spaces in fact provide room to think, to hesitate, to wonder, to pretend or to simply be curious, we could then state that this room may well be crucial for our existence. And we have to foster it with all we have, as it is certainly upon this premise that our futures rely.

While Man Ray was experimenting with his first Rayographs, Aby Warburg began work on his Atlas Mnemosyne. Using panels of roughly 150 x 250cm, he started to compile visual information from his extensive archives. In arranging and rearranging reproductions of renaissance paintings and relating material in specific configurations, correlating them to an array of constantly evolving criteria, he set out to build a panorama of meaning that may have well been closer to the original intentions of their authors than the other scholarly methods from the time had surmised. Looking at gestures expressing emotions, and criteria that he referred to as "Pathos Formula", he established entirely new orders of thought and content. He referred to the orders offered by the Atlas, not as new dogmatic findings, but instead suggested the concept of a *Denkraum*, a tool that works as a room-of-thought and room-to-think. Endless configurations can be mounted here, in front of our inner eyes, and actuated *en face*, present to our visual perception.

In fact, the structure of the Atlas, correlating the different sources and resources in a systematic yet 'open' set, accentuates the potential of multiple associations and analogies. Accordingly, potentials are multiplied and not confined to linear causal reference. I would argue that this specific arrangement and systematic spatial disposition allows for the argument of a parallel structure. Similar to the arrangement of 'natural' elements, a new potential appears *between things, rather than within themselves only.* This potential can be comprehended only if put into spatial situations. The Atlas Mnemosyne does so. Every change and possible reconfiguration can create a new meaning and space of thought: *Denkraum*. In a very literal and parallel analogy, the ichnographic drawing used as a projective tool does a similar thing. It correlates elements of potentials in space and activates gravitational fields of meaning, spatial definitions of enclosures or openness, to be apprehended in living the space between them. In a further iteration of that thought, this will not be confined to the situations of elements in space such as, for instance, buildings and trees, but also to all the interiors that we live in: Floors, walls, interstices, thresholds, windows, all will be of a similar register: Here more related to proprioception, to verticality and our body's movement in space, than to a visual horizon perceptible in the landscape.

Importantly therefore, an ichnographic drawing will not only depict exterior spaces or elements as solids in space: It will also trace the practicable space as a system of continuities and ruptures, of visibilities and obscurities, of barriers and accessibilities.

This is the architectonics of a correlated system of parallel and structured drawings that are not bound in a fixed reference frame: Vitruvius' set of three conceptions opens up an endless space of thought, a *Denkraum*. We have inherited the *Denkraum* as a powerful tool, but it is about to disappear - unless we break the deadlocks that entirely fixed reference frames impose.

This *Denkraum* is in fact the playground of architectonic conception. It is able to activate our *Vorstellungskraft*, the power of imagination. To work with this very flexible and malleable space enables us to navigate between complex concepts without losing sight of the whole. In our complex world, such a tool should not to be neglected. The power of imagination, the *Vorstellungskraft* and the tools we need to scaffold it, are fundamental for our futures. We will depend on imagination to live beyond present day challenges that are closing in. We will need plenty of capacities of the body and of the mind to guide the technologies we have invented. We will need seas of potential to let us project vivid futures for the place in which we live. Unfortunately the powerful technologies that we have invented are for the most part not used to augment our capacities of imagination. But they could be. Just like drawing books for children, where everything is already outlined, ever more encompassing technologies of simulation remove us further from the incredible capacity of our minds and souls: To imagine the worlds that could be other, new, and perhaps not as self-destructive.

Introductory text by Man Ray for
Photographs by Man Ray: 105 Works, 1920–1934:

THE AGE OF LIGHT

In this age, like all ages, when the problem of the perpetuation of a race or class destruction of its enemies, is the all-absorbing motive of civilized society , it seems irrelevant and wasteful still to create works whose only inspirations are individual human emotion and desire. The attitude seems to be that one may be permitted a return to idyllic occupations only after meriting this return by solving the more vital problems of existence. Still, we know that the incapacity of race or class to improve itself is as great as its incapacity to learn from previous errors in history. All progress results from an intense individual desire to improve the immediate present, from an all-conscious sense of material insufficiency. In this exalted state, material action imposes itself and takes the form of revolution in one form or another. Race and class, like styles, then become irrelevant, while the emotion of the human individual becomes universal. For what can be more binding amongst beings than the discovery of a common desire? And what can be more inspiring to action than the confidence aroused by a lyric expression of this desire? From the first gesture of a child pointing to an object and simply naming it, but with a world of intended meaning, to the developed mind that creates an image whose strangeness and reality stirs our

subconscious to its inmost depths, the awakening of desire is the first step to participation and experience.
It is in the spirit of an experience and not of experiment that the following autobiographical images are presented. Seized in moments of visual detachment during periods of emotional contact, these images are oxidized residues, fixed by light and chemical elements, of living organisms. No plastic expression can ever be more than a residue of an experience. The recognition of an image that has tragically survived an experience, recalling the event more or less clearly, like the undisturbed ashes of an object consumed by flames, the recognition of this object so little representative and so fragile, and its simple identification on the part of the spectator with a similar personal experience, precludes all psychoanalytical classification or assimilation into an arbitrary decorative system. Questions of merit and of execution can always be taken care of by those who hold themselves aloof from even the frontiers of such experiences. For, whether a painter, emphasizing the importance of the idea he wishes to convey introduces bits of ready-made chromos alongside his handiwork, or whether another, working directly with light and chemistry, so deforms the subject as almost to hide the identity of the original, and creates a new form, the ensuing violation of the medium employed is the most perfect assurance of the author's convictions. A certain amount of contempt for the material employed to express an idea is indispensable to the purest realization of this idea.
Each one of us, in his timidity, has a limit beyond which he is outraged. It is inevitable that He [or she] who by concentrated application has extended this limit for himself, should arouse the resentment of those who have accepted conventions which, since accepted by all, require no initiative of application. And this resentment generally takes the form of meaningless laughter or of criticism, if not of persecution. But this apparent violation is preferable to the monstrous habits condoned by etiquette and estheticism.
An effort impelled by desire must also have an automatic or subconscious energy to aid its realization. The reserves of this energy within us are limitless if we will draw on them without a sense of shame or of propriety. Like the scientist who is merely a prestidigitator manipulating the abundant phenomena of nature and profiting by every so called hazard or law, the creator dealing in human values allows the subconscious forces to filter through him, colored by his own selectivity, which is universal human desire, and exposes to the light motives and instincts long repressed, which should form the basis of a confident fraternity. The intensity of this message can be disturbing only in proportion to the freedom that has been given to automatism or the subconscious self. The removal of inculcated modes of presentation, resulting in apparent artificiality or strangeness, is a confirmation of the free functioning of this automatism and is to be welcomed.
Open confidences are being made every day, and it remains for the eye to train itself to see them without prejudice or restraint.

MAN RAY

2.c *To Draw into Space*

If drawing is a space to aspire to DESIRE, a true and malleable *Denkraum*, is it then possible to conceive of a construct capable of enacting potentials in space, as the two-dimensional surface of paper does for the actions that pertain to drawing? Can we conceive of a three-dimensional canvas? And would this three-dimensional canvas allow us to project into further dimensions, as does the drawing on paper? If we could imagine and conceive such a three-dimensional canvas, could our gestures become space-defining actions, as were the first cave paintings? Could we project our gestures and signs into space as the first sounds began to vocalize expressions and thoughts? In allusion to the first plates of carved stone or the first rolls of papyrus, such a device will necessarily have a collective dimension, as has language. Tens of thousands of years ago hieroglyphs began to depict ideas and concepts. Thousands of years thereafter abstractions such as the alphabet have brought about further means to converge and differ. Hieroglyphs as a trans-vocal means, the Alphabet as a trans-lingual concept, each brought about revolutionary consequences based on their performative qualities.

Bodily existence however, differs from concepts that are of the mind. If we project an idea into space, we need to consider gravity. Structure is a means to comply with gravity – inevitable in fact, in the context of gravitational forces. Beyond the conceptual, we will constantly be confronted by physics, not in a linear manner, but rather at ever repeated instances. In conveying ideas beyond concepts and diagrams, we will have to imagine structures relating to gravity.

To consider a three-dimensional canvas is daring: It should retain all the basic characteristics of a conventional canvas. It should have a certain neutrality. It has to have a material dimension. It should be able to receive gestures or projections. And it should be able to transform itself entirely in terms of being consumed by the meaning or the purposes it will contain. If finally consumed, it will only be there as a support, as is the paper of a book.

These supports have been invented over and over again in history. The conception of the first poles of a tent, or the virtual grid projected by *cardo* and *decumanus* in the Roman settlements; these are examples of how we can conceive to scaffold concepts into gravitational space. Much further east, the Japanese concept of the *Ma* offers a model of how place is formed following basic principles that transcend the grid or linear structures in emerging negotiation between private and public. Common to those examples is their collective nature. They invent principles that allow us to convey ideas to others and to translate them from a conceptual existence into the material world. They aim at giving us the means to collectively venture through the transformation of ideas into tangible, livable situations or conditions – materially, socially, culturally, economically, spatially.

At an architectural scale, basic structural principles can take on this task. In history they are as much rooted in crafts as in theory. The tent, Laugier's hut, the Greek temple, Japanese carpentry, the European *Strickbau*, or more recently, the balloon frame and concrete or steel skeletons; these are all examples of how humankind has, since the beginning, been inventing principles to project ideas into gravitational space. We dare therefore, in direct analogy, to propose these principles as a metaphor, or as a meta-principle. A meta-principle that will be entirely consumed by its meaning. Such an idea demands a structural support, similar to a piece of paper or a canvas. A structural support that is so basic that you can apply characteristics of a proto-state to it. We have named it the *protostructure*.

The protostructure is not a new invention. The balloon frame, for instance, is a system that allows for the facilitation of almost any program, or almost any form or style. The balloon frame itself will completely disappear in the function, the program or the message it takes on. Its structure is entirely resilient in consisting of a repetition of elements that remain in mutual dependence, such that if one structural element is cut, it will be delegating what is missing in performance to its neighboring structural allies. In a few moves, the system will bring about the answers necessary for a change in form or in functional articulation. Of course, the system has limits and requires a certain integrity that allows for grey zones, until it finally collapses – something that is poetically revealed in Gordon Matta-Clark's work.

The idea of a protostructure provides in its conception a precise principle, open to be transformed by any circumstances that may arise. As such, it lends itself as a pivot between the space of imagination and the gravitational world. It can provide the principle and the physical dimension of a canvas in space. It is the literal construct that will receive the gestures drawn up by many and execute them into physical being. The structural-physical dimension will always ask for responses in gravitational space. It will question any idea about how far it can be absorbed into its system, about how far it can *itself* as a structural principle allow for clear logic, nuances, and perhaps deviations and exceptions thereof. As gravity will always exist in the discourse between idea and its translation, or between one idea and another one coming from our peers, the protostructure acts as a catalyst in communication, exchange and negotiation of spatial practices. Its structural dimension will become the gravitational activator of arguments, ideas and reactions. It will uphold its physical dimension as a reference for any projections: Conceptually weaker ones may only hold up for moments, whereas strong ideas may last. So as lasting thoughts on paper: They will be shared more and more, finally contributing to a collective culture and memory.

Structural principles, spatial logics and physical dimensions in space can be shared collectively. The historic examples mentioned above have all been at work in facilitating social life, in conquering territories or in building cities around the globe. It is our hypothesis that the concept of protostructure may provide ground for a common space to be explored collectively, in a bottom-up approach, where gravity itself and communication take on the task of catalyzing decisions, rather than top-down hierarchy. It provides a conceptual space with physical dimension that we can live and transform together. As the drawing surface provides ground for the sharing and exploring of ideas, protostructure may provide "ground" in space. Similar to gridded paper in a notebook, we envisage protostructure as a three-dimensional canvas capable of negotiating ideas and able to absorb transformation. We see it as a device ready to take on the role of a space of projection for translating conceptions and doubts, structurally and gravitationally. A *Denkraum* engaging our *Vorstellungskraft*, opened up by a drawing that stands in space and in our minds. A protostructure is a spatialized concept that we can begin to inhabit together.

To expand on the metaphor of the canvas we may ask a further question: Is the construct of protostructure as capable as a canvas to receive gestures in space? As the caves that received the first paints by the Neanderthals, or the canvas that absorbs the drops from Jasper John's utensils? Or: Can I be with the drop that falls gravitationally, actuating meaning, expression and material force, in the context of a protostructural condition? Can I, as a human, share gestures in space over time? Slower than drops can drip? Gestures that finally make space, over time?

Perhaps these gestures will never be the expression of a looking-at, but that of a being-in.

But even if we assume that gestures in protostructures may pertain latently to principles of drawing, we have to admit that their translation into space takes on another immediacy. In our previous volume of All About Space, we cited long passages from Richard Sennett's book "Together". We treated the workshop or atelier as a place where people communicate and converge in order to craft specific objects and instruments. There, communication only partially goes through verbal means: The craft itself takes on the major task of making things. If we expand the workshop into the city, from a dedicated space to a transitional situation in the public realm, or if we transfer it to the land, as a specific moment in time that will alter a condition of a place in the landscape, the notion of workshop transmutes into a "worksite" or more commonly "construction site". The French term *chantier* goes back to *cantherius*, the Latin word for rafter, or *chevron* in French. Another translation would be "supporting timber". A parallel to the idea of protostructure opens up again here: The *chevron* is a part of the carpentry of the roof, the rafter, yet another open and resilient system for interpretation in many forms and functions. In the 17th century, the word takes on the meaning of *atelier extérieur*, "exterior workshop". Interestingly the *chantier* is an intermediary concept that supports processes of transition, physically and in time. Further meanings of the word literally take on the meaning of support, still in use today. In fact the notion of an exterior workshop has rich implications. In today's hierarchical production processes, with fewer and fewer crafts and skills performed, the notion of more generalized wisdom and crafts might be helpful to reconsider ways of working together.

In the German language the earliest non-vernacular construction sites, namely of Romanesque and then Gothic cathedrals, were named *Bauhütte*. There is no direct English translation, nor in French. Literally, it means "construction house" or "construction hut". But more importantly, the term includes implicitly the meanings that concern the know-how of the people capable of building a cathedral, and the people themselves as well. The stonemasons had an accentuated knowledge of geometry and drawing, and they had the crafts to translate complex forms into stone, cutting piece by piece. As no elevation drawings of the cathedrals were made at the time, they must have referred to a kind of *imago* of what the architecture will essentially be, without knowing a defined image of it. The Gothic cathedrals emerged based on knowledge, experience and craft, the chemicals, so to speak (to keep with Man Ray's evocations). In fact the *Bauhütte* (earlier just *Hütte* - it was Johann Wolfgang Goethe who supposedly coined the longer term in 1816) was an association of workshops, a *Werkstattverband*. This is another interesting German term. It can be translated as an "association of diverse workshops". However, the term also resonates with "compound". Indeed, the *Bauhütte* comprises a series of highly specialized and knowledgeable professions, bound together in a specific place and location on a *chantier*. They exchanged and collaborated to carry out the most demanding task of mankind at the time: To produce the house of God. The combined unity of people, their knowledge, their crafts, and the place where they act and translate into physical reality the aspiring ideas of their time, may add to our observations of collective action and "drawing into space". It is fascinating to think about the potential of that form of collaboration: That these highest skills in craft and knowledge could produce such magnificent architectures without any drawing, and that the emergent space would only reveal itself over decades of time, is for us today truly hard to grasp. It demands from our imagination a complete turnaround in terms of cultural implications. To not know the outcome at the beginning of a construction would be highly contested by just about any professional in the fields related to architecture today, including myself.

We are curious to see what drawing into space could mean today. Not in a nostalgic way, which is entirely uninteresting, but in making use of our times, sociologically, economically, environmentally and technologically. The facets of the *Werkstattverband* may be a common worksite, a shared place, actual or digital and highly specialized with common perspectives and open to other ways of knowledge: The *Scaenographias* of our times. To go further in the analogy: The plan was first known in the cathedrals. Often drawn one-to-one onto the ground directly, it literally laid their foundations. The *Orthographia*, on the other hand, in profile and personality, remained open to imagination. Research shows that it was not drawn in advance. Only over time those elevations would take on their form, as a drawing into space. Emerging slowly, according to the available knowledge implied by the crafts involved (the two-dimensional drawing in fact appeared later, rather as a byproduct: drawn by Villard de Honnecourt,, around 1220). The *Bauhütte* brings together people who share a common interest, in order to go to the limits of their own knowing: People who together conceive of a space to be shared – and certainly not a predefined object. A place that they, crucially, produce together.

Let us come back to the notion of the *chantier*: As the original Latin term suggests, one of its operational qualities is scaffolding, providing constructs aimed at holding-up processes. The concrete will need support in the process of hardening, or most arches demand supporting structures until they reach their keystone. We may also think of Brunelleschi, who had to invent auto-supportive principles of scaffolding – seemingly defying gravity – to build the dome of Santa Maria del Fiore, a dome that was simply too large for the technologies of the time. It was drawn onto the ground a hundred years earlier. Or we may project ourselves into outer space, inventing a way to fix the mutilated arm of our space ship in order to save our lives. In all those examples the *chantier* is the place where we combine all our efforts, physical and intellectual, to come to terms with a situation in translation: From one state into another, from a state of precariousness to an overcoming – or simply to reach another level in a modest climb across floor platforms.

The *chantier* is then a place where converging energies take form. The *chantier* has physical attributes that need to be well imagined and drawn up. Yet we need to articulate ideas, in advance or in time – in words, in lines, in drawings, in edifying concepts that let us draw into space. From an immersed viewpoint this may imply an interval between the knowing of form and the knowing of making. Theories play their role here. A culture that prefigures results in defined elements differs from a culture that sees the evolution of knowledge as building up over time. Besides informal building, recent examples in architectural practice show that models that have similarities with the idea of a *Werkstattverband* – in India, South-America, the United States, the United Kingdom and across the planet, are proof of the idea that collective working amongst disciplines is again gaining ground. We are convinced that the intelligent articulation of diverse tasks into an overlapping and resilient network of people and skills, provides foundation for true innovation in design-to-production processes.

We are aware that we are emphasizing again and again the importance of structure – precisely to allow for freedom in conception. And as space and gravity demand structure to act upon them, so does time.

The protostructures themselves take on a transient form. They resemble geometric configurations or forms that can easily be altered or consumed. In their physical and structural dimension, protostructures are ideally auto-supportive. They will therefore depend on further elements, not only to be articulated in space but also in structural performance: Articulations need to work in compound with the protostructures, otherwise the system may not perform. In reference to Rosalind E. Krauss, protostructures tend to be open grids and not finite ones.[14] And they rarely provide a closed frame. Rather, they take on other forms as they travel through time in interaction with the people that act on them. Likewise, the timelines that we use in our projects cast out segments of time, structuring activities open in their outcome, but set to take place. Together, protostructures and accompanying timelines form an open system: They project actions into space and offer people a context for interacting with ideas and material.

If we are to draw into space the references we have cited from the domain of the arts and in the form of the *chantier*, we have a ground for the hypotheses we work with. To draw into space, to design-produce not self-confined objects but architectural space beyond the object, will be as much of time and process as it will be of matter employed in the material world. It will be measure, element, inhabitation – always incomplete, unfinished, open in its form. Articulated, but not confined to a single purpose, voicing desire rather that fear, crafting open outlook rather than protected cells. We will draw with our minds open, think of and build porous membranes between the inside and outside and offer access for all, out of respect for the other. We will negotiate space amongst ourselves. We will live through thresholds. New narratives will emerge.

The city itself shall be our *Denkraum*, now gravitational – resonating with our physical gestures.

14 Rosaline Krauss, "Grids", October, Vol. 9, MIT Press, Cambridge Mass., 1979

ARCHITECTURES OF CONTRIBUTION

In the present time, when the perpetuation of a system seems to be the all-encompassing drive of a technological society – closing the system, towards its entropic end – and in view of the all-encompassing scope of the stakes that we are facing, it may seem that small ventures between a few, to build up values of another sort with their minds, their hands and their collective intelligence are irrelevant.

Still, we know of the incapacity of automated systems to attribute values other than calculable ones. Hyper-calculating algorithms fall short when confronted with the mysteries of the human soul, and life as an improbability in itself. As a consequence, evermore standardized, entropic, non-liveable space is about to emerge. This stands in stark contrast to the capacities that we have as noetic and social beings. To quote Man Ray, "*all progress results from an intense individual desire to improve the immediate present, from an all-conscious sense of material insufficiency. In this exalted state, material action imposes itself and takes the form of revolution in one form or another. [...] The emotion of the human individual becomes universal. For what can be more binding amongst beings than the discovery of a common desire? And what can be more inspiring to action than the confidence aroused by a lyric expression of this desire?*" (*Man Ray, 1934*)

It is in the spirit of urgency that we propose to first work on values other than efficiency, profitability, or longstanding knowledge of architectural types and languages, by initiating architecture as the conception and acting on space based on an intrinsic principle of contribution and care, and on individual and collective desire. It is the experience of this very possibility that we wish to share with communities in the most diverse environments – houses as habitats, imagined, thought, conceived, drawn and built by and with many. These spaces that emerge between many souls in constant deliberation are expressions and contributions of desire that traverse far beyond the object and far beyond mere efficiency. They aim, timidly, to make life for all, human or otherwise, better and more liveable.

It is in such a condition that architecture may take other paths. It may emerge, not necessarily as ordinated, coherent and aesthetically legible objects, ready to be consumed as eloquent speech or used as a functional machine serving a specific purpose. Rather, spaces may take on a form resembling organisms akin to whole cities, with their many imperfections and often less obviously ruled development. They may become constructs embodying collective histories rather than the architectural canon. At times they may sound like symphonies – loud reverberations in the streets followed by whispers in the night. Some architects and historians may view such an architecture as a lesser being – babble rather than literature, childish rather than mature. Nevertheless, there are many beauties, with many names, referencing many cultures. Cities such as Hong Kong or Salvador de Bahia may be experienced as being equally beautiful to Paris or Torino. It is often the inexplicable that makes one love a city or not. Attachment is not a primarily intellectual faculty – even if education and intellect contribute vastly.

Structures, rhythms, details and materials may evolve by themselves into new forms through constant deliberation and in the interplay between many. It is the open field of potential that draws out new collective ideas to be brought into material life through intrinsically coordinated open operations. We must think of new canvases and new tools. We must unlearn and relearn architecture. Values will shift and form may be very different, perhaps at times recurring from other times in our histories. Projects and resulting spaces will be material articulations of liminalities – potentials articulated by material and temporal processes – becoming inscribed as values of contribution.

Such an architecture is immersive; it is aimed at an ecology of space. As an immersive architecture it must be phenomenological, where the experiential comprehension of the places and the space that we live in evolves. It becomes where we meet other people and our environment. To survive it must be economical beyond capitalism; it must give us values to live a better life, not alone and fenced off, but together.

Many of us assume that architects know better about how to build our environment. Yet, we know that we have contributed to the same paradigms that govern the present system of values that is ultimately entropic and is about to destroy our entire living environment. The drive for more control finally seems to lead altogether to an entire loss of control. On the other hand, to think of an architecture that is not a top-down linear procedure, but rather an endlessly interwoven process of constant deliberation in appropriation, refusal, conception and articulation of ideas that always must value space as a condition, is a challenging shift. It implies that control cannot reside in a sole superior instance that is unified. That difference, to make a difference, cannot reside in a unidirectional conception of how the world shall be.

Architecture is a political practice. The way we evolve space reconfigures matter, places, people, biological life. To act upon space is a collective responsibility. Our foremost question must therefore be about the values that exercise control in these actions. Who or what governs life and us? What are the values that truly matter?

0 Language

EMBRACE language. Use the etymologies of close and more distant languages, the interstices, multiplicities, vibrating oscillations of sense, of meaning, of outcome, of outburst, of physical manifestations and frictions. LIVE in the spaces of your imagination, in the evocative worlds between making and thinking. Language is a means of articulation, not a place of right or wrong, of better or worse. It is not a divisive condition between skilled and unskilled, vernacular and raw or even one language and another. It is the place of the authentic, of individuation and collective commitment and exchange. It is where we must oppose false pretention and dogmatism. Do not let your language be normalized. It is here where ideas and cultures grow and die. Construct multiplicities of languages in mutual interpenetration, clean and clear at times, resonating with the beat of our hearts, raw and unchiseled echoes at others, tingling our minds and bodies. We are languages – we are syntactic emergences and revolutions, we embody grammatical errors and virtuosity, we may become tectonic poetics.

1 Space of Imagination

EMBRACE imagination. CARE for it as we care for our children. Foster it as we foster our mental and physical offspring. Imagination is in us, and we have to feed it, play with it, educate it, challenge it. Imagination is the way to better lives. Collective imagination is insurmountable. Unless engaged, it will be taken hostage by our animal instincts.

2 Tools of Imagination

EMBRACE tools. LEARN and UNLEARN instruments. Use any tools, from the most advanced to the most archaic, close or not close to the imagined path. Parallel your actions in crafts. Make those actions and material translations imaginative. CARRY imagination beyond. Use tools to articulate space for exchange amongst ourselves and others. CONSTRUCT thought, BUILD visions and LIVE them.

3 Collective Action

EMBRACE collective action. BE CRITICAL of signature-culture and heroic gestures. If the object as an end has seen ever increasing importance since the wake of the modern age, we will shift into apprehensions of potentials of space. A place and life where everything will always be in a stage of becoming, never even thought of as finished, always in transformation. In this condition we will understand ourselves as individuals that are likewise in a constant state of becoming. Our existence as professionals therefore must become transitory, operational rather than focused on an outcome.

4 Scaffolding

INVENT new structures to share and communicate. Invent new canvases for your gestures, new frames and skins to house your desires and shelter your needs. To expand our agency we need tools, we need concepts, we need structures. Conceptual and physical structures that articulate time and space in an intermediary stage will unleash collective processes – hovering between definition and potential. Find and CONSTRUCT ground. Constructed as the lands in the Netherlands. Invented as the frames in timber balloons, or as drawings in steel. The becoming of spatial canvases that are as fragile as a painting by Agnes Martin.

5 Positioning

RETHINK the role of the architect. Reconsider necessities, desires, actions, tools, instruments and operational practices. There is a growing earth-wide movement of new approaches to space and to collective action. TAKE RESPONSIBILITY. TAKE ACTION.

6 Beyond the Object: An Endless Land

A distinction between the constructed environment and nature is obsolete. The planet is affected by us into its outermost atmospheres. The land perhaps, before all, lends itself as a new terminology as a land that holds landscape and culture simultaneously. It is simultaneously original and made. Landscapes, cityscapes, water and land are all senses of the term. It is the continuous and uninterrupted spherical surface that we inhabit. Beyond the object there is space. On earth, this space is paired with the land. IMAGINE land. CONSTRUCT it well.

HOUSE 3 in Brussels would like to consider itself as People and Space in becoming. Becoming beyond the object.

Paris, August 2018

HOUSE 3

Camille Vallet

Rythme. Fréquence. Densité.
Alternance de vides et de pleins, de nœuds, d'interférences, dans une construction qui se lit comme un maillage. Elle vibre en cadence, danse, forte de ses envolées, de sa souplesse, de ses horizontalités et de ses verticalités claires qui dessinent à contre-jour sa silhouette striée.

Matrice. Protostructure. Nombreux sont les noms qu'elle a portés ou plutôt non, qui l'ont portée, elle, simple assemblage de bois et de métal, qui donne vie tour à tour aux villas, aux stoas et aux cathédrales.

TROIS SŒURS

HOUSE, ce sont trois formes. Trois sœurs, similaires en génétique et pourtant différentes de propos. Au commencement, il n'y avait qu'un point. HOUSE 1. Une parcelle dense, insoluble, clairement détachée de son contexte. La première sœur s'élève au milieu des champs, comme issue de ceux-ci, comme abandonnée par le ciel sur quelques monticules de terre.

Puis elle se contextualise. Elle lit le territoire, se fond en lui ; il lui a donné son rythme, ses lignes. Une intention, une direction, même. HOUSE 2. Elle oscille alors sous les ponts de Zürich, forme encore indolente et indécise, qui, en perdant sa qualité ponctuelle, devient linéaire. Lisible, de droite à gauche ou de gauche à droite, au fil des portiques, la deuxième sœur glisse successivement d'un état à un autre, s'offrant tour à tour bar, bassin, cuisine et terrasse. Séduite par cet environnement de béton qui offre un contraste alléchant avec sa dentelle de bois, elle s'est attachée à ses lignes.

Enfin, plus vagabonde, la troisième sœur cherche à pénétrer la matière, à la rompre. À l'envahir jusqu'à ce qu'elle cède, qu'elle se dilate, qu'elle s'adapte à son rythme de pleins et de vide. HOUSE 3. Elle naît d'abord de cette dilatation, de ces écarts, de ces resserrements. Sa structure en horizontales et en verticales se fractionne jusqu'à ce qu'elle soit composée de fibres. Elle s'arc-boute alors comme une chose vivante, craquant comme une forêt de bambous envahie par le vent. Avec HOUSE 3, l'architecture devient organique.

C'est à Bruxelles que la troisième sœur a trouvé racine. Elle croît dans la faille de l'ancien garage Citroën et perce la dalle du KANAL Centre Pompidou pour s'élever, gracile, légère, effrayante de finesse. Sa force est issue de sa multiplicité. Sa qualité spatiale découle de son équilibre entre vide et matière. Ainsi, rythme et affolante densité périphérique s'ouvrent soudainement sur le vide ménagé en son cœur. Parfois, les poutres du garage la traversent de part en part, sursaut du contexte pour se réapproprier l'espace accaparé par la structure diaphane. Le choc des matérialités est à l'image de ce que HOUSE 3 a vu sur son chemin en Belgique, le long des autoroutes : les poutres en béton peintes en noir, où boursouflent, comme des cicatrices, les armatures de métal ; le faux plafond éventré avec une conscience chirurgicale, qui dessine le pourtour chromé de la maison ; dans l'obscurité du vide technique, les lampes et leurs gaines techniques esquissent les organes que l'on maintient trop souvent cachés dans les bâtiments modernes. Là, grâce à HOUSE 3, le showroom Citroën, transformé en garage dans les années 50, se lit à corps ouvert, comme dans les interventions de Gordon Matta Clark. La technique du bâtiment y est exposée de manière brute, intense, essentielle. Les détails d'assemblage de la HOUSE se mêlent à l'infrastructure préexistante dans une juxtaposition qui frise le collage.

L'ESTHÉTIQUE EN MOUVEMENT

Si HOUSE 3 est une maison, elle est avant tout une maison de jeu. Le jeu, le jocus, la plaisanterie, le badinage. Qui a dit qu'on ne badinait pas avec l'architecture ? Mais le jeu de HOUSE 3 est surtout une interprétation. Une œuvre composée de onze parties, onze voix, rythmes et corps qui viennent se plaquer sur la trame existante pour donner vie à des lieux. Chaque partie est une variation sur le jeu musical de la structure : une cadence vive pour certains, toutes en croches et en noires, ou bien plus apaisée, en blanches, en silences et en respirations.

Devant la dense ramure verticale des poteaux de bois de HOUSE 3 – n'entend-on d'ailleurs pas « house three » lorsque l'on se le murmure ? –, on guette l'ouverture qui nous invitera à pénétrer dans sa trame.

Si ses sœurs se lisaient depuis l'extérieur, objets éphémères capables d'être décrits en élévation, HOUSE 3 est une architecture que l'on ne comprend que depuis l'intérieur. Sa façade, c'est celle du showroom Citroën. Ne cherchez pas à la trouver belle en suivant ses tendons, ces armatures de bois qui font saillie contre la brèche du bâtiment. Ou alors appréciez-la comme on aime lire la mécanique de la nature : on se plaît, parfois, à observer attentivement la crispation d'un muscle qui se tend, roide, dans l'action d'un danseur. Rien n'est totalement statique : tout est dépendant du mouvement. Ce n'est que dans le geste accompli que s'exprime la beauté de HOUSE 3.

Guettez-les, sur le pourtour de la structure, ces pas sur le point de s'esquisser.

Un écart, d'abord, qui se tend dans la direction du visiteur, qui nous invite à grimper sur une plateforme, à glisser sous une voûte, à s'attarder autour d'une table.

De l'autre côté une diagonale, parfaitement rectiligne, subtilement inclinée, qui dessine un geste au travers de HOUSE 3 toute entière, pour rejoindre le niveau de la dalle éventrée.

Parfois, le geste n'est pas fait de matière, de lignes, de forces, mais il s'arrondit d'ombre et de lumière. Ce sont ainsi des lampes, points lumineux qui invitent à se rassembler autour d'un disque à la surface abstraite, ou au contraire un totem de crépi, érigé comme un Landmark dans toute la hauteur de la maison.

Certaines voix sont plus complexes à entendre : elles chantent en chœur, sur plusieurs tons différents, à divers points. Un passage, en fréquences hautes et en démultiplications, s'élève peu à peu dans la masse dense de la ramure. Un balcon, horizontale claire en surplomb du grand vide central, calme la densité périphérique.

Rythme et respiration.

Mais le plus important de cette trame architecturale, c'est qu'elle n'est encore qu'une portée gravée de notes, qui appelle les interprètes à s'en saisir. HOUSE 3 : maison-machine, maison-théâtre, maison-jeu, qui rêve d'être incarnée. Incarner. Formé de caro, carnis, la chair, prendre corps. Toucher, aussi. Laisser le corps explorer ce que le regard ne peut qu'effleurer.

Se coucher sur le béton froid d'une poutre horizontale, reflet de la structure du Garage Citroën, ou encore laisser les voiles flottants frôler son visage. S'accouder, le temps d'un verre, à un bar en bois ; plonger la main dans le vert et dans la terre ; caresser, doucement, avec la pointe des doigts, le béton lisse moulé dans le tissu, puis y appliquer franchement la paume comme pour y lire les témoins de la gravité ; jouer, de saut en saut, de passage en passage, dans un dédale de sapin ; tapoter la surface plastique tendue telle une peau sur l'armature de bois.

Comme un décor de théâtre, HOUSE 3 esquisse des possibles : elle forme l'empreinte de spectateurs et d'acteurs ; elle cache des coulisses dans sa ramure et expose des scènes dans sa clairière ; elle est le jeu et l'usage en puissance.

La plus complexe des trois sœurs : durable, joueuse, imprévisible.

Libre.

To build HOUSE 2 and HOUSE 3 has been an experience only possible with the contribution, the will and the imagination of you, the students. ALICE dreams of you at night:

Oria Abbas
Elodie Abbet
Franck Aurel Ahandza Bekolo
Noah Ajani
Harijith Ajithkumar
Amnah Al-Anbaki
Artan Alim
Benjamin Ambühl
Mélodie Amorim Natario
Manon Clémence Amsler
Rita Andrade Viegas
Morgane Angelozzi
Kimberley Meghan Archimi
Marie Thérèse Clémence Aublé
Sadia Avdija
Sofia Ayala Carrasco Garcia
Michaël Armagan Aydogan
Florian Baeriswyl
Antonine Elisa Baert-Yue
Zoé Christiane Herta Bahy
Simon Léo Gilles Ballester
Audrey Marie Balmat
Mélanie Baptista de Sousa
Samuel Barbey
Julie-Anna Marie Barès
Daniel Filipe Barradas Grade
Arnaud Georges Yvon Henri Barrail
Meryl Louise Barthe
Lisa Baseggio
Léo Bastianelli
Henri Shalon Baudet
Mélanie Bauer
Violetta Bayramova
Yonah Belaich
Téo Belgeri
Raphaël Belogi
Nathan Jacob Benarroch
Léo Benjamin
Alia Bennani Hamdouch
Aurélie Gabrielle Berdat
Pauline Lucie Berger
Capucine Miën Vérone Berger
Paola Marine Bergier
Lara Carole Nadège Bernath
Lara Marie-Claire Bertholet
Marion Beuchat
Zora Beyeler
Stanisław Jan Bezençon
Schaeleen Bhatch
Alice Carole Biber
Arthur Basile Billotte
Léa Binggeli
Kim Céline Bitterlin
Kathleen Bitz
Milena Blagojevic
Mélanie Sophie Blaser
Eléonore Garance Bleeker
Joséphine Marie Meije Bonnotte
François Nicolas Emmanuel Born
Erica Katharina Bossard
Cédric Grégory Bosshard
Katerina Botsis
Mourad Boumlik
Céline Anne Bourban
Nada Bousseta
Julie Bovier
Carlotta Maria Boxebeld
Helin Bozu
Basile Antoine Brun
Nikita Rachel Brunner
Baptiste Burget
Léo Ram Sovath Burnand
Mandy Burnier
Alex Burri
Zacharie Arnaud Charles Marie Cabaud
Matteo Cadei
Kevin Campigotto
Gaspar Candil Garcia
Nicolas Vincent Robert Carlier
Lisa Alice Fanny Carminati
Céline Antonine Carrière
Antoine Claude Elliot Casile
Manon Caroline Cathelain
Carolina Cerchiai
Elena Cereghetti
Basile Chabbey
Nolwenn Aude Fare Françoise Chamorel
Chaza Chawa
Alain Gabriel Cheneval
Bénédicte Marion Chenevard
Baptiste Chevalier
Amélie Marie Chiffelle
Elisa Nadia Christen
Christina Cibeira Lachmann
Adrien Clairac
Margaux Clivaz
Carolina Contreras Alvarez
Alexandre Conus
Kevin Corazza
Raoul Cordoba
Héloïse Roxane Corpataux
Pauline Morgane Alicia Cosandier
Kilian Adrien Cossali
Pierre Edmond Courvoisier
Basile Frank Crelier
Tiago Joaquim Da Silva Teixeira
Frederik Alex Anderson Dahlqvist
Myriam Daiz
Raphael Sina Darabi
Alice Charlotte Marguerite Léa Dareys
Pablo Valentin De Britto Tavares
Maria Donata De Ieso
Enzo Marie Renaud Balthazar De Moustier
Thibault Jean De Oliveira
Laura De Oliveira Guerreiro Beutler
Claire Alice Debons
Melchior Dominique Marie Dechancé
Laure Melati Dekoninck
Estelle Erna Betty Delavy
Timothée Stéphane Marie Delcourt
Léa Delessert
Luca Della Bruna
Clara Demuynck
Florian Seraphin Dervishaj
Julie Anne Maud Dessoude
Sylvain Destouches
Gaëtan Détraz
Caroline Vanessa Dorothea Dhellin
Lydia Anjali Di Munno
Tiguidanké Diallo
Marine Dominé
Nadia Vérène Doriot
Luca Dos Santos
Kastriot Dragusha
Isabeau Joséphine Margaux Dubey
Charles François Dubois
Lise Mathilde Duchamp
Aurelien Louis André Duchier
Flavien André Christian Ducor
Romain Dupertuis
Camille Cécile Sylvie Duriez
Leon Lucas Economidis
Paulina Fotini Efthymiopoulos
Etienne Léonard Eich
Brigitte Eichenberger
Chada El Alami
Benessa El Daccache
Allae-Eddine El Farrah
Adam El-Hamadeh
Mohamed Amine Elbouhdidi
Mihaela Andreea Enciu
Shadia Errassas
Charlotte Chloé Escher
Elodie Louise Marie Fabre
Manon Fame
Alicia Fankhauser
Marie-Ange Farrell
Théo Alf Christian Feldmann
Alvina Ferrara
Luana Ferrari
Rafael Ferreira Da Silva
Sonia Lorena Ferreiro Gomez
Pablo Joseph Adam Fillit
Yan Roman David Fleury
Loïc Michael Flury
Antoine Foehrenbacher
Cédric Vincent Follonier
Lina Hélène Formica
Sabrina Patricia Forsell
Edward Louis Forsey
Duncan Fouchet
Marine Annette Frey
Teodor Gacic
Estelle Gagliardi
Amélie Gaillet
Johann Gandolfo
Théo Fernando Manuel Gaspar
Gilles Benjamin Theo Gasser
Joakin Sébastien Gebert
Julien Frédéric Genin
Nikita Giaccari
Kenzo Giaccari
Gimmi Giacuzzi
Eliane Amina Gigon
Sven Zuo Yue Gillet
Federico Maria Giorgi
Lara Giorla
Noémie Anissa Girardet
Loïc Clément Girod
Leonita Gjocaj
Maximilian Thomas Glaus
Elliot Jules Gobet
Lea Nina Iris Goldhirsch
Carolina Gonçalves Videira
Flavio Mario Gorgone
Catherine Alexandra Goy
Eléonor Lily Gras
Céliane Eliane Malou Grenier
Loïc Jean Grétillat
Karina Grigoryeva
Albane Grimont
Lucas Antoine Gublin
Eléonore Sixtine Laurence Marie Solange Gueyffier
Alysée Graziella Claire Gugler
Fabian Guillaume
Serayu Gujja
Mikail Gün
Johan Manuel Olivier Gurba
Fabio Manuel Gysler
Maya Souheil Haddad
Sarah Roxane Hahusseau
Rafael Halilovic
Aya Hamine
Axelle Hamm
Sébastien Maxime Hasler
Gilliane Hasler
Madina Hassan Moallin
Eva Hauswirth
Julien Heil
Dylan Ulrich Heim
Héloïse Laurie Merry Suzanne Héloïse Lauret
Laetitia Chloé Hirt
Camille-Marie Hochar
Luca Hoser
Eliott Gaston François Hounieu
Laureen Menglian Océane Hu
Aline Katharina Hübner
Romain Iff
Francesca Marie-Reine Igowa
Giada Martina Ilacqua
Matthias Gabriel Venceslas

Jammers
Doriand Andrzej Jaton
Youssef Jeddi
Charlotte Flavie Judith Jianoux
Victoire Joëssel
Alberto Johnsson
Océane Juillerat
Aysu Kadayifci
Ilona Laurence Anna Kaeser
Lundrim Karameta
Dimitri Kasparian
Jonathan Kiener
Chiara Kocis
Gleb Kolesnikov
Tadeusz Jozef Kondracki
Tristan Kramer
Samuel Marc Labhard
Marine Lena Lachat
Lauriane Marie-Clémence Renée Lagrange
Bryan Lam
Lorenzo Rudolf Lamarche
Allan Anthony Lambelet
Marco Landert
Pierrot Michel Zin-Zan Lankry
Emma Christine Joelle Larcelet
See Hoi Hosea Lau
Catherine Elsie Jacqueline Leyland
Roxane Li Sen Lié
Jana Annina Liebi
Alexandre Tristan Bénédict Lombardi
Chiara Suzanne Mathilde Lombardi--Dellamonica
Carmen Lonfat
Thibaud Clément Louet
Vincent Luetto
Loïc Lugrin
Sean Bernard Raymond Lusti
Maxime Bertrand Luthy
Rémi Esteban Trinh Madrona
Valérie Anne Maillard
Andrea Sthefania Marmolejo Valdez
Bryan Rafael Marques Soares
Patricia Martins Ferreira
Hibiki Masaki
Anthony Giovanni Paul Masini
Agathe Marguerite Caroline
Marie Mauvais
Marina Medic
Eugénie Ségolène Mégevand
François Nicolas Bernard Megret
Fadwa Mehdaoui
Albin Mehmeti
Kaltrina Mehmeti
Lino Mattia Mercolli
Sam Fernand Mettraux
Kyra Lea Michel
Inès Marie Thérèse Michelin
Judith Michellod
Ferdinand Michon
Yoann Guillaume Sacha Miéville
Louis Marie Pierre Maurice Milhac
Loris André Millius
Isabelle Christina Miodonski
Amélie Mischler
Theresa Moeller Genannt Gosoge
Camille Emma Monnard
Claire Isabelle Montégudet
Matteo Simon Morais Marques
Emilie Rita Alice Morales Fernandez-Brandt
Julie Margot Morel
Hugo Morel
Simone Morelli
Philippe Mourelle
Idriss Mouti
Lionel Maxime Mudry
Victor Oskar Rudolph Müller
Giulia Murgia
Pierre Pascal Erwin Musy
Lea Muttoni
Diana Rami Michel Nabky
Shalin Nalumansi
Mathias Narbel
Malak Nasreldin
Thelma Nassisi
Fabio Angelo César Neuenschwander
Thuy Thanh Nguyen
Tuong-Vy Tiffany Nguyen
Sacha Philippe Christophe Nicolas
Dimitri Nicole
Camille Manon Imelda Nicolet
Flavio Junio Nogueira Pereira
Nicolas Emile Noth
Gabriel Ihechimnemerem Ogbonna
Klea Ott
Ghita Ouassini
Valérie Ovadia
Timur Emre Özcan
Antonio Pagano
Quentin Paillat
Lorenzo Palacio
Jonathan Joseph Panakal
Carina Pannatier
Melinda Papi
Ncuti Arnaud Paris
Joséphine Parlier
Sean Pasquier
Grégoire Hugo Pauvert
Fanny Pavillard
Lucie Marie Emilie Peccoux
Catherine Pedroni
Elisa Pellissier
Fiona Marie Lara Pèpe
Laura Périat
Alina Mara Perozzo
Lucie Perretten
Chiara Pezzetta
Quang Vinh Pham
Achille Félix Pidoux
Vincent Irénée Pignard
Julien Pignat
Maylis Françoise Marie Pillet
Daniel Louis Pilsworth
Luana Alexandra Pimenta Santos
Bruno Daniel Pinto De Oliveira
Sarah Catherine Amélie Planchamp
Oana Emma Popescu
Theodor Popescu
Valentin Popescu
Julien Alexandre Porret
Nicolas Albert André Pralong
Antoine Gabriel Damien Prat
Chloé Marie Léopoldine Cathy Prévot
Louis Queloz
Bastien Evan Rabaglia
Lucien Eric Rahm
Claudia Alexandra Ramalhoto Penela
Lia Giovanna Laura Rampazzi
Roman Ramseyer
Roman Ramseyer
Filippo Rattazzi
William Pelham Rawlingson Plant
Léna Carola Reesink
Tina Amandine Regelin
Elodie Rey
Julien Rey
Elina Marie Nadia Reymond
Jonas Charlélie Reymondin
Miranda Charlotte Reynolds
Evan François Jacques Ribadeau Dumas
Antoine Matthieu Ricard-Gauthier
Alessandra Ricci
Quentin Rickli
Julie Riondel
Cyril Adrien Robert
Tiphaine Elisa Robert
Justine Anne Françoise Rognon
Alex Roman
Roberto Rossi
Manuel Rossi
Anna Rouviere
Antoine Charles Michel Rudaz
Gabriel Nicolas Saez Araya
Aude Sahli
Árpád Salamin
Maylis Salihu
Yassine Ahmed Sam
Zelal Sari
Mathilde Savary
Flore Ondine Schaerrer
Abigaël Schaller
Fabio Alfred Gino Scheggia
Siena Scheidegger Tobias
Laurent Scherwey
Lionel Scherz
Chloé Eva Louise Schindler
Jacques Schmidt
Sandrine Schneuwly
Mathias Schopfer
Mélanie Estelle Schroff
Fanny Olivia Schröter
Karen Kim Schuler
Laura Vanessa Schwendimann Monasterios
Clara Marie Anne Seffacene
Yasmine Sefraoui
Vlora Seljmani
Stefania Semenova
Matthieu Seppey
Christine Ashraf Kamal Shehata
Maria Sienko
Alice Thina Amanda Sikiaridis
José Gabriel Silva
Emma Simonin
Victor Sitavanc
Anastasia Skorik
Basile Quentin Sordet
Pablo Ricardo Stadelmann
Natalia Stavrovskaja
Luca Stefanelli
Arthur Henryk Stepczynski
Anne Gabrielle Steullet
Angelina Stevanovic
Mathieu Antoine Stoppa
Emmanuel Théo Stump
Pierluigi Surano
Valentina Daria Takatch
Davide Tarditi
Ella Léonie Täube
Zehra Susanna Ter
Ghita Terrab
Romane Terrien
Charlotte Thallinger
Maxime Francis Nicolas Theubet
Manon Danièle Thévenaz
Issa Marah Ananda Thévenaz
Julie Alodie Agnès Theytaz
Alessandro Tiezzi
Sözdar Toktas
Salimat Toturbieva
Tuong Vy Sarah Tran
Roberto Trivelli
Luca Truscello
Noémie Tschabold
Gaël Corentin Tuchschmid
Sarah Ulrich
Karl Agust Valfells
Stéphane Ganesh Vallon
Luna Sunita Valls-Haenni
Tanguy Pierre Vandenberghe
Prudence Marie Sybille Vanpoulle
Samuel Pierre Varrin
Eliott Vaucher
Luana Veraguth
Gianni Verrillo
Driss Veyry
Louis Joseph Viandier
Carina Soraia Vidal Martins
Cyrielle Noémi Vié
Pauline Marie Viennot-Bourgin
Leonne-Zoë Vögelin
Timon Voide
Alan Von Arx Carrascal
Sarah Helene Von Steiger
Laura Nadine Vuffray
Sibylle Marie Cécile Katherine Vuillemin
Elise Aline Maric Vulliez
Héloïse Philomène Joyce Vust
Jivan Waber
Ziad Wahida
Naomy Walther
Loïs Phyllis Weber
Corentin Raphael Nathan Weber
Alexander Robert Jan Wegener
Mehdi Wermuth
Céline Audrey Widmer
Sidney Wirth
Arno Léon Oreste Alfred Wust
San Yun
Paola Saskia Zanchi
Deborah Zanolo
Arnaud Loick Zbinden
Emma Maria Zeindl Cronin
Samara Rigoberta Zuber Vasile

ALL ABOUT SPACE VOL. 3
BEYOND THE OBJECT

Edited by Dieter Dietz, Matthias Michel & Daniel Zamarbide
For ALICE (Atelier de la conception de l'espace) at the Ecole polytechnique fédérale de Lausanne (EPFL), Switzerland

1st edition, 2018

Concept, translations, historical and cartographical research:
Matthias Michel

Original Photography:
Dylan Perrenoud,
Katalin Deér (HOUSE 2),
Studio ALICE (HOUSE 3),
Drone Photography:
Alexa den Hartog, Yves Seiler
Topographical Rendering (p. 200):
Céline Stephanie Tran

Translation, copy-editing & proof-reading:
Teresa Cheung, Ingrid Fichtner, Emma Jones, Francesca Leibowitz, Matthias Michel

Graphic Design:
Hubertus-Design
Jonas Voegeli, Benoit Brun

Lithography:
Marjeta Morinc

Print & Binding:
Druckerei Kösel GmbH

Paper:
Munken Cream

Typeface:
Janson Max Neue @abcdinamo

Quoted text (pp. 281–82, 291):
Man Ray, "The Age of Light", in: Man Ray, *Photographs by Man Ray: 105 Works, 1920–1934*, New York: Dover Books, 1979, p. 9 (Reprint of *Photographs by Man Ray: 105 Works, 1920–1934*, Hartford: James Thrall Soby, 1934).

All historical photo and pictorial material replicated in *A Brief History of Space* is either in the public domain or free content that is explicitly not subjected to any copyright restrictions, unless noted otherwise. The availability of a considerable part of this material is owed to the many contributors to free studies and knowledge on Wikimedia Commons (wikimedia.org).

Thanks to Claude Huber for her indispensable assistance in creating the historical cartography of the Circles of Space and Time.

This publication was generously supported by Faculté de l'environnement naturel, architectural et construit (ENAC), École polytechnique fédérale de Lausanne (EPFL).

The editors would like to thank Jonas Voegeli for his initiative and his uncompromised optimism to invite ALICE to Zurich Toni-Areal: Without his persuasiveness in convincing Zurich Art University ZHdK and the many partners necessary for this adventure, HOUSE 2 would never have seen the day. Furthermore this project would not have been possible without the help of the direction and staff of the school. In particular Andrea Roca was essential for the success of the project, and special thanks to Hansueli Matter, Tobias Gugg, Ronny Paschen, Matthias Wyssmann of the City of Zurich was crucial for the opening of doors at the right place and time.

Thanks to Nicole Cueni and Reto Stäubli of SBB for their open-minded and uncomplicated agreement to construct HOUSE 2 on their premises. Christoph Gemperle for a precise expertise on combustion behavior of HOUSE 2 on fire. Albert Kunz for his insight and his precise instruction regarding fire security. Alain Parratte for silent support in the background.

For HOUSE 3 in Brussels we would like to extend our most sincere thanks to Cédric Libert and Yves Goldstein, who invited ALICE to the showroom in the Citroën Garage. The experience at KANAL / Centre Pompidou is unparalleled and would equally not have happened without support of Bernard Blistène and his team of the Center Pompidou. The whole team of Civa and KANAL Foundation was crucial at every moment of the process, in particular Marine Urbain, Tania Garduno, Géraldine de Brouwer, André Verstraeten, Baptiste Delhauteur, Jennifer Beauloye, Younes Zarhoni, Redouan & Abdel, Dieter Vanthournout and Pieter Van Damme always were there when it was necessary.

Special thanks are owed to Rémy Meylan and Kenny Verbeek, far-looking engineers in timber constructions, and Jaime Ruiz, fearless coordinator of the entire ALICE team.

For the HOUSES Stéphane Grandgirard, Laurent Chassot and Thibault Smith were crucial in all phases of their transition from idea to physical existence, without them the HOUSES would not have seen the day as they did. We cannot overemphasize the crucial contributions of all the studio directors and members of the ALICE's team with their visions, patience and skills: Raffael Baur, Arthur Blanc, Laurent Chassot, Elena Chiavi, Jorge Christie, Margherita Del Grosso, Dieter Dietz , Marcia Dos Reis, Aurélie Dupuis, Camille Fauvel, Thomas Favre-Bulle, Stéphane Grandgirard, Sébastien Grosset, Patricia Guaita, Emma Jones, Shin Koseki, Clarisse Labro, Julien Lafontaine, Victor Maréchal, Agathe Mignon, François Nantermod, Dario Negueruela Del Castillo, Rudi Nieveen, Laura Perez Lupi, Myriam Perret, Aurèle Pulfer, Aurélien Reymond, Jaime Ruiz, Javier Saez, Thibault Smith, Céline Tran, Lucas Uhlmann, Ruben Valdez, Daniel Zamarbide.

We like to particularly thank our student-assistants, airborns and intern team: Emma Ammeter, Luciano Antonietti, Sadia Avdija, Semere Berhe, Vincent Bianchi, Cedric Bosshard, Alex Burri, Sophie Deckers, Adam El-Hamadeh, Marie-Ange Farrell, Pablo Fillit, Alice Fiorini, Gilles Gasser, Maximilian Glaus, Julien Heil, Selen Karakoc, Tomislav Levak, Antonin Mack, Bastian Marzoli, Kyra Michel, Judith Michellod, Maxence Milhau, Marion Moutal, Gabriel Ogbona, Antonio Pagano, Quentin Paillat, Ella Pham, Piet Pham, Daniel Pilsworth, Valentin Popescu, Antoine Ricard-Gauthier, Yann Salzmann, Chloé Schindler, Karen Schuler, Basile Sordet, Ziad Wahida, Arno Wust, Arnaud Zbinden, Noémie Zurbriggen.

Park Books
Niederdorfstrasse 54
8001 Zurich
Switzerland
www.park-books.com

Park Books is being supported by the Federal Office of Culture with a general subsidy for the years 2016–2020.

ISBN 978-3-03860-112-8